LINEAR ALGEBRA

WITH

MATHEMATICA

BROOKS/COLE
SYMBOLIC
COMPUTATION
SERIES

ohnson

Mathematica Command List

LINEAR ALGEBRA
WITH
MATHEMATICA®

LINEAR ALGEBRA
WITH
MATHEMATICA®

Eugene W. Johnson
University of Iowa

Brooks/Cole Publishing Company

I(T)P™ An International Thomson Publishing Company

Pacific Grove • Albany • Bonn • Boston • Cincinnati • Detroit • London • Madrid • Melbourne
Mexico City • New York • Paris • San Francisco • Singapore • Tokyo • Toronto • Washington

Sponsoring Editor: *Robert Evans*
Marketing Team: *Patrick Farrant, Margaret Parks*
Editorial Associate: *Elizabeth Barelli Rammel*
Production Editor: *Marlene Thom*
Manuscript Editor: *Donald W. DeLand*

Permissions Editor: *Carline Haga*
Cover Design: *Roy Neuhaus*
Typesetting: *Scratchgravel Publishing Services*
Printing and Binding: *Malloy Lithographing, Inc.*

For more information, contact:

BROOKS/COLE PUBLISHING COMPANY
511 Forest Lodge Road
Pacific Grove, CA 93950
USA

International Thomson Publishing Europe
Berkshire House 168–173
High Holborn
London WC1V 7AA
England

Thomas Nelson Australia
102 Dodds Street
South Melbourne, 3205
Victoria, Australia

Nelson Canada
1120 Birchmount Road
Scarborough, Ontario
Canada M1K 5G4

International Thomson Editores
Campos Eliseos 385, Piso 7
Col. Polanco
11560 México D. F. México

International Thomson Publishing GmbH
Königswinterer Strasse 418
53227 Bonn
Germany

International Thomson Publishing Asia
221 Henderson Road
#05–10 Henderson Building
Singapore 0315

International Thomson Publishing Japan
Hirakawacho Kyowa Building, 3F
2–2–1 Hirakawacho
Chiyoda-ku, Tokyo 102
Japan

Printed in the United States of America

10   9   8   7   6   5   4   3   2   1

Library of Congress Cataloging-in-Publication Data

Johnson, Eugene W., [date]–
    Linear algebra with Mathematica / Eugene W. Johnson.
      p.   cm.
    Includes index.
    ISBN 0-534-13068-2
    1. Algebras, Linear—Data processing. 2. Mathematica (Computer file) I. Title.
QA185.D7J65   1995
512'.5'078—dc20
                           94-38614
                            CIP

Preface

This book began several years ago when I was asked to teach a two semester hour linear algebra course to engineering students. This was a challenge, because it meant I had reduced class time (two semester hours instead of the usual four) to discuss the number of examples I generally like to cover in my linear algebra courses.

The solution was to use the computer, specifically a computer algebra system. In class we would develop the basic processes for problem solving and then use the computer to implement those processes in examples. Doing so reduced the time spent on tedious and uninstructive calculation and enabled us to focus on applications and other enhancements.

There are, of course, many paths one can travel in linear algebra with the aid of a computer. For example, numerical methods could be studied. However, it is my opinion that the first course in linear algebra is best taught with exact methods, which requires the use of a computer algebra system capable of exact calculations. *Mathematica*® has the capability to do exact numerical calculations and is therefore a natural choice. That it can also work with variables, polynomials, and functions is further incentive to use the program.

Despite the large number of examples given, this book is not designed to stand alone. It does not contain formal statements or proofs of theorems. Rather, it should be used either as a supplement to a standard introductory text on linear algebra or by those who already have a working knowledge of the subject and wish to off-load some of the drudgery of the calculations to the computer. The book begins with a short but self-contained introduction to *Mathematica*, and then it proceeds to use *Mathematica* as a tool to work with vectors, matrices, and linear transformations.

Mathematica's ability to do symbolic computation is frequently exploited to develop computational proofs of special cases of important properties. The basic approach of this text, however, is to develop a topic and one or more applications and then give exercises and problems that illustrate the topic.

Acknowledgments

In the course of preparing this book, I have had the pleasure of sharing ideas with a number of talented people; it is my hope that the reader will also find some enjoyment in its use.

I would like to thank Robert Evans, Elizabeth Rammel, Nancy Conti, and Jeremy Hayhurst for their encouraging cheerfulness, assistance, and support on this project.

Thanks also go to the many students at the University of Iowa who have participated in the development of this book by sharing their impressions. Special thanks to Asuman Oktac and Alin Cârsteanu for their careful reading of the manuscript and for their solutions to the exercises.

Finally, I thank the following reviewers for their helpful comments: Richard Alo, University of Houston–Downtown; Thomas Fournelle, University of Wisconsin–Parkside; Judy Holdener, U.S. Air Force Academy; Myron Hood, California Polytechnic; Phil McCartney, Northern Kentucky University; Robert Moore, University of Washington; Mo Tavakoli, Chaffey College; and John Wicks, North Park College.

Eugene W. Johnson

Contents

1   Matrices and Linear Systems   35

2   The Algebra of Vectors   71

3 Eigenspaces   108

4 Linear Transformations   149

LINEAR ALGEBRA WITH
MATHEMATICA®

0 Introduction

Linear algebra is the primary tool for working with mathematical systems. The elements of such a system might be numbers, equations, functions, or other algebraic objects. Because such systems arise in the solution of problems in all scientific disciplines, linear algebra is one of the most central topics in mathematics.

By collecting the related components of a problem into a system that can be dealt with as a single algebraic entity, an extremely important conceptual simplification is obtained. This simplification can often turn a confusing maze of information into a compact mathematical problem for which there is a straightforward, well-defined solution process. This is the appeal of linear algebra.

Unfortunately, even straightforward, well-defined solution processes are not necessarily either short or quick. But there now exist excellent computer programs that can assist dramatically by handling the routine calculations, freeing you to concentrate on the strategy for solving the problems. This book is based on the use of one such system called *Mathematica*.

Mathematica is a powerful computer program for doing mathematical computations.[1] *Mathematica* "knows" virtually all standard mathematical functions and operations. Further, *Mathematica* graphs functions and equations and can be "taught" things it did not originally know.

In some respects, *Mathematica* can be likened to a super-programmable graphing calculator. However, unlike most calculators, *Mathematica* is not restricted to performing its calculations with decimal approximations. *Mathematica* is quite capable of doing approximate calculations with *approximate numbers* if that is your choice. On the other hand, *Mathematica* can also do *exact* arithmetic with *exact* data—including unknowns and variables—as is typically done in the mathematics classroom.

Using *Mathematica*, you can relegate routine calculations to the computer without having to sacrifice accuracy. This is no minor gain, as the cumulative effect of rounding errors in problems involving systems of equations is

---

[1]*Mathematica* is subtitled "A System for Doing Mathematics by Computer."

easily substance for a separate course. (However, if you wish to use floating-point routines, *Mathematica* is also well equipped to assist you there.)

The breadth and flexibility of *Mathematica* can serve you well. The time you spend learning the program will pay dividends far beyond your study of linear algebra.

0.1 Getting Started with *Mathematica*

Mathematica is available for a large variety of computers, and the exact method of starting *Mathematica* varies from system to system. We assume that you are familiar with the general principles of operating the computer on which you will use *Mathematica*. Whatever the computer, *Mathematica* is launched in the same way as other applications on that system.

As a warm-up, enter the examples in the "tour" (0.3) to get a feel for the way things work. You might also try a little experimenting on your own. There are four key points to keep in mind.

1. In *Mathematica* all built-in function or command names begin with a capital letter. Any arguments are enclosed in square brackets rather than parentheses. For example, you use `Sin[x]` to represent sin (*x*).
2. You tell *Mathematica* to execute a command by typing the command and then "entering" it. You enter your command by pressing the appropriate key or key combination, generally either **Enter, Return, Shift-Enter,** or **Shift-Return.** For example, on the Apollo Computer®, you can use either **Enter** or **Return.** On the Macintosh®, either **Enter** or **Shift-Return** works. Some experimentation may be required on your part. If there is nobody available who can tell you what works, try **Enter** or **Return** and see what happens. If *Mathematica* seems to have paid no attention, chances are you need to use a different key or key combination. We will refer to the key that enters your command as the **Enter** key.
3. If *Mathematica* ignores your commands, reread steps 1 and 2. If *Mathematica* reads your commands but does not understand them, it usually responds with an error message.
4. Some systems do not load the bulk of the *Mathematica* program until you enter your first command. For this reason, *Mathematica* may take a long time to respond the first time you enter a command in a new session.

0.2 Editing, Saving, and Retrieving Your Work

Some file-handling commands provided by *Mathematica* are common across all systems. However, most systems provide additional capabilities based on their own hardware and operating systems. Editing operations are also quite system specific.

Specific, system-dependent information is available in the *User's Guide* that accompanied the program for your system.

0.3 An Introductory Tour of *Mathematica*

Although *Mathematica* is a powerful program for doing mathematical computations, for many purposes it is no more difficult to operate than a pocket calculator. Unlike most pocket calculators, however, *Mathematica* gives you the ability to do *exact* calculations if you prefer.

0.3.1 Arithmetic in *Mathematica*

Mathematica's Arithmetic Notation

Standard Notation	*Mathematica* Notation
$x + y$	x + y
$x - y$	x - y
xy	x y (or x * y)
x/y	x / y
x^y	x ^ y

Throughout this "tour," commands entered by the user and *Mathematica*'s responses are shown in Courier type. The margin notes comment on the displayed *Mathematica* session, which is formatted to simulate an actual *Mathematica* session. The exact appearance of your screen during a *Mathematica* session may vary somewhat from that shown, depending on the computer and operating system you are using.

Regardless of the computer system, arithmetic can be done in *Mathematica* in either exact or approximate mode.

Exact Calculations with *Mathematica*

Unlike most calculators and computer programs, *Mathematica* has an exact mode. For example, when numbers are entered in rational form, exact answers are given.

This computes the sum $\frac{1}{3} + \frac{4}{5}$. Mathematica's response always begins on a new line.

```
In[1]:= 1/3 + 4/5

Out[1]= 17
        --
        15
```

This computes the difference $\frac{34}{55} - \frac{114}{27}$.

```
In[2]:= 34/55 - 114/27

Out[2]= -(1784)
          ----
          495
```

This computes the product $\frac{24}{47} \times \frac{94}{96}$. Here a space is used to indicate multiplication.

```
In[3]:= 24/47   94/96
```
$$Out[3] = \frac{1}{2}$$

Alternatively, you can use the asterisk (*) for multiplication if you prefer.

```
In[4]:= 24/47 * 94/96
```
$$Out[4] = \frac{1}{2}$$

Use the forward slash (/) for division as well as for fractions.

```
In[5]:= (1/2) / (1/2)
Out[5]= 1
```

Note the important difference if parentheses are not used here.

```
In[6]:= 1/2/1/2
```
$$Out[6] = \frac{1}{4}$$

This gives 2^{64}. (You also can use the double asterisk (**) instead of "^".)

```
In[7]:= 2^64
Out[7]= 18446744073709551616
```

If numbers are entered in rational form, *Mathematica* operates in *exact mode*.

Mathematica also works with unknowns and variables using general rules of algebra.

This tells Mathematica to "compute"

$$\frac{x(x + x - y - x)}{x}.$$

Note that Mathematica cancels the x terms; the two rational expressions are equal, but the functions they define are not.

```
In[1]:= x(x + x - y - x)/x
Out[1]=  x - y
```

This is the command that tells Mathematica to factor the polynomial $x^3 - 3x^2y + 3xy^2 - y^3$.

```
In[2]:= Factor[x^3 - 3 x^2 y + 3 x y^2 - y^3]
Out[2]=  (x - y)³
```

This is the command that tells Mathematica to expand the polynomial $(x + 1)(x - 1)^3$.

$In[3]:= \text{Expand}[(x+1)(x-1)^3]$

$Out[3]= x^4 + 2\ x - 2\ x^3 - 1$

Mathematica does not automatically simplify all expressions. Here it leaves $\frac{x^3 - y^3}{x - y}$ *in unsimplified form.*

$In[4]:= (x^3 - y^3)/(x - y)$

$Out[4]= \dfrac{x^3 - y^3}{x - y}$

This is the command that tells Mathematica to simplify the expression $\frac{x^3 - y^3}{x - y}$.

$In[5]:= \text{Simplify}[(x^3 - y^3)/(x - y)]$

$Out[5]= x^2 + x\ y + y^2$

Note the capitalization of the command names `Expand`, `Factor`, and `Simplify`. All *Mathematica* function and command names begin with capital letters. Also note the use of square brackets instead of parentheses. In *Mathematica*, all commands and functions are used with square brackets in the form `Command[x]`. Parentheses are used in *Mathematica* exclusively for grouping terms.

Sometimes you may decide to apply a function or command such as `Simplify` as an afterthought. *Mathematica* also supports a postfix notation for this.

This also simplifies the expression $\frac{x^3 - y^3}{x - y}$.

$In[6]:= (x^3 - y^3)/(x - y)//\text{Simplify}$

$Out[6]= x^2 + x\ y + y^2$

Mathematica can do exact calculations with some special numbers and virtually all standard mathematical functions. The following shows *Mathematica*'s awareness of the square root, natural log, and exponential functions.

This computes the product $\sqrt{3}\sqrt{4}$.

$In[1]:= \text{Sqrt}[3]\ \text{Sqrt}[4]$
$Out[1]= 2\ \text{Sqrt}[3]$

Mathematica uses I for the complex number $i = \sqrt{-1}$. *This computes* i^2.

$In[2]:= I^2$
$Out[2]= -1$

Here Mathematica calculates the 10th power of the complex number $2 + 3i$.

$In[3]:= (2 + 3\ I)^{10}$
$Out[3]= -341525 - 145668\ I$

This demonstrates Mathematica's awareness of the properties of the log and exponential functions.

$$In[4]:= \text{Log[Exp[3/5]]}$$

$$Out[4]= \frac{3}{5}$$

This repeats the same calculation with postfix notation.

$$In[5]:= \text{Exp[3/5]//Log}$$

$$Out[5]= \frac{3}{5}$$

Note again the capitalization of the function names and the use of square brackets.

Simplify
    All built-in function names and command names in *Mathematica* begin with capital letters.

F[x]
    Square brackets are used to apply any function or command in *Mathematica*.

x//F
    Mathematica supports postfix notation as well as the more standard prefix notation.

Approximate Calculations

When you use decimal notation, *Mathematica* acts like a standard calculator by rounding the output to a default or specified number of significant digits. This is *Mathematica*'s *approximate mode*.

This computes a decimal approximation of $\frac{1}{3}+\frac{6}{7}$. Note the rounding error.

$$In[1]:= \quad .333333 + .857143$$
$$Out[1]= \quad 1.19048$$

This computes an approximation of $\sqrt{2}$.

$$In[2]:= \quad \text{Sqrt[2.0]}$$
$$Out[2]= \quad 1.41421$$

This squares the approximation of $\sqrt{2}$.

$$In[3]:= \quad \text{Sqrt[2.0]^2}$$
$$Out[3]= \quad 2$$

This computes a decimal approximation of 2^{64}. Compare this to the exact answer obtained earlier.	`In[4]:=  2.0^64` `Out[4]=  1.84467*10`^{19}

> When functions are applied to data in approximate form, approximate answers are usually returned.

0.3.2 Prompts and Labels

When *Mathematica* is ready for you to enter a command, some systems print a *prompt* of the form `In[n]:=` where *n* is a positive integer. A prompt is simply an indicator that *Mathematica* is waiting for you to give it an instruction. Some systems do not prompt you for a command but prepend the label `In[n]:=` to the *n*th command *after* you have entered it. In either case, your command ends up with a label of the form `In[n]`. You have probably also noted that *Mathematica* attaches labels of the form `Out[n]=` to its responses.

0.3.3 Previous Results

Mathematica uses the percent sign (`%`) to refer to the result of the previous calculation. Similarly, the double percent (`%%`) refers to the result immediately preceding `%`, and so on. You also can refer to the result labeled `Out[n]` with `Out[n]` or `%n`.

`%`	the previous result
`%%`	the result preceding `%`
`%%...%` (*k* times)	the *k*th preceding result
`Out[n]`	the *n*th result of the session
`%n`	the result labeled `Out[n]`
`In[n]`	the *n*th command

After this calculation, 5 is the result that immediately precedes the next calculation.	`In[1]:= 2+3` `Out[1]= 5`
This subtracts 12 from 5, the result of the immediately preceding calculation.	`In[2]:= %  -  12` `Out[2]= -7`

This subtracts –7 from 5. –7 is the result of immediately preceding calculation and 5 is the result immediately preceding it.

```
In[3]:= %% - %
Out[3]=  12
```

This computes the product 5(–7 + 12). %%% refers to 5, %% refers to –7, and % refers to 12.

```
In[4]:= %%% (%% + %)
Out[4]= 25
```

Here the results Out[1] *and* Out[2] *are added.*

```
In[5]:= Out[1] + Out[2]
Out[5]= -2
```

This repeats the calculation Out[1] + Out[2] *using the* %n *notation.*

```
In[6]:= %1 + %2
Out[6]= -2
```

0.3.4 Assigning Your Own Names

Any *Mathematica* expression—numerical, symbolic, or mixed— can be assigned a name by using the assignment operator "equal" (=). Once a name is assigned to an expression, the name can be used any time you want to refer to the expression. This greatly expands the type of functionality provided by the %n and Out[n] labels but requires that you implement it.

Here the number $119 \times (476 + 23!)$ *is assigned the name* numer.

```
In[1]:= numer = 119 * (476 + 23!)
Out[1]= 3076389991927312220216644
```

Here the number $12^{23} + 1936$ *is assigned the name* denom.

```
In[2]:= denom = 12^23 + 1936
Out[2]= 662473726694923701122064
```

Here the names numer *and* denom *are used to calculate the quotient* $\frac{\text{numer}}{\text{denom}}$. *Note the simplification.*

```
In[3]:= numer/denom
```

$$Out[3]= \frac{10987107114026115072023}{236597759533901321825788}$$

Names you assign can be used in conjunction with percent signs. Unlike the percent signs, the names you assign retain the same values until you change them.

$In[4]:= $ %/numer

$$Out[4]= \frac{1}{66247372669492370011122064}$$

Here the fourth calculation is repeated using the built-in names %1 *and* %3.

$In[5]:= $ %3/%1

$$Out[5]= \frac{1}{66247372669492370011122064}$$

Here Mathematica's ability to work with named quantities is used effectively in combination with its ability to work with symbolic quantities; recall that feet^2 is the standard scientific abbreviation for square feet.

$In[6]:= $ height = 23 feet
$Out[6]= $ 23 feet
$In[7]:= $ width = 14 feet
$Out[7]= $ 14 feet
$In[8]:= $ area = height width
$Out[8]= $ 322 feet^2

0.3.5 Multiple-Line Commands

It may sometimes be necessary to enter a *Mathematica* command that exceeds the available line space. In this case, *Mathematica* will either "wrap" the input (in the same way most word-processing programs would) or horizontally scroll the screen, depending on your system. Either way *Mathematica* makes room for you to complete your command.

If, on the other hand, you want to begin a new line to control the format of your command, you do not have to rely on line wrapping; rather, you may be able to use a key combination to begin a new line. If you use **Enter** to tell *Mathematica* to evaluate your expression, try **Return**. If you use **Return**, try **Enter**. If you can't find a key combination that works for you, you may be able to use the backslash (\) character in conjunction with some other key or key combination.

*Under Microsoft Windows™, the **Enter** key is used after the first line to continue the input; **Shift-Enter** is used with the second line to evaluate the expression. On a Macintosh, you would use **Return** at the end of the first line and **Enter** at the end of the second.*

```
In[1]:= 123+
          234

Out[1]= 347
```

Note that a complete command is not formed until the second command fragment is entered.

*On a Macintosh, you can also use the line continuation character (\) and **Return** at the end of the first line and **Enter** at the end of the second line.*

```
In[2]:= 123\
          +234

Out[2]= 347
```

Throughout this book, new lines are begun without further mention of the method. You may have to test your system to see what works.

0.3.6 The Command Separator and Silent Terminator

More than one command can be entered on a line in *Mathematica* if the commands are separated by a semicolon (;). When this is done, the results of the commands followed by semicolons are not displayed—the semicolon suppresses the output of the command it follows. This property of the semicolon can be used to suppress the output of single commands.

```
com1; com2
```
   The semicolon (;) can be used to separate multiple commands on the same line.

```
Command;
```
   The semicolon suppresses *Mathematica*'s output.

You can place more than one command on a line.

```
In[1]:= 1+3; 2
Out[1]= 2
```

You can use the semicolon to suppress the display of results you do not wish to see.

```
In[2]:= 10!;
```

The label Out[2] *is assigned even though it is not displayed.*

```
In[3]:= %2
Out[3]= 3628800
```

0.3.7 Getting Help

Mathematica has an extensive help system. You access the help system with a command of the form ?*topic*.

Help is even available on getting help.

```
In[1]:= ??
Information::basic:
    ?Name gives information on Name, ?Ab* on all
symbols starting with Ab. ??Name gives more
information.
```

The command ?* *lists all functions, commands, and defined variables but not arithmetic and other operators. However,* ?+ *will give help on +, for example.*

```
In[2]:= ?*
Abort
$Aborted
.
.
.
ZeroTest
Zeta
```

?topic	give information on *topic*
??topic	give all information on *topic*
??A*z	list names of commands and functions with names beginning with *A* and ending with *z*

0.3.8 Built-in Functions and Constants

Mathematica has an extensive library of built-in mathematical functions. Most are used as they would normally be written on paper, except that the function names are capitalized and square brackets are used around the argument instead of parentheses, as in Sin[x]. *Mathematica* also knows the standard mathematical constants **e**, π, and **i** $(= \sqrt{-1})$.

Built-in Mathematical Constants

Standard Notation	*Mathematica* Notation
e	Exp[1] or E
π	Pi
i	I or Sqrt[-1]

Mathematica recognizes the mathematical constant e as Exp[1] *and as* E.

```
In[1]:= Log[E]
Out[1]= 1
```

Mathematica is also aware of the number π.

```
In[2]:= Sin[Pi]
Out[2]=  0
```

Mathematica is aware of i (= √−1) as I.

```
In[3]:= I^2
Out[3]=  -1
```

0.3.9 Changing Assignments

Once a name is assigned a value, it can always be assigned a different value using the assignment operator (=). However, there are several special ways in which assignments are changed—and with sufficient frequency—that *Mathematica* offers special operators for those purposes. First, consider the need to unassign outdated variable names.

Here x is assigned the value 3 and y is assigned the value 5.

```
In[1]:=  x = 3
Out[1]= 3
In[2]:= y = 5
Out[2]= 5
```

This "unassigns" x with the =. operator.

```
In[3]:=  x =.
```

This unassigns y with the Clear *command. The command* Clear[x,y] *would have cleared the definitions of both x and y at the same time.*

```
In[4]:=  Clear[y]
```

We will use "unassign" and "clear" interchangeably. However, there are small differences between =. and Clear that will be explained later.

```
x =.                        unassign x
Clear[x₁,…,x₂]              unassign x₁, . . . , xₙ
```

It is a good idea to clear all variable names as soon as they are no longer needed. Another strategy is to clear any variable names immediately before using them; it is easy to forget that a variable is assigned and then misinterpret the meaning of a result.

Some Special Operators in *Mathematica*[2]

Some operators change the value of an assigned variable in particularly useful ways.

Here x is assigned the value 3.

```
In[1]:=  x = 3
Out[1]= 3
```

Here the value of x is incremented by 1 *with the ++ operator.*

```
In[2]:=  x++
Out[2]= 3
In[3]:=  x
Out[3]= 4
```

There is also a -- operator. It does what you would expect.

```
In[4]:=  x--
Out[4]= 4
In[5]:=  x
Out[5]= 3
```

Here 2 is added to the value of x.

```
In[6]:=  x += 2
Out[6]= 5
```

This subtracts 3 from the value of x.

```
In[7]:=  x -= 3
Out[7]= 2
```

This multiplies the value of x by 4.

```
In[8]:=  x *= 4
Out[8]= 8
```

This divides the value of x by 2.

```
In[9]:=  x /= 2
Out[9]= 4
```

The operators ++, --, +=, -=, *=, and /= can be applied only to an assigned variable. Attempting to apply them to an unassigned variable results in an error message.

---

[2]This optional section is intended mostly for those who enjoy programming with compact code, as in the programming language C.

Here ++ is applied to an
unassigned variable.

```
In[1]:=   x++
Increment::rvalue:
        x has not been assigned a value.
```

x++	increment the value of x by 1
x--	decrement the value of x by 1
x += k	increment the value of x by k
x -= k	decrement the value of x by k
x *= k	multiply the value of x by k
x /= k	divide the value of x by k

0.3.10 Delayed Assignments

In addition to the assignment operator (=), there is also a delayed assignment operator (:=).

   If, following the assignment of a numerical value to a variable x, you then use the assignment operator = to assign y the value of an expression that involves x, then the value of y is unchanged by a later change in the value of x.[3] The variable y keeps the value of the expression *at the time of the assignment.* For this reason, = is sometimes called the *immediate assignment operator.* If, on the other hand, you use := to assign y the value of an expression that involves x, then the value of y *is* changed by a change in the value of x. In fact, if := is used in the assignment of y, then the value of y is calculated each and every time the name is used, and the current value of x is used in the calculation.

Here "=" is used to
assign x.

```
In[1]:= x = 1
Out[1]= 1
```

Here ":=" is used to assign
y *a value that depends on*
x. *Note that there is no*
output.

```
In[2]:=   y := x^2 + 1
```

Note the effect of changing
the value of x.

```
In[3]:= y
Out[3]= 2
In[4]:= x = 0
Out[4]=   0
In[5]:= y
Out[5]= 1
```

[3]Note that this statement assumes that x is assigned a value before y is assigned a value.

Use the delayed assignment operator with care.

Here the value of y *changes*
with every input.

```
In[1]:= 5
Out[1]= 5
In[2]:= y := %
```

The value of y *is now* 5.

```
In[3]:= y
Out[3]= 5
```

This changes the reference
of %.

```
In[4]:= 2
Out[4]= 2
```

The value of y *is now* 2.

```
In[5]:= y
Out[5]= 2
```

y = x	immediately give *y* the value of *x*
y := x	evaluate *y* each time it is used, using the current value of *x*.

A note of caution: If the assignment y = x is made before x has been as-signed a value, then y will change with x, much as if y := x had been used.

0.3.11 Extending *Mathematica*

When you assign a name in *Mathematica*, you extend the domain of things known to the program in a useful but rather minor fashion. *Mathematica* also allows you to make more substantial extensions, particularly by defining new functions.

Although *Mathematica* has an extensive library of built-in functions, it does not have every function you might want. For example, simple functions such as $f(x) = x^2 + 1$ are not built in.

A function such as $f(x) = x^2+1$ is called an *expression-based function* be-cause its definition involves evaluation of the same expression regardless of the value of *x*. Compare this with the function

$$g(x) = \begin{cases} x^2 & \text{if } x < 2 \\ x & \text{otherwise} \end{cases}$$

where the rule applied to *x* depends on the value of *x*.

Mathematica has an easy way for you to define new expression-based functions.

This defines the function $f(x) = x^2 + 1$. *Here it is necessary to use* x_ *on the left side of the assignment operator to tell Mathematica that* x *is the variable.*

```
In[1]:= f[x_] = x^2+1
Out[1]= x^2 + 1
```

This evaluates f at $x = -1$ *and at* $x = 2$.

```
In[2]:= f[-1]
Out[2]= 2
In[3]:= f[2]
Out[3]= 5
```

Note that you can use ? *to get information about functions you define as well as built-in functions.*

```
In[4]:= ?f
Global `f
f[x_] = 1 + x^2
```

Alternatively, you can define functions with *Mathematica*'s Function command.

This uses the Function *command to define the function* $f(x) = x^3 - 3$, *and then evaluates f at* $x = 1$.

```
In[1]:= f = Function[x, x^3 - 3]
Out[1]= Function[x, x^3 - 3]
In[2]:= f[1]
Out[2]= -2
```

The general form for a function of one variable is

Function[variable, *rule*]

For a function of two variables, you would use the form Function[{var$_1$,var$_2$}, *rule*], and so on. Use ?Function in a *Mathematica* session for more information.

It is not necessary to name functions to use them. Unnamed functions are called *pure functions* in *Mathematica*. Here is a sample application of a pure function.

Here the square function is applied to the set {2,3,4}.[4]

```
In[1]:= Function[x, x^2][{2,3,4}]
Out[1]= {4, 9, 16}
```

It is also possible to define pure functions without using the Function command. The notation is unusual but quite useful. In the following example,

---

[4]*Mathematica*'s data types are explained in Section 0.3.17.

#1 refers to the first variable. If there were more variables, they would be denoted #2, #3, and so forth. You can use # instead of #1 but not ## instead of #2.

Here the cube function is applied to each of 2, 3, *and* 4. *The* & *is necessary with the* # *notation.*

```
In[1]:= (#1^3)&[{2,3,4}]
Out[1]= {8, 27, 64}
```

---

f[x_] = *rule*
    define the function $f(x)$

f = Function[x, *rule*]
    define the function $f(x)$

f = Function[{x, y}, *rule*]
    define the function $f(x,y)$[5]

Function[{x}, *rule*][z]
    Applies *rule* to z

rule &[z]
    applies *rule* to z

0.3.12 Branching and Multipart Functions

You also can define functions that are not based on a single rule, as demonstrated in the following.

This defines the function

$$f(x) = \begin{cases} x^3 & if\ x < 2 \\ x^2 & otherwise \end{cases}.$$

The function rule is: If $x < 2$ *(the first entry in the* If *part), then use* x^3 *(the second entry in the* If *part); otherwise, use* x^2 *(the third entry in the* If *part).*

```
In[1]:= f[x_] := If[x<2,x^3,x^2]
In[2]:= f[-2]
Out[2]= -8
In[3]:= f[3]
Out[3]= 9
```

---

[5]Type ?Function for more information on the Function command.

The `If` command has the general form

`If[test, if_test_true, if_test_false]`

Generally, *test* checks the value of the variable to see what rule to apply. In the test, the following relations are frequently used.

Standard Notation	Mathematica Notation
$x > k$	`x > k`
$x \geq k$	`x >= k`
$x < k$	`x < k`
$x \leq k$	`x <= k`
$x = k$	`x == k`

Mathematica's `Which` command is even more versatile than `If` for defining multipart functions.

`Which` *makes it easy to define functions with several part definitions. This defines the function*

$$g(x) = \begin{cases} x^3 & \text{if } x < 0 \\ 5 & \text{if } x = 0 \\ x^2 & \text{otherwise} \end{cases} .$$

```
In[1]:= g[x_] := Which[x<0,x^3,x==0,5,x>0,x^2]
In[2]:= g[-2]
Out[2]= -8
In[3]:= g[0]
Out[3]= 5
In[4]:= g[3]
Out[4]= 9
```

The `Which` command has the general form

`Which[test_1, action_1, ..., test_k, action_k]`

Use `If` to define a two-part function.
Use `Which` to define a multipart function.

0.3.13 Equations

In *Mathematica*, an equation is two expressions with two equal signs (==) between them. If both sides of the equation have numerical values, the equation evaluates to either `True` or `False`. If the left side of the equation involves an unassigned variable, the equation is not evaluated by *Mathematica*.

Mathematica has routines that solve many types of equations. Its most basic equation solver is called `Solve`. The `Solve` command returns exact solutions. It returns all exact solutions that it finds, but it may not always find all possible solutions and sometimes reports extraneous solutions.

Here the Solve *command solves the equation* $2x + 3 = 5$ *for x. Note the form of the solution.*

```
In[1]:= Solve[2 x + 3 == 5, x]
Out[1]= {{x -> 1}}
```

Here Solve *is used to find the roots of a quadratic equation. Mathematica reports both solutions.*

```
In[2]:= Solve[x^2 - 3 x + 1 == 0, x]
```
$$Out[2]= \{\{x \to \frac{3 + \text{Sqrt}[5]}{2}\},$$
$$\{x \to \frac{3 - \text{Sqrt}[5]}{2}\}$$

Here Solve *is used to solve the equation* $\sin(x) = 0$ *for x. Only the value* 0 *is returned. This time a warning is issued.*

```
In[3]:= Solve[Sin[x] == 0, x]
Solve::ifun:
    Warning: Inverse functions are
being used by Solve, so some solutions
may not be found.
Out[3]= {{x -> 0}}
```

In this case, Mathematica returns an answer that begs the question. (There are no rules or formulas for the roots of a polynomial degree six or greater.)

```
In[4]:= Solve[x^6 - x - 1 == 0, x]
```
$$Out[4]= \{\text{ToRules}[\text{Roots}[-x + x^6 == 1, x]]\}$$

Solve[*expr*$_1$ == *expr*$_2$, x]
    solve *expr*$_1$ = *expr*$_2$ for *x*

0.3.14 Approximate Solutions

Sometimes *exact* answers are not possible, and sometimes the expression of an answer in exact form is so complicated that a decimal approximation is more desirable. *Mathematica has facilities to help in both cases.*

  Mathematica has a number of built-in numerical routines for obtaining approximate solutions. For example, you can use NSolve to obtain a numerical approximation of the solution to an equation.

Use NSolve *to obtain an approximate solution.*

```
In[1]:= NSolve[x^6 - x - 1 == 0, x]
```

Note that both real and
complex approximate
solutions are reported.

```
Out[1]=
  {{x -> -0.77809},
   {x -> -0.629372 - 0.735756 I},
   {x -> -0.629372 + 0.735756 I},
   {x -> 0.451055 - 1.00236 I},
   {x -> 0.451055 + 1.00236 I},
   {x -> 1.13472}}
```

For a more detailed description of the options you can use with NSolve, enter ??NSolve.

> NSolve[*expr$_1$* == *expr$_2$*, x]
>   numerically solve *expr$_1$* = *expr$_2$* for *x*

Mathematica's N command converts expressions to decimal form. This often allows you to get an approximate answer if there is no satisfactory exact answer.

Here Mathematica fails to
find an exact solution to
$x^5 - 2x + 3 = 0$. The N
command is then used to
convert the response to an
approximate solution.

```
In[1]:= Solve[x^5 - 2 x + 3 == 0, x]
Out[1]= {ToRules[Roots[-2 x + x^5 == -3, x]]}

In[2]:= N[%]
Out[2]=
  {{x -> -1.42361},
   {x -> -0.246729 - 1.32082 I},
   {x -> -0.246729 + 1.32082 I},
   {x -> 0.958532 - 0.498428 I},
   {x -> 0.958532 + 0.498428 I}}
```

Any numeric expression can be converted to a floating-point approximation in *Mathematica* using the N command.

Here N *is used in postfix*
notation to get a decimal
approximation of π.

```
In[1]:= Pi//N
Out[1]= 3.14159
```

You can also specify the
number of digits for a
particular calculation. Note
Mathematica's use of the
backslash (\ ) to indicate
continuation of the output.

```
In[2]:= N[Pi, 100]
Out[2]=
3.1415926535897932384626433832795028841971169\
   9937510582097494459230781640628620899862\
   8034825342117068
```

Many functions work in approximate mode when applied to expressions in decimal form.

Here N *(used in postfix notation) converts the polynomial to decimal form, and then* Solve *returns an approximate solution.*

```
In[1]:= Solve[x^5 - 2 x + 3 == 0//N, x]
Out[1]=
{{x -> -1.42361},
  {x -> -0.246729 - 1.32082 I},
  {x -> -0.246729 + 1.32082 I},
  {x -> 0.958532 - 0.498428 I},
  {x -> 0.958532 + 0.498428 I}}
```

NSolve[*expr*₁ == *expr*₂]
    give an approximate solution of $expr_1 = expr_2$

N[*expr*]
    give a numerical approximation of *expr*

N[*expr*, n]
    give an *n*-digit numerical approximation of *expr*

expr//N
    give a numerical approximation of *expr*

0.3.15 Calculus with *Mathematica*

If you have not previously used *Mathematica*, you may be surprised by its ability to solve calculus problems. There are many interesting problems that involve both calculus and linear algebra.

This is the Mathematica equivalent of $\frac{d}{dx}\sin(x)$.

```
In[1]:= D[Sin[x], x]
Out[1]= Cos[x]
```

This computes the second derivative of $\sin(x)$.

```
In[2]:= D[Sin[x], {x, 2}]
Out[2]= -Sin[x]
```

You also can use the prime notation for derivatives.

```
In[3]:= Sin'[x]
Out[3]= Cos[x]
```

This computes the second derivative.

```
In[4]:= Sin''[x]
Out[4]= -Sin[x]
```

This is the Mathematica equivalent of $\int \cos(x) dx$.

```
In[5]:= Integrate[Cos[x], x]
Out[5]= Sin[x]
```

Here is an example that shows more of Mathematica's power.

```
In[6]:= Integrate[1/(x^3 + 1), x]
```

$$Out[6]= \frac{\text{ArcTan}[\frac{-1 + 2x}{\text{Sqrt}[3]}]}{\text{Sqrt}[3]}$$

$$+ \frac{\text{Log}[1 + x]}{3} - \frac{\text{Log}[1 - x + x^2]}{6}$$

This evaluates the definite integral $\int_{1}^{e} \frac{1}{x} dx$.

```
In[7]:= Integrate[1/x, {x, 1, E}]
Out[7]= 1
```

Integrate[*expr*, x]
    give an antiderivative of *expr* with respect to *x*

Integrate[f, {x, a, b}]
    evaluate $\int_{a}^{b} f(x) dx$

D[y, x]
    evaluate $\dfrac{dy}{dx}$

D[y, {x, n}]
    evaluate $\dfrac{d^n y}{dx^n}$

F'[x]
    evaluate f'(x)

If you ever solve differential equations, you will appreciate *Mathematica*'s DSolve command.

This solves the differential equation $f''(x) - f(x) = 0$. Here C[1] and C[2] are arbitrary constants.

```
In[1]:= DSolve[f''[x] - f[x] == 0, f[x], x]
```

$$Out[1]= \{\{f[x] \to \frac{C[1]}{E^x} + E^x C[2]\}\}$$

This solves the initial-value problem $f'(x) = f(x)$, $f(0) = 3$.

```
In[2]:= DSolve[{D[f[x], x] - f[x] == 0,
  f[0] == 3}, f[x], x]
Out[2]= {{f[x] -> 3 E^x}}
```

DSolve[*expr*$_1$ == *expr*$_2$, f[x], x]
   solve the differential equation *expr*$_1$== *expr*$_2$

DSolve[{*expr*$_1$ == *expr*$_2$, f[a]==b}, f[x], x]
   solve the initial-value problem *expr*$_1$ = *expr*$_2$
   for $f(x)$ with $f(a) = b$

0.3.16 Graphing in *Mathematica*

It is often helpful to get a picture of the problem you are trying to solve. *Mathematica* can assist in this regard by drawing graphs of mathematical expressions.

This is the command to generate the graph of the equation $y = x^3 - x + 1$ for x in the interval [−10,10].

```
In[1]:= Plot[x^3 - x + 1, {x, -10, 10}]
```

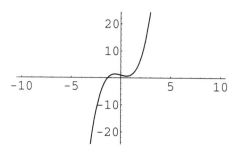

```
Out[1]= -Graphics-
```

This graphs the same equation on the interval [−2, 2]. Notice how this clarifies some of the key features of the graph (see the following page).

```
In[2]:= Plot[x^3 - x + 1, {x, -2, 2 }]
```

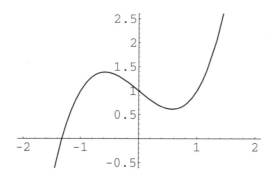

Out[2]= -Graphics-

This generates a three-dimensional plot of $z = \sin(x) + \cos(y)$ for x and y in the interval $[-\pi, \pi]$.

In[3]:= Plot3D[Sin[x] + Cos[y],
{x, -Pi, Pi}, {y, -Pi, Pi}]

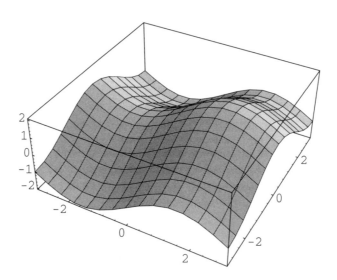

Out[3]= -SurfaceGraphics-

```
Plot[expr, {x, a, b}]
    graph y = expr on the interval a ≤ x ≤ b

Plot3D[expr, {x, a, b}, {y, c, d}]
    graph z = expr on the intervals a ≤ x ≤ b, c ≤ y ≤ d
```

0.3.17 Object Types in *Mathematica*

Mathematica can work with many different types of objects; functions, symbols, exact numbers, decimal numbers, graphs, and equations are just a few. Some other important types of objects *Mathematica* uses are illustrated here.

L[1] *and L*[2] *are lists, one of the most basic data types in Mathematica. Lists are used in many commands. Notice that Mathematica does not remove the redundant entries and that the order of the entries is maintained as given.*

```
In[1]:= L[1] = {1, 1, 2, 2, x, y, z}
Out[1]= {1, 1, 2, 2, x, y, z}
In[2]:= L[2] = {1, 1, 3, 4, w, x}
Out[2]= {1, 1, 3, 4, w, x}
```

Lists are also used as sets. Here the intersection L[1] ∩ *L*[2] *is calculated.*[6] *Any redundant entries are removed by this calculation.*

```
In[3]:= Intersection[L[1], L[2]]
Out[3]= {1, x}
```

Here the set union L[1] ∪ *L*[2] *is computed.* Union *also removes redundant entries.*

```
In[4]:= Union[L[1], L[2]]
Out[4]= {1, 2, 3, 4, w, x, y, z}
```

The empty set is denoted by {}.

```
In[5]:= Intersection[{1, 2}, {3, 4}]
Out[5]= {}
```

The Join *command is similar to* Union *but preserves order and repeated entries.*

```
In[6]:= Join[{3, 2, 1}, {1, 2, 3}]
Out[6]= {3, 2, 1, 1, 2, 3}
```

---

[6]You also can use L[1]~Union~L[2] for the union and L[1]~Intersection~L[2] for the intersection.

You can use Union *or* Intersection *on a list to remove the repeated entries.*

```
In[7]:= Union[%]
Out[7]= {1, 2, 3}
```

Most built-in functions distribute over lists. Applying sine *to the list L applies it to each of the entries in L.*

```
In[8]:= S = {0, Pi/4, Pi/2, 3 Pi/4, Pi}
```

$Out[8]= \{0, \dfrac{Pi}{4}, \dfrac{Pi}{2}, \dfrac{3Pi}{4}, Pi\}$

```
In[9]:= Sin[S]
```

$Out[9]= \{0, \dfrac{1}{Sqrt[2]}, 1, \dfrac{1}{Sqrt[2]}, 0\}$

L[[i]] *denotes the i*th *element of a list L. Recall that* % *refers to the previous result, in this case to* Out[9].

```
In[10]:= %[[2]]
```

$Out[10]= \dfrac{1}{Sqrt[2]}$

Multiplication by numbers and unassigned variables distributes over lists. The same is true for division.

```
In[11]:= k{a, b, c}
Out[11] = {a k, b k, c k}
```

```
In[12]:= {a, b, c}/k
```

$Out[12]= \{\dfrac{a}{k}, \dfrac{b}{k}, \dfrac{c}{k}\}$

The sum of two lists is the list of sums. The analogous statement is true for products, quotients, and powers.

```
In[13]:=  {a, b, c} + {d, e, f}
Out[13]= {a + d, b + e, c + f}
```

Sometimes lists of lists are useful. This sets up a table of selected values of the sine function.

```
In[14]:= A = {S,Sin[S]}
```

$Out[14]= \{\{0, \dfrac{Pi}{4}, \dfrac{Pi}{2}, \dfrac{3Pi}{4}, Pi\},$

$\{0, \dfrac{1}{Sqrt[2]}, 1, \dfrac{1}{Sqrt[2]}, 0\}\}$

You can use MatrixForm *to format the output into a more readable form.*

```
In[15]:= MatrixForm[A]
Out[15]//MatrixForm=
```

$$\begin{matrix} 0 & \dfrac{Pi}{4} & \dfrac{Pi}{2} & \dfrac{3Pi}{4} & Pi \\ 0 & \dfrac{1}{Sqrt[2]} & 1 & \dfrac{1}{Sqrt[2]} & 0 \end{matrix}$$

Length *counts the number of terms in a list.*

```
In[16]:= Length[A]
Out[16]= {2}
```

Dimensions *gives all dimensions of a multi-dimensional array.*

```
In[17]:= Dimensions[A]
Out[17]= {2, 5}
```

A[[i,j]] *denotes the entry in the i*th *row and j*th *column of the rectangular array A.*

```
In[[18]]:= A[[1, 2]]
```

$$Out[18]= \frac{Pi}{4}$$

You can use Flatten *to change a list of lists into a simple list.*

```
In[19]:=  Flatten[A]
Out[19]=
```

$$\{0, \frac{Pi}{4}, \frac{Pi}{2}, \frac{3Pi}{4}, Pi, 0, \frac{1}{Sqrt[2]}, 1, \frac{1}{Sqrt[2]}, 0\}$$

Partition *is the opposite of* Flatten.

```
In[20]:= Partition[%, 5]
Out[20]=
```

$$\{\{0, \frac{Pi}{4}, \frac{Pi}{2}, \frac{3Pi}{4}, Pi\},$$

$$\{0, \frac{1}{Sqrt[2]}, 1, \frac{1}{Sqrt[2]}, 0\}\}$$

`L = {a,b,c}`	assign the list {a,b,c} the name L
`list[[n]]`	the nth element of *list*
`Length[list]`	give the length of *list*
`Dimensions[list]`	give the dimensions of *list*
`MatrixForm[A]`	print A in matrix form
`TableForm[A]`	print A in table form[7]

0.3.18 Substitution and Replacement

In mathematics, it is frequently desirable to substitute one quantity for another, perhaps to simplify an expression or for other reasons—such as to obtain a definite integral from an antiderivative. Substitution is called *replacement* in

---

[7]Roughly the same as MatrixForm. MatrixForm uses uniform horizontal spacing, which can force line folding if there is a long term. TableForm may help organize the data in such cases.

Mathematica. The replacement operator is "slash-period" (/ .). In use, the / . operator is followed by a list of replacement rules $\{x_1 \rightarrow a_1, \ldots, x_n \rightarrow a_n\}$ to be applied to the expression. The minus and greater than characters are used to form the composite arrow-like character "->".[8]

This gives

$$\int_a^b (x^2 - 1)dx.$$

```
In[1]:= F = Integrate[x^2 - 1, {x, a, b}]
```

$$Out[1]= a - \frac{a^3}{3} - b + \frac{b^3}{3}$$

This replaces a by 1 *and b by* 2 *to give*

$$\int_1^2 (x^2 - 1)dx.$$

```
In[2]:= F/.{a -> 1, b -> 2}
```

$$Out[2]= \frac{4}{3}$$

0.3.19 Automating Repetitive Procedures: Loops

It is often necessary to repeat the same operation on a sequence of objects. Loops provide the mechanism needed to automate the process, and *Mathematica* provides several forms of loops. One of the principal forms is

```
Do[expr, {index, indexmin, indexmax}]
```

Here, `index`, `indexmin`, and `indexmax` are integers. In this case, *expr* is evaluated once for each integer value of `index` from `indexmin` to `indexmax`. This is called a Do loop. If `indexmin` = 1, you can also use the shorter form

```
Do[expr, {index, indexmax}]
```

Consider the following example.

This simple loop prints each of the first five natural numbers. In this case, the index is i, `indexmin` *and* `indexmax` = 5.

```
In[1]:= Do[Print[i], {i, 1, 5}]
1
2
3
4
5
```

Another useful form of the loop, called a For loop, is the following.

```
For[index = start,
test,
index = index + incr,
what_to_do]
```

---

[8]If only one replacement rule is given, it need not be enclosed in braces.

where `index` is a counter (*i, j, m,* and *n* are common choices), `indexmin` is the beginning value of `index`, and `incr` is the amount by which `index` is incremented on each pass through the loop. The loop will terminate (and `what_to_do` will not be executed) the first time `test` evaluates to `False`. If `incr = 1`, you can use `index++` in place of `index + incr`. It should be noted that For loops leave the index with an assigned value when the loop is terminated.

Consider the following simple example.

This simple loop prints each of the first three odd numbers and their squares. In this case, `index` *is i,* `indexmin` *is 1,* `incr` *is 2, and* `test` *is i ≤ 5.*

```
In[1]:= For[i = 1, i <= 5, i = i + 2, Print[i, "   ",
i^2]]
1   1
3   9
5   25
```

The index[9] is left with the value 7.

```
In[2]:= i
Out[2]= 7
```

It is a good habit to unassign variables if the assignment is no longer needed. The index `i` *is unassigned here.*

```
In[3]:= i =.
```

```
For[start, test, incr, body]
    beginning with start, repeat the sequence
        execute body and increment the counter
    until test fails

Do[expr, {i, imax}]
    beginning with i = 1, repeat the sequence
        evaluate expr and increment i by 1
    until imax is reached

Do[expr, {i, imin, imax}]
    beginning with i = imin repeat the sequence
        evaluate expr and increment i by 1
    until imax is reached
```

[9]The index is sometimes called the counter.

0.3.20 Sums and Products

Mathematica has special commands for generating sums and products from formulas.

This computes $\displaystyle\sum_{i=1}^{10} i!$, *the sum of the factorials of the first ten natural numbers.*

```
In[1]:= Sum[i!, {i, 1, 10}]
Out[1]= 4037913
```

This gives $\displaystyle\prod_{j=1}^{10} 2i$, *the product of the first ten even natural numbers.*

```
In[2]:= Product[2i, {i, 1, 10}]
Out[2]= 3715891200
```

> Sum[*expr*,{i,imin,imax}]
>   sum the values of *expr* for $i = imin$ to $i = imax$
>
> Product[*expr*,{i,imin,imax}]
>   multiply the values of *expr* for $i = imin$ to $i = imax$

0.3.21 Simplification and Evaluation

In Section 0.3.1, the Simplify command was used to force cancellation of a common factor in the numerator and denominator of a quotient. As this demonstrates, *Mathematica* does not always reduce expressions to their simplest form. There are a number of reasons for this: one is to save time when simplification is not required; another is that sometimes it is not clear what is desired or how to proceed.

Because expressions are not always put in a simplified or standard form, *Mathematica* has a number of special-purpose commands that can be used to change the form of an answer. You have already seen Simplify used. Here is a list of some other commands you may find particularly useful.

> Expand[*expr*]   expand *expr*
> Factor[*expr*]   factor *expr*
> N[*expr*]   evaluate approximation of *expr*
> Simplify[*expr*]   write *expr* with as few terms as possible
> Together[*expr*]   write *expr* in the form $\dfrac{numer}{denom}$

Use the help system for more detailed information.

0.3.22 Parts of Things

Mathematical expressions have parts: a product has factors, a sum has summands, a fraction has a numerator and a denominator, a list has entries, and so on. Parts of expressions are addressed in a uniform way in *Mathematica*. If *expr* is an expression (and everything is an expresson in *Mathematica*), then *expr* [[i]] is the *i*th part of *expr*. The *j*th part of the *i*th part of *expr* (if it exists) can be addressed either as *expr*[[i]][[j]] or as *expr*[[i,j]].

    Consider the list A = {{1, 2, 3}, {2, 3, 4}}. It has two parts, each of which has three parts. A[[i]] is the *i*th part of A and A[[i,j]] is the *j*th part of the *i*th part.

Define A.	```In[1]:= A = {{1, 2, 3}, {2, 3, 4}}``` ```Out[1]= {{1, 2, 3,}, {2, 3, 4}}```
A[[2]] *is the second part of A.*	```In[2]:= A[[2]]``` ```Out[2]= {2, 3, 4}```
A[[2, 3]] *is the third part of the second part of A.*	```In[3]:= A[[2, 3]]``` ```Out[3]= 4```
A[[2, {1, 3}]] *gives the first and third parts of the second part of A.*	```In[4]:= A[[2, {1, 3}]]``` ```Out[4]= {2, 4}```

Now consider the sum $S = a\,b\,c + d\,e\,f$.

Define S.	```In[1]:= S = a b c + d e f``` ```Out[1]= a b c + d e f```
S[[2]] *is the second part of S.*	```In[2]:= S[[2]]``` ```Out[2]= d e f```
S[[2, 3]] *is the third part of the second part of S.*	```In[3]:= S[[2, 3]]``` ```Out[3]= f```
S[[2, {1, 3}]] *gives the first and third parts of the second part of S.*	```In[4]:= S[[2, {1, 3}]]``` ```Out[4]= d f```

The FullForm command shows you how *Mathematica* has stored an expression internally. Consider the quotient $Q = a/b$. Quotients are stored internally by *Mathematica* as products.

Define q.	```In[1]:= q = a/b``` $Out[1]= \dfrac{a}{b}$

This shows how Math-
ematica has stored the
quotient internally. It has
the form a b⁻¹.

```
In[2]:= FullForm[q]
Out[2]FullForm= Times[a, Power[b, -1]]
```

The numerator of q is $q[[1]]$ and its denominator is $q[[2,1]]$. However, it is easier to access the parts of a quotient q with the Numerator and Denominator commands.

This gives the numerator
of q.

```
In[3]:= Numerator[q]
Out[3]= a
```

This gives the denominator
of q.

```
In[4]:= Denominator[q]
Out[4]= b
```

When working with a polynomial $p = a_n x^n + \cdots + a_1 x + a_0$, it is often convenient to address the coefficient of a particular power of x. This can be done by picking out the parts; however, it is more convenient to use *Mathematica*'s Coefficient command.

Define p.

```
In[1]:= p = 2 - 7 x^3 + 11 x^5
Out[1]= 2 - 7 x³ + 11 x⁵
```

This gives the coefficient
of x^3.

```
In[2]:= Coefficient[p, x, 3]
Out[2]= -7
```

Here is another example that arises when solving equations.

Solve the equation
$2x + 3 = 5$.

```
In[1]:= Solve[2 x + 3 == 5, x]
Out[1]= {{x -> 1}}
```

This assigns s the value
returned by Solve.
%[[1, 1, 2]] *is the*
second part of x -> 1,
which is the first part of
{x -> 1}, *which is the*
first part of %.

```
In[2]:= s = %[[1, 1, 2]]
Out[2]= 1
```

This uses replacement in
combination with part
selection to assign s the
value returned by Solve.

```
In[3]:= s = x /. %1[[1]]
Out[3]=  1
```

---

expr[[i]]
 the *i*th part of *expr*

expr[[i, j]]
 the *j*th part of the *i*th part of *expr*

Numerator[q]
 the numerator of a quotient q

Denominator[q]
 the denominator of a quotient q

Coefficient[p, x, i]
 The coefficient of x^i in p

0.3.23 Quitting a *Mathematica* Session

You end the session with the
Quit *command.*

In[1]:= Quit

Quit   quits the *Mathematica* session

  This "tour" has touched on only the basic capabilities of *Mathematica*. For further reading of a general nature, refer to the book *Mathematica: A System for Doing Mathematics by Computer* by Stephen Wolfram.[10]

EXERCISES _____

Use the examples in the "tour" and the *Mathematica* help system to guide you in the following.
1. a. Compute the sum *s* and product *p* of the first 20 odd integers. (Note that an odd integer is of the form $2n + 1$.)
  b. Compute the quotient *s*/*p* and the power p^s. (You will have to wait for *Mathematica* to complete the latter calculation.)
  c. Try to compute s^p.
  d. Unassign the variables *s* and *p*.

2. Differentiate and integrate the quotient $\dfrac{1}{(x^2 + 1)^2}$.

---

[10]Stephen Wolfram, *Mathematica: A System for Doing Mathematics by Computer*, 2nd ed. (New York: Addison-Wesley, 1991).

3. Plot the equation $y = \dfrac{1}{(x^2 + 1)^2}$ for x in the interval $[-5, 5]$.

4. By experimentation, determine the smallest integer n for which $n! > 10^n$. (You may be able to put loops to good use here.)

5. The function $\gamma(x) = \int\limits_{0}^{\infty} e^{-t} t^{x-1} dt$ is a built-in *Mathematica* function, denoted Gamma[x]. Compare $\gamma(n)$ to $(n - 1)!$ for several values of n. What do you guess the relation is between the two? Use a loop to verify your guess for $n = 1, \ldots, 50$.

6. a. Assign the value 20! to the variable fact.
    b. Assign the number of seconds in a billion years to the variable time.
    c. Compute the ratio fact/time.
    d. Unassign the variables fact and time.

7. Define the function $f(x) = x^3 - 3x + 1124$ and evaluate it at $x = -1234$, $-123, -12, 0, 12, 123, 1234$.

8. Define the function $g(x) = \dfrac{x^3 - x + 2}{x^5 - 3x + 27}$ and graph it over the interval $[-10, 10]$. Estimate the vertical asymptotes and the local maxima and minima.

9. Use the Plot3D command to plot the graph of the expression 4 sin(4x) + 10 cos(y) for x and y in $[-\pi, \pi]$. (Recall that π is denoted Pi in *Mathematica*.)

10. If you are so inclined, you can use the Unprotect command for some skullduggery. Unprotect Sum and assign the variable Sum the value Product. Enter the command Sum[i, {i, 0, 50}]. Do you know what happened? Can you now redefine Sum so you don't fall victim to your own dirty deed? (Fortunately, virtually all things you do in a *Mathematica* session—including this one—are forgotten when the session is ended.)

1 Matrices and Linear Systems

Beginning in this chapter, the keywords displayed in square brackets [...] immediately following a section head are *Mathematica* commands that are used for the first time in that section.

1.1 The Packages

```
[ << , LinearAlgebra`Master`, Remove]
```

Mathematica has a number of special-purpose "packages." There are several useful linear algebra commands made available to you with the command

```
<<LinearAlgebra`Master`
```

We will refer to this command as "loading the LinearAlgebra package." *Mathematica* will probably show no response to this command. If there is a response, read it carefully to determine whether the package was found. If the package was not found, carefully check your typing. Be sure what you have typed agrees completely with what is shown. Be sure you use back quotes (`` ` ``) (accent grave) around `Master` rather than the more common closed quote (').

A word of warning: Using a command from a package before you load the package can cause difficulties. See Exercise 10 of Section 1.2 if you get into this situation.

1.2 Matrices, Gaussian Elimination, and Row-Reduction

The great philosopher and mathematician René Descartes advocated a simple two-step strategy for the solution of problems:

1. Break the problem into solvable components.
2. Solve the components.

In linear algebra, a surprising number of problems can be broken into components that require the solution of a system of linear equations, giving special prominence to this rather elementary procedure. Solving systems of linear equations is a straightforward but time-consuming, error-prone task when done by hand. *Mathematica* can be very helpful to you here: It is quick and it does not make arithmetic errors.

A common strategy for solving a system of linear equations

$$
\begin{aligned}
a_{11}x_1 + a_{12}x_2 + \cdots + a_{1n}x_n &= b_1 \\
a_{21}x_1 + a_{22}x_2 + \cdots + a_{2n}x_n &= b_2 \\
&\ \ \vdots \\
a_{m1}x_1 + a_{m2}x_2 + \cdots + a_{mn}x_n &= b_m
\end{aligned}
$$

is to augment the coefficient matrix $A = [a_{ij}]$ by the array $B = [b_i]$ of constants to form the augmented matrix of the system

$$
[A, B] =
\begin{bmatrix}
a_{11} & a_{12} & . & . & . & a_{1n} & b_1 \\
a_{21} & a_{22} & . & . & . & a_{2n} & b_2 \\
 & & & . & & & \\
 & & & . & & & \\
 & & & . & & & \\
a_{m1} & a_{m2} & . & . & . & a_{mn} & b_m
\end{bmatrix}
$$

Then use Gaussian elimination (row-reduction) and back-substitution to obtain the solution.

You can follow this same strategy in *Mathematica*.

1.2.1 Manual Row-Reduction

`[AppendRows`[1]`, {}, =, +=, -=, *=, /=]`

Given the linear system

$$
\begin{aligned}
2x_1 + \quad x_2 + \quad 4x_3 &= \frac{41}{4} \\
3x_1 + \frac{3}{2}x_2 + \frac{34}{5}x_3 &= \frac{41}{12} \\
\frac{2}{3}x_2 + \quad 5x_3 &= \frac{35}{4}
\end{aligned}
\tag{1.2.1}
$$

you can form the augmented matrix of the system as follows.

In[1]:= `<<LinearAlgebra`Master` `

[1]This is one of the commands in the `LinearAlgebra` package.

Define the coefficient matrix A. In Mathematica, a matrix is a list of lists. The inner lists are the rows.

```
In[2]:= A =
    {{2, 1, 4},
     {3, 3/2, 34/5},
     {0, 2/3, 5}}
```

$$Out[2]= \{\{2, 1, 4\}, \{3, \frac{3}{2}, \frac{34}{5}\}, \{0, \frac{2}{3}, 5\}\}$$

Define the matrix B of constants.

```
In[3]:= B = {{41/4},{41/12},{35/4}}
```

$$Out[3]= \{\{\frac{41}{4}\}, \{\frac{41}{12}\}, \{\frac{35}{4}\}\}$$

Form the augmented matrix R with the `AppendRows` *command.*

```
In[4]:= R = AppendRows[A,B]
```

$$Out[4]= \{\{2, 1, 4, \frac{41}{4}\}, \{3, \frac{3}{2}, \frac{34}{5}, \frac{41}{12}\},$$

$$\{0, \frac{2}{3}, 5, \frac{35}{4}\}$$

Here we chose to use R for "reduction matrix." The value of R will change several times during the row-reduction.

You can step through the Gaussian elimination procedure manually.

Divide the first row by 2.[2] We denote this operation by "/=".[3]

```
In[5]:= R[[1]] = R[[1]] / 2; R
```

$$Out[5]= \{\{1, \frac{1}{2}, 2, \frac{41}{8}\}, \{3, \frac{3}{2}, \frac{34}{5}, \frac{41}{12}\},$$

$$\{0, \frac{2}{3}, 5, \frac{35}{4}\}\}$$

The semicolon following `R[[1]]/2` suppresses the output from the first command. The second command tells *Mathematica* to display the new value of R. The output format is not optimal, but you can see that 1 is now the (1,1) entry of R.

Replace the second row by the sum of row$_2$ and $-3 \times$ row$_1$ to zero the (2,1) entry. We denote this row operation by "+=".[4]

```
In[6]:= R[[2]] = R[[2]] - 3 R[[1]]; R
```

$$Out[6]= \{\{1, \frac{1}{2}, 2, \frac{41}{8}\}, \{0, 0, \frac{4}{5}, -(\frac{287}{24})\},$$

$$\{0, \frac{2}{3}, 5, \frac{35}{4}\}\}$$

Again, the semicolon is used to suppress the output of the row operation, and the new value of R is displayed.

---

[2]This would not work if R had been defined with the delayed assignment operator ":=".
[3]The command `R[[1]] /= 2` could be used here.
[4]You could use `R[[2]] += -3 R[[1]]` here.

Interchange the second and third rows of R. We denote this row operation by "={}". Note that the rows are listed on the right-hand side in their desired order.[5]

$In[7]:= R = R[[\{1,3,2\}]]$

$Out[7]= \{\{1, \frac{1}{2}, 2, \frac{41}{8}\}, \{0, \frac{2}{3}, 5, \frac{35}{4}\},$

$\{0, 0, \frac{4}{5}, -(\frac{287}{24})\}\}$

Continue until you reach row-echelon form.

$In[8]:= R[[2]] = 3/2\ R[[2]]; R$

$Out[8]= \{\{1, \frac{1}{2}, 2, \frac{41}{8}\}, \{0, 1, \frac{15}{2}, \frac{105}{8}\},$

$\{0, 0, \frac{4}{5}), -(\frac{287}{24})\}\}$

$In[9]:= R[[3]] = 5/4\ R[[3]]; R$

$Out[9]= \{\{1, \frac{1}{2}, 2, \frac{41}{8}\}, 0, 1, \frac{15}{2}, \frac{105}{8}\},$

$\{0, 0, 1, -(\frac{1435}{96})\}\}$

In standard matrix form,

$$R = \begin{bmatrix} 1 & \frac{1}{2} & 2 & \frac{41}{8} \\ 0 & 1 & \frac{15}{2} & \frac{105}{8} \\ 0 & 0 & 1 & -\frac{1435}{96} \end{bmatrix}$$

You now see that the original system is equivalent to the "upper triangular" system

$$x_1 + \frac{1}{2}x_2 + 2x_3 = \frac{41}{8}$$

$$x_2 + \frac{15}{2}x_3 = \frac{105}{8}$$

$$x_3 = -\frac{1435}{96}$$

Complete the solution with back-substitution, as follows.

[5]Alternatively, we could have used the command $\{R[[2]], R[[3]]\} = R[[\{3,2\}]]$. This approach is often more useful for large matrices.

The value of x_3 is obvious.

$In[10]:= \text{x[3]} = \text{R[[3,4]]}$

$Out[10]= -(\dfrac{1435}{96})$

This solves for x_2.

$In[11]:= \text{x[2]} = \text{R[[2,4]]} - 15/2 \text{ x[3]}$

$Out[11]= \dfrac{8015}{64}$

And this completes the solution.

$In[12]:= \text{x[1]} = \text{R[[1,4]]} - 1/2 \text{ x[2]} - 2 \text{ x[3]}$

$Out[12]= -(\dfrac{10597}{384})$

Here is a list of the solution values.

$In[13]:= \text{S} = \{\text{x[1]},\text{x[2]},\text{x[3]}\}$

$Out[13]= \{-(\dfrac{10597}{384}), \dfrac{8015}{64}, -(\dfrac{1435}{96})\}$

This verifies the solution for the first equation.

$In[14]:= \text{Print[Sum[A[[1,j]]x[j],\{j,1,3\}],}$
" ", B[[1,1]]]

$\dfrac{41}{4} \quad \dfrac{41}{4}$

The pair of spaces enclosed in double quotes is included in the `Print` command to separate the two values in the output. You can verify the second and third equations similarly.

The variables x_1, x_2, x_3 retain their values throughout the remainder of the session unless they are reassigned. We unassign them using the equal-dot operator (=.). `Clear` will not work with variable names such as `x[i]`.[6]

Unassign the variables.

$In[15]:= \text{x[1]} =. \text{ ; x[2]} =. \text{ ; x[3]} =. \text{ ;}$

A typical row-reduction of an $m \times n$ matrix requires approximately $\dfrac{m(m-1)}{2}$ applications of the "`+=`" operator, m applications of "`*=`", and few, if any, row interchanges. Most of the work is done using "`+=`".

1.2.2 Automated Row-Reduction
`[RowReduce, Do]`

In addition to the manual elementary row operations "`+=`", "`*=`", and "`={ }`" (for row interchanges), *Mathematica* also offers an automated procedure for row-reduction. The `RowReduce` command can be used to take a matrix to reduced row-echelon form.

---

[6]The command `Clear[x]` could be used.

Recall that a matrix F is in reduced row-echelon form if the following criteria are all satisfied.

1. The first nonzero entry of any row of F is a one (called the *leading one* of the row).
2. Above and below any leading one, all entries of F are zero.
3. If $i < j$, and if row_i and row_j do not consist entirely of zeros, then the leading one of row_i is to the left of the leading one of row_j.
4. All rows consisting entirely of zeros are grouped at the bottom of F.

Consider, once again, the linear system (1.2.1):

$$2x_1 + \quad x_2 + \quad 4x_3 = \frac{41}{4}$$

$$3x_1 + \frac{3}{2}x_2 + \frac{34}{5}x_3 = \frac{41}{12}$$

$$\frac{2}{3}x_2 + \quad 5x_3 = \frac{35}{4}$$

In Section 1.2.1 the matrix of the system was called R.

```
In[1] := M =
{{2,1,4,41/4},
{3,3/2,34/5,41/12},
{0,2/3,5,35/4}};
```

The RowReduce *command applies row operations to arrive at a matrix that is in reduced row-echelon form.*

```
In[2] := R = RowReduce[M]
```
$$Out[2]= \{\{1, \ 0, \ 0, \ -(\frac{10597}{384})\}, \ \{0, \ 1, \ 0, \ \frac{8015}{64}\},$$
$$\{0, \ 0, \ 1, \ -(\frac{1435}{96})\}\}$$

Note that the result is not quite the same as that obtained by row-reduction in the previous section, where row-reduction was stopped as soon as an echelon form was reached.

The situation is clearer if the result is displayed in matrix form.

```
In[3] := %//MatrixForm
Out[3]//Matrixform=
```

$$\begin{array}{cccc} 1 & 0 & 0 & -(\frac{10597}{384}) \\ 0 & 1 & 0 & \frac{8015}{64} \\ 0 & 0 & 1 & -(\frac{1435}{96}) \end{array}$$

The solution is now completely obvious. However, you may want to automate the assignment of the values to variables. This is especially helpful for larger matrices, though slightly more difficult in general than this case. Here is one strategy for doing this.

Make a list of the leading variables in the order you will solve for them.

```
In[4]:= v = {3,2,1}
Out[4]= {3, 2, 1}
```

Use back-substitution to complete the solution. This solves for x_3, then x_2, and finally x_1.[7]

```
In[5]:= Do[x[v[[i]]] = R[[v[[i]],4]], {i,1,3}]
```

Here is a list of the solution values. You can check this against the list of solutions found in Section 1.2.1.

```
In[6]:= S = {x[1],x[2],x[3]}
```
$$Out[6]= \{-(\frac{10597}{384}), \frac{8015}{64}, -(\frac{1435}{96})\}$$

Consider the following linear system. This provides an example in which there are nonleading variables, so back-substitution is less trivial.

$$-\frac{142}{35}x_1 \quad - \frac{284}{35}x_2 \quad + \frac{32}{5}x_3 \quad + \frac{194}{35}x_4 \quad = \frac{134}{35}$$
$$-\frac{3}{2}x_1 \quad - \quad 3x_2 \quad + \quad 2x_3 \quad + \frac{3}{2}x_4 \quad = \frac{1}{2} \qquad (1.2.2)$$
$$\frac{24}{7}x_1 \quad + \frac{48}{7}x_2 \quad - \quad 4x_3 \quad - \frac{18}{7}x_4 \quad = \frac{2}{7}$$

The augmented matrix of the system is

$$M = \begin{bmatrix} -\dfrac{142}{35} & -\dfrac{284}{35} & \dfrac{32}{5} & \dfrac{194}{35} & \dfrac{134}{35} \\ -\dfrac{3}{2} & -3 & 2 & \dfrac{3}{2} & \dfrac{1}{2} \\ \dfrac{24}{7} & \dfrac{48}{7} & -4 & -\dfrac{18}{7} & \dfrac{2}{7} \end{bmatrix}$$

Enter the matrix M. Notice that the output is generated by the command `M//MatrixForm`.[8]

```
In[1]:= M =
{{-142/35, -284/35, 32/5, 194/35, 134/35},
 {-3/2, -3, 2, 3/2, 1/2},
 {24/7, 48/7, -4, -18/7, 2/7}}; M//MatrixForm
```

[7]If there are nonleading variables, you need to solve for the leading variables.
[8]Note that `M = {{...},...,{...}}//MatrixForm` is not equivalent to `M = {{...},...{...}}; M//MatrixForm`. You may want to test this for yourself.

$Out[1] =$

$$-(\frac{142}{35}) \quad -(\frac{284}{35}) \quad \frac{32}{5} \quad \frac{194}{35} \quad \frac{134}{35}$$

$$-(\frac{3}{2}) \quad -3 \quad 2 \quad \frac{3}{2} \quad \frac{1}{2}$$

$$\frac{24}{7} \quad \frac{48}{7} \quad -4 \quad -(\frac{18}{7}) \quad \frac{2}{7}$$

Row-reduce M and display
the result.

$In[2] := R = RowReduce[M]; R//MatrixForm$
$Out[2] =$

$$1 \quad 2 \quad 0 \quad 1 \quad 3$$

$$0 \quad 0 \quad 1 \quad \frac{3}{2} \quad \frac{5}{2}$$

$$0 \quad 0 \quad 0 \quad 0 \quad 0$$

Parameterize the
nonleading variables x_2
and x_4.[9]

$In[3] := x[2] = t[2]; x[4] = t[4];$

Solve the equation

$$\sum_{j=1}^{4} x_j r_{2j} = r_{25} \text{ for } x_3, \text{ where}$$

$R = [r_{ij}]$, *and assign x_3 the*
value returned.

$In[4] := Sum[x[j] R[[2,j]], \{j,1,4\}] == R[[2,5]]$
$Out[4] = \frac{3\ t[4]}{2} + x[3] == \frac{5}{2}$

$In[5] := Solve[\%,x[3]]$
$Out[5] = \{\{x[3] \rightarrow \frac{-(-5 + 3\ t[4])}{2}\}\}$

$In[6] := x[3] = \%[[1,1,2]]$
$Out[6] = \frac{-(-5 + 3\ t[4])}{2}$

Solve the equation

$$\sum_{j=1}^{4} x_j r_{1j} = r_{15} \text{ for } x_1.$$

Here x_1 is assigned the
value returned by Solve *in*
one step.

$In[7] := Sum[x[j] R[[1,j]], \{j,1,4\}] == R[[1,5]]$
$Out[7] = 2\ t[2] + t[4] + x[1] == 3$

$In[8] := x[1] = Solve[\%,x[1]][[1,1,2]]$
$Out[8] = 3 - 2\ t[2] - t[4]$

[9]If you are not in a new session, you should clear *x* before proceeding.

It may be convenient to generate a list of the x values.

```
In[9]:= S = {x[1],x[2],x[3],x[4]}
Out[9]=
```

$$\{3 - 2\ t[2] - t[4],\ t[2],\ \frac{-(-5 + 3\ t[4])}{2},\ t[4]\}$$

The reduced row-echelon form of a matrix is often preferred over an arbitrary row-echelon form because of its uniqueness. Many matrices that are in row-echelon form can be obtained from R using elementary row operations, but only one matrix can be obtained that is in reduced row-echelon form. It is particularly easy to do manual back-substitution from reduced row-echelon form. On the other hand, many numerical analysts argue that it is more efficient to do only the forward elimination before applying back-substitution.

EXERCISES 1.2 _____

1. Use *Mathematica* to solve the linear system (1.2.1). Verify that the solution satisfies the three original equations.
2. Use *Mathematica* to solve the linear system (1.2.2). Verify that the solution satisfies the three original equations.

In Exercises 3–6, use *=, += , ={}, and back-substitution to solve the following systems with *Mathematica*. Verify your solutions.

3.
$$3x_2 - 4x_3 + \frac{5}{3}x_4 = \frac{23}{12}$$

$$2x_1 + 7x_2 + \frac{4}{3}x_3 + 3x_4 = \frac{41}{4}$$

$$\frac{1}{2}x_1 - 3x_2 + 2x_3 + \frac{13}{3}x_4 = \frac{41}{12}$$

$$\frac{7}{6}x_1 + \frac{7}{3}x_2 - \frac{14}{9}x_3 + 7x_4 = \frac{35}{4}$$

4.
$$\begin{aligned}
3x_1 + 2x_2 - 3x_3 + 4x_4 &= 5 \\
2x_1 + 7x_2 + 11x_3 - 3x_4 &= 41 \\
2x_1 - 5x_2 + 3x_3 + 5x_4 &= 12 \\
6x_1 + 3x_2 - 49x_3 + 2x_4 &= 34
\end{aligned}$$

5.
$$\begin{aligned}
3x_1 + 2x_2 - 3x_3 + 4x_4 &= 5 \\
2x_1 + 7x_2 + 11x_3 - 3x_4 &= 41
\end{aligned}$$

6.
$$\begin{aligned}
2x_1 + 3x_2 + 3x_3 - 2x_4 &= 3 \\
x_1 + 2x_2 + x_3 - x_4 &= 1 \\
4x_1 + 7x_2 + 5x_3 - 4x_4 &= 12
\end{aligned}$$

In Exercises 7–9, use row-reduction and back-substitution to solve the linear system with coefficient matrix A and constant matrix K.

7. $A = [a_{ij}]$ is the 3×5 matrix with $a_{ij} = (i + j)/j$ and $K = [k_{ij}]$ is the 3×1 matrix with $k_{ij} = 1$ for $i = 1, \ldots, 3$ and $j = 1$. Verify the solution.

8. $A = [a_{ij}]$ is the 5×4 matrix with $a_{ij} = i/j$ and $K = [k_{ij}]$ is the 5×1 matrix with $k_{ij} = i$ for $i = 1, \ldots, 5$ and $j = 1$.

9. $A = [a_{ij}]$ is the 4×6 matrix with $a_{ij} = \max(i, j)$ and $K = [k_{ij}]$ is the 4×1 matrix with $k_{ij} = i!$ for $i = 1, \ldots, 4$ and $j = 1$.

10. In a *Mathematica* session in which you have not loaded the `LinearAlgebra` package, enter the definitions `A = {{1,2}}` and `B = {{3,4}}`. Then enter the command `AppendRows[A,B]`. You will get the response `AppendRows[{{1, 2}, {3, 4}}]`, which is not what you wanted. The `AppendRows` command is defined in the `LinearAlgebra` package, to which *Mathematica* does not yet have access. Now enter the command

    `<<LinearAlgebra`Master`

    and reenter the command `AppendRows[A,B]`. Again, you get the response `AppendRows[{{1, 2}, {3, 4}}]`. The problem is that your use of `AppendRows` in your working context (usually `Global`) defined `AppendRows` in that context so that `AppendRows` simply refers to itself. To get yourself out of this dilemma, enter the command `Remove[AppendRows]`, which removes the definition from your current working context.[10] The next time you use the command, *Mathematica* will look beyond the current context for the command and find the definition you want in the `LinearAlgebra` package.

1.3 More on Matrices in *Mathematica*

Matrices are two-dimensional arrays so their entries are addressed by two subscripts, as in

$$A = \begin{bmatrix} a_{11} & a_{12} \\ a_{21} & a_{22} \end{bmatrix}$$

where a_{ij} denotes the entry in the ith row and jth column. In *Mathematica*, the (i, j) entry is denoted `A[[i,j]]`. This is sometimes called "computer subscript notation."

In Section 1.2, we used the form $A = \{\{a_{11}, \ldots, a_{1n}\}, \ldots, \{a_{m1}, \ldots, a_{mn}\}\}$ to define a matrix A as a list of lists. *Mathematica* provides two commands to

---

[10]The command `$Context` will return your current context. Use `?Context`, or see the *Mathematica* book for more information on the advanced topic of contexts.

assist you in defining matrices or other tables or arrays: the `Table` command and the `Array` command. Their use is summarized in the following.

- `Table[`*expr*`, {i, imin, imax}, {j, jmin, jmax}]`
- `Table[`*expr*`, {i, imax}, {j, jmax}]`
- `Array[`*function*`, {m, n}]`

The following demonstrates the use of these commands.[11]

This defines the 4×3 matrix

$$A = \begin{bmatrix} 11 & 12 & 13 \\ 21 & 22 & 23 \\ 31 & 32 & 33 \\ 41 & 42 & 43 \end{bmatrix}$$

using the `Table` *command.*

```
In[1]:= A = Table[10i+j, {i,4}, {j,3}]
Out[1]=
   {{11, 12, 13}, {21, 22, 23},
    {31, 32, 33}, {41, 42, 43}}
```

The first argument of `Table` is an expression in i and j. The second and third arguments give the bounds on i and j. The (i, j) entry is computed by evaluating the expression for all i and j in the specified bounds. If a range has the form $\{i, 1, m\}$ you can use $\{i, m\}$ in place of $\{i, 1, m\}$. However, the bounds on i and j do not have to be of the form $1, \ldots, m$ and $1, \ldots, n$, and variables other than i and j can be used.

Here is another example.

```
In[2]:= B = Table[r^2 - s^2, {r,-2,2}, {s,-1,1}]
Out[2]= {{3, 4, 3},
   {0, 1, 0},
   {-1, 0, -1},
   {0, 1, 0},
   {3, 4, 3}}
```

The entries of B are addressed as `B[[i,j]]` for $1 \le i \le 5$ and $1 \le j \le 3$.

The `Array` command uses a function rather than an expression to compute its entries. `Array` can be used with either built-in functions or user-defined functions.

Here Mathematica's built-in maximum function is used to generate the matrix

$$M = \begin{bmatrix} 1 & 2 & 3 \\ 2 & 2 & 3 \end{bmatrix}.$$

```
In[1]:= M = Array[Max, {2,3}]
Out[1]= {{1, 2, 3}, {2, 2, 3}}
```

Note that the (i, j) entry, `M[[i,j]]`, is the maximum of the subscripts i and j.

---

[11]None of the commands from `LinearAlgebra`Master`` are used in this session.

Recall from Section 0.3.11 that *Mathematica* supports three methods for writing user-defined functions. Their use is demonstrated in the following.

Here the function
$g(i, j) = i^2 - j$
is defined and used to
generate a 3 × 4 matrix.

```
In[2]:= g[i_,j_] = i^2 - j
Out[2]= i² - j

In[3]:= Array[g, {3,4}]
Out[3]= {{0, -1, -2, -3}, {3, 2, 1, 0},
    {8, 7, 6, 5}}
```

Note that the (i, j) entry of the matrix is $i^2 - j$.

Here the function

$$f(i, j) = \begin{cases} i^j & \text{if } i < j \\ j^i & \text{otherwise} \end{cases}$$

is defined and used to
generate a 2 × 3 matrix in
which the (i, j) entry is $f(i, j)$.

```
In[4]:= f = Function[{i, j}, If[i<j, i^j, j^i]]
Out[4]= Function[{i, j}, If[i < j, iʲ, jⁱ]]

In[5]:= Array[f, {2,3}]
Out[5]= {{1, 1, 1}, {1, 4, 8}}
```

It is also possible to define a matrix using an unnamed generating function. The definition of the function is given as the first argument.

Here a simple pure function
is used with the `Array`
command.

```
In[1]:= Array[(10 #1 + #2) &, {2,3}]
Out[1]= {{11, 12, 13}, {21, 22, 23}}
```

Here the 7 × 7 matrix
Id[7] = [δ$_{ij}$] defined by

$$\delta_{ij} = \begin{cases} 1 & \text{if } i = j \\ 0 & \text{otherwise} \end{cases}$$

is defined using a pure
function known as the
Kronecker delta function.

```
In[2]:= Id[7] = Array[If[#1 == #2, 1, 0] &, {7,7}]
Out[2]= {{1, 0, 0, 0, 0, 0, 0},
    {0, 1, 0, 0, 0, 0, 0},
    {0, 0, 1, 0, 0, 0, 0},
    {0, 0, 0, 1, 0, 0, 0},
    {0, 0, 0, 0, 1, 0, 0},
    {0, 0, 0, 0, 0, 1, 0},
    {0, 0, 0, 0, 0, 0, 1}}
```

Here the 2 × 2 matrix with
(i, j) entry a[i,j] is
generated using an unde-
fined function. We will call
such a matrix a symbolic
matrix.

```
In[3]:= Clear[a]
In[4]:= A = Array[a, {2,2}]
Out[4]= {{a[1,1], a[1,2]}, {a[2,1], a[2,2]}}
```

Editing Matrices

At some point you will almost certainly want to change one or more of the entries of a matrix you have already defined rather than redefine the matrix. You do this simply by reassigning the entry.

Consider the matrix A as an example.	`In[1]:= A = {{11,21,13}, {21,22,23}}` `Out[1]= {{11, 21, 13}, {21, 22, 23}}`

To modify an entry, you simply "reassign" it.	`In[2]:= A[[1,2]] = 12`
	`Out[2]= 12`
	`In[3]:= A`
	`Out[3]=  {{11, 12, 13}, {21, 22, 23}}`

Automatic `MatrixForm`

You have seen the `MatrixForm` command used to show a matrix in standard rectangular form. You can configure your *Mathematica* session so that all matrices are automatically output in standard rectangular form. This is done using the *Mathematica* variable `$Post`, as follows.

`$Post` *controls the printing of the output.*	`In[1]:= $Post := If[MatrixQ[#], MatrixForm[#], #] &`

The value assigned to `$Post` is a function. `MatrixQ[#]` tests whether the output is a matrix. If `MatrixQ[#]` evaluates to `True`, then the second entry of the `If` command tells *Mathematica* to use `MatrixForm`. The third entry of the `If` command tells *Mathematica* to pass through the output if `MatrixQ` returns `False`.

Now you have customized output for matrices.	`In[2]:= A = Array[Max, {3,3}]`
	`Out[2]=//MatrixForm=`
	　　1　2　3
	　　2　2　3
	　　3　3　3

If you change your mind, use `Clear` *to return the output to Mathematica's default notation.*	`In[3]:= Clear[$Post]`
	
	`In[4]:= A`
	`Out[4]= {{1, 2, 3}, {2, 2, 3}, {3, 3, 3}}`

EXERCISES 1.3

1. Define the following matrices using *Mathematica*.

    a. The 5×5 matrix $M = [m_{ij}]$ with

    $$m_{ij} = \begin{cases} 1 & \text{if } i \geq j \\ 2 & \text{otherwise} \end{cases}$$

    (*Mathematica* uses `>=` for $\geq$.)

    b. The 5×5 matrix $N = [n_{ij}]$ with

    $$n_{ij} = \begin{cases} 0 & \text{if } i = j \\ 1 & \text{otherwise} \end{cases}$$

c. The 5×1 matrix $F = [f_{ij}]$ defined by $f_{ij} = 1/i$.

2. Define the 10×10 matrix $N = [n_{ij}]$ in your *Mathematica* session, where $n_{ij} = i^2 + 3i - j^3 + 2j - 1$.

3. In standard mathematical notation, the symbol 3 is used to denote both the number 3 and the constant functions $f(x) = 3$, $f(x,y) = 3$, and so on. Given this, what would you expect to be *Mathematica*'s response to the command `M = Array[3, {2,2}]`? What would you expect to be *Mathematica*'s response to the command `M = Array[3 &, {2,2}]`? Check your answers in a *Mathematica* session.

4. Assume $L[1] = \{1,2,3,4\}$, $L[2] = \{2,3,4,5\}$, $L[3] = \{3,4,5,6\}$, and $LL = \{L[1],L[2],L[3]\}$. Explain *Mathematica*'s response to the command `Array[LL[[#1,#2]] &, {2,2}]`.

1.4 Matrix Arithmetic

```
[., *, +, -, ^, /, Inverse, MatrixPower]
```

Mathematica uses the same notation for most arithmetic operations with matrices that it uses with numbers. One exception is that the symbol "." is used for matrix multiplication. The arithmetic operators are summarized in the following table.

Matrix Arithmetic

Operation	Standard Notation	*Mathematica* Notation
addition	$A + B$	A + B
subtraction	$A - B$	A - B
scalar multiplication	kA	k A
		k * A
	$\dfrac{1}{k}A$	1/k A
		1/k * A
		A/k
matrix multiplication	AB	A . B
powers	A^n	MatrixPower[A,n]
inverse	A^{-1}	Inverse[A]
		MatrixPower[A,-1]

Enter the following matrices A and B to use as examples.

Semicolons are used to suppress the output.

```
In[1]:= A = Array[Min, {3,3}];
In[2]:= B = Array[Max, {3,3}];
```

You build an arithmetic matrix expression just as you would any arithmetic expression, using " . " for matrix products and `Inverse[A]` *in place of* A^{-1}.[12]

```
In[4]:= F = A . B + B;
In[5]:= G = A . A . B - B;
In[6]:= 1/2 Inverse[A] . (F + G)
```

$$Out[6] = \{\{\frac{7}{2}, \frac{9}{2}, 6\},$$

$$\{\frac{13}{2}, 7, 9\},$$

$$\{\frac{17}{2}, 9, \frac{21}{2}\}\}$$

Note that definitions made in one session are valid only for that session. Definitions can be saved to disk and loaded into a new session, but they will be unknown to *Mathematica* after the session in which they are defined is closed.

1.4.1 A Few Pitfalls to Avoid

Don't use "**" or an equivalent for matrix products.[13]* `A * B` *multiplies corresponding entries of A and B, whereas* `A . B` *computes the standard matrix product.*

```
In[1]:= A = Array[3 &, {2,2}];

In[2]:= B = Array[2 &, {2,2}];

In[3]:= A . B - A B
Out[3]= {{6, 6}, {6, 6}}
```

Don't use `A^(-1)` *for the inverse of A.* `A^(-1)` *computes the inverses of the individual entries of A.*

```
In[4]:= A^(-1)
```

$$Out[4] = \{\{\frac{1}{3}, \frac{1}{3}\}, \{\frac{1}{3}, \frac{1}{3}\}\}$$

Don't use " . " for scalar multiplication. For example, `1/3 . B` *is interpreted by Mathematica as* $\frac{1}{3.0}$ B, *which evaluates in decimal form.*

```
In[5]:= 1/3 . B
Out[5]= {{0.666667, 0.666667},
   {0.666667, 0.666667}}
```

---

[12]The names `C`, `D`, and `E` are *protected*. *Mathematica* will not let you use them unless you `Unprotect` them.

[13]Recall that * is equivalent to a blank space. The same warning applies for both notations.

1.4.2 Legal Names

You are free to use as many characters in a name as you choose. For example, you could use SumOfAandB for the sum of two matrices *A* and *B*. However, for built-in functions *Mathematica* uses names that begin with capital letters, so you are less likely to have a conflict with a built-in name if you use names that begin with lowercase letters. You need to avoid the single-letter names C, D, E, I, N, and O.[14] If you try to use one of these, *Mathematica* will not make the assignment; rather, it will report that the name is protected. You can temporarily remove *Mathematica*'s protection for any protected name using the Unprotect command. For example, Unprotect[C] would allow you to assign a value to C. The effect of the Unprotect command lasts only as long as the current *Mathematica* session.

Mathematica will not accept names that contain spaces or names that begin with numbers. There are also certain reserved characters that should not or cannot be used. You will have no problem if you stick to standard names such as those used in the text. On the other hand, if you use characters like %, @, and so on, *Mathematica* usually responds with an error message, which is the program's way of saying you have violated its rules. This does no harm to the system.

The most common convention for naming matrices is to use single upper-case letters *A, B, F,* and so forth. If a family or related matrices is defined, subscripts are commonly used. You may choose to do this with a notation like *A*[1], *A*[2], ... The effect is to create a function *A* that has a small domain. You have a wide choice of indices using this notation. For example, you can name a matrix *A*[red]. Alternatively, you can use names like *A*1, *A*2, ...

Here are three points to note regarding the use of indexed names.

- You cannot introduce a name of the form A[i] if A has been defined as a matrix. In this case, an attempt to assign A[i] results in an error message.
- If you have assigned A[1], A[2],... and then assign the name A, you will not be able to access A[1],A[2],... until you unassign the name A using the =. operator. If you use Clear to unassign A you will lose the definitions of A[1],A[2], ...
- The function created by assigning values to A[1],A[2], . . . , is named A. You can view its table of values using ??A.

1.4.3 Random Matrices

If you are testing a hypothesis and want to work with random examples, you can use *Mathematica*'s Random command to generate pseudorandom matrices. You can also specify the type and range of the entries.

---

[14]Loading some packages protects other names. For example, the DiscreteMath package protects the name M.

This generates a "random" 3 × 3 integer matrix that has entries in the range [–100,100].

```
In[1]:= Array[Random[Integer, {-100,100}] &, {3,3}];
```

You could use `Random` to generate matrices to test the probability that $A B = B A$, for example.

1.4.4 Symbolic Matrices

You can do arithmetic with matrices having entries that are unassigned variables or values of an undefined function. We call these *symbolic matrices.* In many cases, symbolic matrices can be used to prove results in low dimensions.

Here m is used as an undefined function.

```
In[1]:= M = Array[m, {2,2}]
Out[1]= {{m[1, 1],  m[1, 2]}, {m[2, 1], m[2, 2]}}
```

This defines a 2 × 2 matrix that has undefined variables as entries.

```
In[2]:= S = {{a,b},{c,d}}
Out[2]= {{a, b}, {c, d}}
```

If *a, b, c,* or *d* had an assigned value, the symbol would be replaced by its value.
Symbolic matrices can be used in all the same ways as numerical matrices.

This gives the standard formula for the inverse of a 2 × 2 matrix.

```
In[3]:= Inverse[S]
```
$$Out[3]= \left\{\left\{ \frac{d}{-(b\ c) + a\ d} , -\left(\frac{b}{-(b\ c) + a\ d} \right)\right\},\right.$$
$$\left.\left\{-\left(\frac{c}{-(b\ c) + a\ d} \right), \frac{b}{-(b\ c) + a\ d} \right\}\right\}$$

Here is the product of S and its computed inverse.

```
In[4]:= S . Inverse[S]
```
$$Out[4]= \left\{\left\{ \frac{b\ c}{-(b\ c) + a\ d} + \frac{a\ d}{-(b\ c) + a\ d} , 0\right\},\right.$$
$$\left.\left\{0, \frac{b\ c}{-(b\ c) + a\ d} + \frac{a\ d}{-(b\ c) + a\ d} \right\}\right\}$$

Here is a simplified answer. It proves the standard formula for the inverse of a 2 × 2 matrix.

```
In[5]:= Simplify[%]
Out[5]= {{1, 0}, {0, 1}}
```

The following uses symbolic matrices to give a computational proof of the associative law $A(BC) = (AB)C$ for 3×3 matrices. The same technique can be used to establish other properties for matrices of a fixed size.

Define three 3×3 matrices for the proof.[15]

```
In[1]:= F = Array[f, {3,3}];
In[2]:= G = Array[g, {3,3}];
In[3]:= H = Array[h, {3,3}];
```

Calculate the two sides of the equation.

```
In[4]:= lhs = F .(G . H);
In[5]:= rhs = (F . G). H;
```

The descriptions of the matrices are quite long and not required, so the "silent terminator" (;) is used.

This picks out the (2,3) entry of lhs.

```
In[6]:= lhs[[2,3]]
Out[6]= (f[2, 1] g[1, 1] + f[2, 2] g[2, 1] +
f[2, 3] g[3, 1]) h[1, 3] +
  (f[2, 1] g[1, 2] + f[2, 2] g[2, 2] +
f[2, 3] g[3, 2]) h[2, 3] +
  (f[2, 1] g[1, 3] + f[2, 2] g[2, 3] +
f[2, 3] g[3, 3]) h[3, 3]
```

This picks out the (2,3) entry of rhs. *Perhaps a comparison will generate an idea.*

```
In[7]:= rhs[[2,3]]
Out[7]= (f[2, 1] g[1, 1] + f[2, 2] g[2, 1] + f[2, 3]
g[3, 1]) h[1, 3] +
  (f[2, 1] g[1, 2] + f[2, 2] g[2, 2] +
f[2, 3] g[3, 2]) h[2, 3] +
  (f[2, 1] g[1, 3] + f[2, 2] g[2, 3] +
f[2, 3] g[3, 3]) h[3, 3]
```

The (2,3)-terms of lhs and rhs are large, but small enough to compare. However, *Mathematica* can determine easily if the two are the same by checking whether their difference is 0.

This shows that the (2,3) entries of lhs *and* rhs *are the same.*

```
In[8]:= lhs[[2,3]] - rhs[[2,3]]
Out[8]=  0
```

Matrix subtraction establishes the equality $F(GH) = (FG)H$.

```
In[9]:= lhs - rhs
Out[9]= {{0, 0, 0}, {0, 0, 0},
    {0, 0, 0}}
```

[15]For this to work properly, f, g, and h must be unassigned variables. If in doubt, use Clear[f,g,h].

EXERCISES 1.4_____

Throughout this text, we use *C, D,* and other protected names for matrices, as would be done in any standard linear algebra book. You can either use the `Unprotect` command to make the name available to *Mathematica* or use another, perhaps related name. For example, you might use *c* or *CC* in place of *C.*

1. Let $A = [a_{ij}]$ be the 5×5 matrix defined by the equation $a_{ij} = 1/(i + j - 1)$. Let $B = [b_{ij}]$ be the 5×6 matrix defined by the equation $b_{ij} = i + j - 1$. Let $C = [c_{ij}]$ be the 5×6 matrix defined by the equation $c_{ij} = 1/(j + 1)$. Determine which of the following are defined and evaluate those that are. (We use *Id* for the appropriate identity matrix.)

    a. $A\,B$ b. $A\,(B + C)$ c. $A\,B + A\,C$
    d. $A\,(B - C)$ e. $A\,B - A\,C$ f. $A\,(B\,C)$
    g. $(A\,B)\,C$ h. A^5 i. $A^{-1}A^6$
    j. $A + 3\,Id$ k. $Id\,A$ l. $A^3 - 3A + Id$

2. Let $L = [l_{ij}]$ be the 2×2 matrix defined by $l_{ij} = \min(i, j)$. Let $M = [m_{ij}]$ be the 2×2 matrix defined by $m_{ij} = \max(i, j)$. Show that $ML \neq LM$. Repeat the exercise for the $n \times n$ analogs of *L* and *M* for $n = 3, 10$, and 11.

3. Let $A = [a_{ij}]$ be the 3×3 matrix defined by $a_{ij} = i^2 - j^2$. Let $p(x) = x^3 + 98x$. Compute $p(A)$ using matrix multiplication for the powers.[16] Note that the answer implies that $A(A^2 + 98I) = 0$, and hence that *A* is not invertible. (Why?) What happens in this case if you try to compute the inverse in *Mathematica* using the `Inverse` command?

4. If $p(x) = a_0 + a_1x + \cdots + a_nx^n$, then for a matrix *A*, $p(A)$ is taken to be $a_0I + a_1A + \cdots + a_nA^n$, where *I* is the identity matrix. Let $A = [a_{ij}]$ be the 5×5 matrix defined by $a_{ij} = \max(i,j)$, and let $p(x)$ be the polynomial generated by the *Mathematica* command `Det[x Id - A]`. Show that $p(A) = 0$, and use this to find the inverse of *A*. (Be sure to use `MatrixPower[A,n]` for the *n*th power of *A*. You will later investigate the polynomial $p(x)$ in more detail.

5. Estimate the probability that an arbitrary square, real matrix is invertible by randomly generating ten square matrices and trying to invert them. Based on your calculations, what do you estimate the probability to be?

6. Use symbolic matrices to give a computational proof of the 3×3 case of the distributive law

    $$(A + B)C = AC + BC$$

7. Use symbolic matrices to give a computational proof for 5×5 matrices that $(kI)A = kA = A(kI)$, for all scalars *k*.

Exercises 8, 9, and 10 use *Mathematica*'s `Random` command.

_____

[16]For example, for A^3 you can use either `A . A . A` or `MatrixPower[A,3]`.

8. You can use *Mathematica*'s Random command to generate pseudo-random decimal numbers or to define a function that generates pseudo-random numbers in a given range or of a given type. The command Random[], for example, generates a decimal between 0 and 1. The command F := Random[Integer, {m,n}]& generates a function that will generate random integers in the range $m, \ldots, n$ (where m and n are integers with $m < n$).

    Use the Random command to generate a 5×5 matrix with pseudorandom rational entries a/b with both a and b between -100 and 100 and $b \neq 0$.

9. A matrix $A = [a_{ij}]$ having the property that $a_{ij} = 0$ whenever $i > j$ is said to be upper triangular.

    a. Define a function $f(i, j)$ that returns random integer entries if $i \leq j$ and 0 otherwise. (See Exercise 8.)

    b. Use the function f to generate two pseudorandom upper-triangular 6×6 matrices L and M.

    c. Verify that the product LM is upper triangular.

10. A matrix $A = [a_{ij}]$ having the property that $a_{ij} = 0$ whenever $i \geq j$ is said to be *strictly* upper triangular.

    a. Define a function $g(i, j)$ that returns random integer entries if $i < j$ and 0 if $i \geq j$. (See Exercise 8.)

    b. Use the function g to generate a 5×5 matrix A.

    c. Compute A^5.

    d. Repeat parts b and c for a variety of matrices and exponents. Can you form a conjecture regarding the nth power of a strictly upper-triangular matrix?

11. A matrix M that satisfys $M^n = 0$ and $M^{n-1} \neq 0$ is said to be *nilpotent of index n*. Based on experimentation, what would you conjecture about the index of nilpotency of a strictly upper-triangular $n \times n$ matrix?

12. As you have seen, the generating function for a matrix can place undefined variables as well as numbers in the matrix.

This function generates a matrix that is partially symbolic and partially numeric.

```
In[1]:= ut:= Function[{i,j},
If[i<j,x[10i+j],0]]
```

Use ut *to generate a 5×5 matrix. Note that T is strictly upper triangular.*

```
In[2]:= T =
Array[ut,{5,5}]
```

    a. What can you say about T^2, T^3, and T^4?

    b. Use the matrix T to give a computational proof that the fifth power of a 5×5 strictly upper-triangular matrix is 0.

13. Show that every strictly upper-triangular $n \times n$ matrix T is nilpotent of index $\leq n$ (i.e., satisfies $T^n = 0$).

1.5 **Det** and Other Built-in Matrix Functions

[Det, IdentityMatrix, Transpose, SubMatrix[17],
BlockMatrix[18]]

Many of the standard matrix commands and functions are built into *Mathematica*. Others are contained in the LinearAlgebra package.

If you have not already done so, load the LinearAlgebra package.

```
In[1]:= <<LinearAlgebra`Master`
```

Define the matrix M as an example.

```
In[2]:= M = Table[10i + j, {i,4}, {j,4}]
Out[2]=
    {{11,12,13,14},
     {21,22,23,24},
     {31,32,33,34},
     {41,42,43,44}}
```

You can compute the determinant of M.

```
In[3]:= Det[M]
Out[3]=
    0
```

The Transpose *command interchanges the rows and columns of M.*

```
In[4]:= Transpose[M]
Out[4]=
    {{11,21,31,41},
     {12,22,32,42},
     {13,23,33,43},
     {14,24,34,44}}
```

You can extract submatrices. This gives the 3×3 upper left-hand corner of M.[19]

```
In[5]:= SubMatrix[M,{1,1},{3,3}]
Out[5]=
    {{11,  12,  13},
     {21,  22,  23},
     {31,  32,  33}}
```

You can build a matrix out of other matrices using the BlockMatrix *command.*

```
In[6]:= A = {{a,b},{c,d}};
In[7]:= B = {{e,f},{g,h}};
In[8]:= BlockMatrix[{{A,B},{B,A}}]
Out[8]= {{a, b, e, f}, {c, d, g, h},
         {e, f, a, b}, {g, h, c, d}}
```

---

[17]You must load LinearAlgebra`Master` before using SubMatrix.
[18]You must load LinearAlgebra`Master` before using BlockMatrix.
[19]SubMatrix is one of the commands in LinearAlgebra`Master`.

This generates the 5 × 5
identity matrix.

```
In[9]:= IdentityMatrix[5]
Out[9]= {{1, 0, 0, 0, 0},
         {0, 1, 0, 0, 0},
         {0, 0, 1, 0, 0},
         {0, 0, 0, 1, 0},
         {0, 0, 0, 0, 1}}
```

You can use the Det command to investigate the properties of the determinant function. These are explored in the exercises, along with the adjoint (adj) command.

EXERCISES 1.5 _____

1. For an $n \times n$ matrix A, $(-1)^{i+j}$ times the determinant of the $(n-1) \times (n-1)$ submatrix A_{ij} obtained by deleting the *ith* row and *jth* column of A is called the (i, j) cofactor of A.[20] That is, the (i, j) cofactor of A is $(-1)^{i+j} \det(A_{ij})$. The cofactors of A are used to define the adjoint of A, which we will use in some of the exercises that follow. The adjoint of A is frequently denoted adj(A).

    Clear x, i, and j and enter the following definition.

    ```
    cofactor[x_,i_,j_]:=(-1)^(i+j)*
    Det[Transpose[Drop[Transpose[
    Drop[x,{i,i}]],{j,j}]]]
    ```

    The command Drop[A, {i,i}] removes the *ith* row of a matrix A, so the cofactor command returns the determinant of A_{ij}.

    Now enter the definition.

    ```
    adj[x_]:=
    Transpose[Table[cofactor[x,i,j],
    {i,Length[x]},
    {j,Length[x]}]]
    ```

    Use the adj and Det commands to verify that the 3×3 matrix $A = [a_{ij}]$ defined by $a_{ij} = i + j$ satisfies A adj$(A) = \det(A)I$.

2. Verify the identity A adj$(A) = $ adj$(A) A = \det(A) I$ for a pseudorandom 5×5 matrix of integers.

3. Verify the identity adj$(A)^T = $ adj(A^T) for a pseudorandom 4×4 matrix of integers.

4. For a pseudorandom 8×8 matrix A of integers, verify that the matrix B obtained by interchanging the first two rows of A satisfies $\det(B) = -\det(A)$.

_____

[20]Sometimes the determinant of this submatrix is called the (i,j) minor.

5. For a pseudorandom 6×6 integer matrix A, verify that any matrix obtained by adding a multiple of the first row to the second has the same determinant.

6. For a pseudorandom 7×7 integer matrix A, verify that $\det(A) = \det(A^T)$.

7. Let K_{ij} denote the (i, j) cofactor of A. (See Exercise 1.) Verify the following, which are known as the Lagrange identities.

   a. $\det(A) = \displaystyle\sum_{j=1}^{n} a_{ij} K_{ij}, \, i = 1, \ldots, n$

   b. $\det(A) = \displaystyle\sum_{i=1}^{n} a_{ij} K_{ij}, \, j = 1, \ldots, n$

   c. $\displaystyle\sum_{j=1}^{n} a_{rj} K_{sj} = \sum_{i=1}^{n} a_{ir} K_{is} = 0$ if $r \neq s$

   for a pseudorandom 4×4 matrix A of integers.

8. Use a symbolic matrix to prove that a 4×4 matrix and its transpose have the same determinant.

9. Use a symbolic matrix to verify the identity $\mathrm{adj}(A)^T = \mathrm{adj}(A^T)$ for all 4×4 matrices.

10. Use mathematical induction to verify the identities

$$\mathrm{adj}(A)^T = \mathrm{adj}(A^T)$$
$$\det(A) \;\; = \det(A^T)$$

for all square matrices.

11. Use a symbolic matrix to prove that interchanging the first two rows of a 4×4 matrix changes the sign of the determinant.

12. Use a symbolic matrix to prove that adding a multiple of the first row to the second row of a 4×4 matrix does not affect the determinant.

13. Use a symbolic matrix to prove that multiplying the first row of a 4×4 matrix by a scalar k changes the determinant by a multiple of k.

1.6 Applications

Curve Fitting and Interpolation

Virtually everyone is aware that two points determine a line. You also know that the equation of a (nonvertical) line has the form $y = a_0 + a_1 x$. Hence, two points (x_1, y_1) and (x_2, y_2) (with $x_1 \neq x_2$) determine a linear equation $y = a_0 + a_1 x$ such that

$$\begin{cases} y_1 = a_0 + a_1 x_1 \\ y_2 = a_0 + a_1 x_2 \end{cases}$$

This system is easily solved for a_0 and a_1 using row-reduction and back-substitution.

In general, $n + 1$ points (x_1,y_1), (x_2,y_2), . . . , (x_{n+1},y_{n+1}) (with $x_i \neq x_j$ whenever $i \neq j$) determine a polynomial equation of the form $y = a_0 + a_1x + \cdots + a_nx^n$ that satisfies

$$\begin{cases} y_1 = a_0 + a_1x_1 + \cdots + a_nx_1^n \\ y_2 = a_0 + a_1x_2 + \cdots + a_nx_2^n \\ \quad . \\ \quad . \\ \quad . \\ y_{n+1} = a_0 + a_1x_{n+1} + \cdots + a_nx_{n+1}^n \end{cases}$$

Again, this system is easily solved for the unknowns $a_0, a_1, \ldots, a_n$ using row-reduction and back-substitution.

For example, assume you know that the graph of a polynomial $p(x)$ of degree 5 or less passes through the six points (1,2), (2,3), (3,6), (4,7), (5,9), and (6,13), and you want to know the value of $p(x)$ at $x = 30$.

Make a list X of the x values.

```
In[1]:= X = {1,2,3,4,5,6};
```

Note that an uppercase X is used. The ith entry of X is denoted X[[i]], so X[[i]] = x_i.

Enter the matrix M = $[x_i^{j-1}]$. (We use the convention here that $x_i^0 = 1$.) A matrix of this form is called a Vandermonde matrix.

```
In[2]:= M = Table[X[[i]]^(j-1),
   {i,6}, {j,6}]; M//MatrixForm
Out[2]//MatrixForm=
1   1    1     1      1
1   2    4     8      16     32
1   3    9     27     81     243
1   4    16    64     256    1024
1   5    25    125    625    3125
1   6    36    216    1296   7776
```

Define the column Y of y values.

```
In[3]:= Y = Transpose[{{2,3,6,7,9,13}}];
```

Solve for the coefficients a_i.[21]

```
In[4]:= AppendRows[M,Y];
In[5]:= RowReduce[%]//MatrixForm
```

---

[21]You must load LinearAlgebra`Master` before using AppendRows.

Out[5]=

1	0	0	0	0	0	23
0	1	0	0	0	0	$-(\frac{667}{15})$
0	0	1	0	0	0	$\frac{385}{12}$
0	0	0	1	0	0	$-(\frac{239}{24})$
0	0	0	0	1	0	$\frac{17}{12}$
0	0	0	0	0	1	$-(\frac{3}{40})$

Place the coefficients in a list for easy reference.

```
In[6]:= a = Table[%[[i,7]], {i,6}]
```

Out[6]= $\{23, \; -(\frac{667}{15}), \; \frac{385}{12}, \; -(\frac{239}{24}), \; \frac{17}{12}, \; -\frac{3}{40}\}$

Now **a** = (a_i) is a one-dimensional array and a_i is denoted a[[i]].

Define the polynomial p having coefficients a_i. You might prefer to use the Sum *command to do this.*

```
In[7]:= p = a[[1]] + a[[2]]x + a[[3]]x^2 +
    a[[4]]x^3 + a[[5]]x^4 + a[[6]]x^5;
```

You can use the replacement operator (/.) to find the value of p for any particular value of x.

```
In[8]:=  p /. {x -> 5}
Out[8]= 9
```

In functional notation, p /. {x -> 5} is $p(5)$.
If you wish, you can define p so it is a polynomial function rather than a polynomial expression.

The Sum *command provides a compact form of the definition.*

```
In[9]:= p =.
In[10]:= p[x_] := Sum[a[[i]]x^(i-1), {i,1,6}]
```

You can now easily find the value of p for any value of x using a style that more closely follows standard mathematical notation.

```
In[11]:= p[5]
Out[11]= 9
```

If you wish, you can Plot
the function p over an
interval of interest.

In[12]:= Plot[p[x], {x,1,10}]

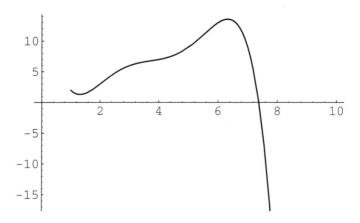

Out[12]= -Graphics-

Problems on Curve Fitting

1. Find the polynomial $p(x)$, of degree at most 8, having a graph that passes through the nine points (–8,12), (–6,23), (–4,16), (–2,23), (1,0), (2,23), (4,16), (6,23), and (8,12). Plot its graph and find $p(7)$.

2. Find the polynomial $p(x)$, of degree at most 3, having a graph that passes through the four points (–4,112), (11,–128), (2,70), and (5,–140). Plot its graph and find $p(10)$.

3. Assume that in the years 1971–1988, water samples were tested in a community in the midwestern portion of the United States to determine their content of alphagen, and that the contents, in parts per million, are given in the following table.

Alphagen: 1971–1988

1971	1972	1973	1974	1975	1976
85	55	37	35	45	50

1977	1978	1979	1980	1981	1982
59	56	49	53	57	59

1983	1984	1985	1986	1987	1988
55	51	44	54	61	63

Environmentalists are concerned about the future concentration of alphagen. They hypothesized that the alphagen content is a polynomial function of degree 17 of time. Based on this table, what do you expect the contents of alphagen to be in the year 1995? (Assume that it is given by the polynomial determined by the data points for the years 1971–1988.) Plot the graph of the function. Do the environmentalists have cause for concern?

Leontief Economic Model

The following is an introduction to the mathematical modeling of Wassily Leontief, who was awarded the Nobel prize in 1973 for his work in mathematical models.

Assume a conglomerate consists of four industries—M_1 = coal, M_2 = steel, M_3 = energy, and M_4 = transportation and heavy equipment (bulldozers, cranes, and so on). Assume each of the industries buys all of its needs from the conglomerate and that all of its needs can be met from within the conglomerate. Let p_i be the total value, in millions or dollars, of the production of M_i. Let k_{ij} be the dollar value of M_i required to produce one dollar's worth of M_j. Let u_i be the value, in millions of dollars, of M_i consumed outside of the conglomerate over some convenient period of time. Assume that k_{ij} and u_i are given by the following table.

	M_1	M_2	M_3	M_4		u
M_1 (coal)	.00	.42	.75	.00	u_1	12
M_2 (steel)	.01	.02	.01	.55	u_2	14
M_3 (energy)	.11	.40	.02	.27	u_3	38
M_4 (transportation and heavy equipment)	.21	.12	.05	.05	u_4	55

The problem is to determine the unknowns p_i so that each product is used in exactly the same quantity it is produced. This leads to the following system of equations.

$$\begin{cases} k_{11}p_1 + k_{12}p_2 + k_{13}p_3 + k_{14}p_4 + u_1 = p_1 \\ k_{21}p_1 + k_{22}p_2 + k_{23}p_3 + k_{24}p_4 + u_2 = p_2 \\ k_{31}p_1 + k_{32}p_2 + k_{33}p_3 + k_{34}p_4 + u_3 = p_3 \\ k_{41}p_1 + k_{42}p_2 + k_{43}p_3 + k_{44}p_4 + u_4 = p_4 \end{cases}$$

The matrix $K = [k_{ij}]$ is called the *consumption matrix*, the matrix

$$P = \begin{bmatrix} p_1 \\ p_2 \\ p_3 \\ p_4 \end{bmatrix}$$

the *output matrix*, and the matrix

$$U = \begin{bmatrix} u_1 \\ u_2 \\ u_3 \\ u_4 \end{bmatrix}$$

the *demand matrix*. Rearranging the terms produces the equivalent system

$$\begin{cases} (1 - k_{11})p_1 & - k_{12}p_2 & - k_{13}p_3 & - k_{14}p_4 & = u_1 \\ - k_{21}p_1 & + (1 - k_{22})p_2 - k_{23}p_3 & - k_{24}p_4 & = u_2 \\ - k_{31}p_1 & - k_{32}p_2 & + (1 - k_{33})p_3 - k_{34}p_4 & = u_3 \\ - k_{41}p_1 & - k_{42}p_2 & - k_{43}p_3 & + (1 - k_{44})p_4 = u_4 \end{cases}$$

The problem proceeds as follows. (Decimals are avoided to prevent cumulative rounding errors.) We assume the LinearAlgebra package has been loaded.

This defines the consumption matrix K.

```
In[1]:= K =
  1/100{{0,42,75,0},
  {1,2,1,55},
  {11,40,2,27},
  {21,12,5,5}};
```

This defines a generating function for the coefficient matrix of the linear system to be solved.

```
In[2]:= f[i_,j_]:=
  If[i==j, 1 - K[[i,j]], -K[[i,j]]]
```

Use f to generate the coefficient matrix of the system.

```
In[3]:= M = Array[f, {4,4}]
Out[3]=
```

$$\{\{1, \qquad -(\frac{21}{50}), \quad -(\frac{3}{4}), \qquad 0\},$$

$$\{-(\frac{1}{100}), \quad \frac{49}{50}, \qquad -(\frac{1}{100}), \quad -(\frac{11}{20})\},$$

$$\{-(\frac{11}{100}), \quad -(\frac{2}{5}), \qquad \frac{49}{50}, \qquad -(\frac{27}{100})\},$$

$$\{-(\frac{21}{100}), \quad -(\frac{3}{25}), \quad -(\frac{1}{20}), \quad \frac{19}{20}\}\}$$

Define the demand matrix U of the system.

```
In[4]:= U = Transpose[{{12,14,38,55}}];
```

Create the augmented matrix of the system.

$In[5]:=$ M$U = AppendRows[M,U]
$Out[5]=$

$$\{\{1, \quad -(\frac{21}{50}), \quad -(\frac{3}{4}), \quad 0, \quad 12\},$$

$$\{-(\frac{1}{100}), \quad \frac{49}{50}, \quad -(\frac{1}{100}), \quad -(\frac{11}{20}), \quad 14\},$$

$$\{-(\frac{11}{100}), \quad -(\frac{2}{5}), \quad \frac{49}{50}, \quad -(\frac{27}{100}), \quad 38\},$$

$$\{-(\frac{21}{100}), \quad -(\frac{3}{25}), \quad -(\frac{1}{20}), \quad \frac{19}{20}, \quad 55\}\}$$

Use Gaussian elimination to reduce the matrix to row-echelon form.

$In[6]:=$ R = RowReduce[M$U]; R//MatrixForm
$Out[6]//MatrixForm=$

$$\begin{array}{ccccc} 1 & 0 & 0 & 0 & \dfrac{175689300}{1398239} \\[2ex] 0 & 1 & 0 & 0 & \dfrac{102395850}{1398239} \\[2ex] 0 & 0 & 1 & 0 & \dfrac{154538900}{1398239} \\[2ex] 0 & 0 & 0 & 1 & \dfrac{140855100}{1398239} \end{array}$$

Define the output values p_i.

$In[7]:=$ p = Table[%[[i,5]], {i,4}]
$Out[7]=$

$$\{\frac{175689300}{1398239}, \quad \frac{102395850}{1398239}, \quad \frac{154538900}{1398239}, \quad \frac{140855100}{1398239}\}$$

You can now convert to floating-point form without concern for cumulative rounding errors.

$In[8]:=$ p//N
   {125.65, 73.232, 110.524, 100.737}

The N command is used to convert fractions to decimals. Here it is used in postfix form.

Problems on the Leontief Model

1. Assume the economy of the country Elpmis consists of four distinct commodities $M_1 =$ food, $M_2 =$ shelter, $M_3 =$ transportation, and $M_4 =$ clothing, and that the consumption and demand matrices of the economy are given by

$$K = \frac{1}{100} \begin{bmatrix} 55 & 45 & 53 & 34 \\ 5 & 2 & 1 & 1 \\ 10 & 11 & 8 & 9 \\ 20 & 35 & 29 & 50 \end{bmatrix} \quad \text{and} \quad U = \frac{1}{10} \begin{bmatrix} 8 \\ 10 \\ 3 \\ 6 \end{bmatrix}$$

Find the output matrix in both exact and decimal form.

2.   The economy of Orcam consists of ten industries, $M_1, M_2, \ldots, M_{10}$. The consumption matrix is given by the generating function

```
F[i_,j_]:= Min[Mod[i+j,20],10]/100
```

and the demand matrix is given by the generating function

```
f[i_,j_]:= Abs[20-i^2]
```

Find the output matrix in both exact and decimal form.

Problems on Matrix Arithmetic
`[Length, Map, Partition]`

Incidence Matrices

An $n \times n$ matrix M consisting entirely of zeros and ones is called an *incidence matrix*. Incidence matrices arise naturally, for example, in transportation problems where a one in the (i, j) entry signifies a connection from the ith to the jth location, and a zero in the (i, j) entry indicates the lack of a connection from the ith to the jth location.

Consider an airline that serves ten states $S_1, S_2, \ldots, S_{10}$. Assume the following array contains a one in the ith row and jth column if there is a (direct) flight from S_i to S_j, and a zero otherwise.

	S_1	S_2	S_3	S_4	S_5	S_6	S_7	S_8	S_9	S_{10}
S_1	0	1	0	0	0	0	0	0	0	1
S_2	0	0	1	0	0	0	0	0	0	0
S_3	1	0	0	0	0	0	0	0	0	0
S_4	0	0	0	0	1	0	0	0	0	1
S_5	0	0	0	0	0	1	0	0	0	0
S_6	0	0	0	1	0	0	0	0	0	0
S_7	0	0	0	0	0	0	0	1	0	1
S_8	0	0	0	0	0	0	0	0	1	1
S_9	0	0	0	0	0	0	1	0	0	0
S_{10}	1	0	0	1	0	0	1	0	0	0

One of the easiest ways to set up such a matrix is to set up the 10×10 zero matrix and then edit it. The editing can be automated as follows.

Define a 10×10 *zero matrix.*	`In[1]:= M =` `  Array[0 &, {10,10}];`

Set up a list of the nonzero entries.	`In[2]:= L =`
	`{{1,2},{1,10},{2,3},{3,1},`
	`  {4,5},{4,10},{5,6},{6,4},`
	`   {7,8},{7,10},{8,9},{8,10},`
	`{9,7},{10,1},{10,4},{10,7}};`

Change the entries of M to ones in the positions listed in L.	`In[3]:= Do[M[[L[[i,1]],`
	`L[[i,2]]]] = 1,`
	`{i,1,Length[L]}]`

Let M denote the matrix of entries. Because M^2 contains a nonzero entry in the (i, j) position if and only if $\sum_{r=1}^{10} M_{ir}M_{rij} \neq 0$, and because this occurs precisely when there is a flight from S_i to an intermediate state S_r from which there is a flight to S_j, it follows that the (i, j) entry of M^2 is nonzero precisely if it is possible to get from S_i to S_j with exactly two flights. Similarly, the (i, j) entry of M^n is nonzero precisely if it is possible to get from S_i to S_j with exactly n flights.

The states in a connection-type problem need not be geographic states. An interesting example of this is obtained by considering airports as a means of connecting from one plane to another, so the planes take on the role of the states. In other situations, a state might be a state of affairs or a configuration of pieces in a game.

A variation of a famous (though fairly simple) problem has a shepherd, a boat, a wolf, a sheep, and a cabbage on the left side of a river. The shepherd is to get everything—himself, the boat, the animals, and the cabbage—to the right side. He cannot leave the wolf and the sheep or the sheep and the cabbage together unattended, and he can carry at most one occupant (in addition to himself) in the boat at one time. In this problem, a state might be represented by a list of the inhabitants of the left bank. The potential residents are the boat, the shepherd, the wolf, the sheep, and the cabbage. Of course, the boat cannot cross without the shepherd. The potential states are then $S_1 = \{$boat, shepherd, wolf, sheep, cabbage$\}$, $S_2 = \{$boat, shepherd, wolf, sheep$\}$, $S_3 = \{$boat, shepherd, wolf, cabbage$\}$, $S_4 = \{$boat, shepherd, sheep, cabbage$\}$, $S_5 = \{$boat, shepherd, sheep$\}$, $S_6 = \{\}$, $S_7 = \{$cabbage$\}$, $S_8 = \{$sheep$\}$, $S_9 = \{$wolf$\}$, and $S_{10} = \{$cabbage, wolf$\}$.

Another famous problem is known as the missionary/cannibal problem. In this problem there are n missionaries, n cannibals and a boat on the left bank of a river. The problem is to get all $2n$ people across the river. They can cross in any order—one or two at a time—but at no time can the cannibals on either side outnumber the missionaries on that side (unless there are no missionaries on that side). Everyone is considered to be on one bank or the other; nobody is counted as being in the boat.

For the missionary/cannibal problem, a state might be represented by an inventory $\{B,M,C\}$ of the left bank, where $B = 1$ if the boat is on the left bank and 0 otherwise, M is the number of missionaries on the left bank, and C is the number of cannibals on the left bank. Following this scheme for $n = 2$ gives the legal states $S_1 = \{1,2,2\}$, $S_2 = \{1,2,1\}$, $S_3 = \{1,2,0\}$, $S_4 = \{1,1,1\}$, $S_5 = \{1,0,2\}$, $S_6 = \{1,0,1\}$, $S_7 = \{1,0,0\}$ (unattainable but legal), $S_8 = \{0,2,2\}$ (unattainable but legal), $S_9 = \{0,2,1\}$, $S_{10} = \{0,2,0\}$, $S_{11} = \{0,1,1\}$, $S_{12} = \{0,0,2\}$, $S_{13} = \{0,0,1\}$, and $S_{14} = \{0,0,0\}$. S_1 is the initial state, and the object is to get to S_{14}. You may find it easier to do the $n = 2$ case by hand than with the computer. For larger values of n, the problem is more difficult.

Problems on Incidence Matrices

1. Enter the incidence matrix of the shepherd, boat, and wolf problem.
    a. Determine the smallest number of crossings in which the deed can be done—if, indeed, it can be done.
    b. Explain why the matrix is symmetric.
2. Construct the incidence matrix for the missionary/cannibal problem for $n = 2$.
    a. Determine the minimum number of (one-way) trips required to get all four across the river—if it is possible.
    b. Determine a strategy for getting all four across the river (without breaking the rules, of course).
3. Repeat Problem 2 for $n = 3$. (This will take a bit longer.)
4. Repeat Problem 2 for $n = 4$. (This will take quite a bit longer.) There are 26 states. If S_1 is the initial state and S_{26} is the desired terminal state, one incidence matrix M can be obtained using the following list LR of paths from the left bank to the right bank and the fact that M is symmetric.

    LR = {{1,15}, {1,16}, {1,19}, {2,16}, {2,17}, {2,19}, {3,17}, {3,18}, {3,20}, {4,18}, {6,20}, {7,21}, {8,25}, {8,26}, {9,23}, {9,24}, {10,24}, {10,25}, {11,25}, {11,26}, {12,26}}.

    As explained in Problem 5, it is necessary to look only at the first 26 powers of M.
5. Enter the incidence matrix A for the airport problem into your *Mathematica* session.
    a. Determine the minimum number of flights required to get a passenger from S_3 to S_7.

    A question of potential interest to a traveler in the region served by this airline is whether it is possible to get between every pair of states. Since all entries of the matrix A (and therefore all its powers) are nonnegative, it is possible to get from state i to state j with (say) five or fewer flights if and only if the (i, j) entry of the matrix $\sum_{i=1}^{5} M^i$ is nonzero. While it might appear that this is potentially an infinite problem, as it turns out the $(n + 1)$st power of an $n \times n$ matrix M can always be written in the form

$$M^{n+1} = a_1M + a_2M^2 + \cdots + a_nM^n$$

This follows from the fact that M is a root of the polynomial generated by the *Mathematica* command `Det(x Id - M)`, which can be verified for A with the code

```
In[1]:= p =
    Det(x IdentityMatrix[10] - A);
In[2]:= Sum[Coefficient[p,x,i]\
    MatrixPower[A,i],{i,0,10}]²²
```

This decreases the number of matrix multiplications from 45 to 9. This result, known as the Cayley-Hamilton Theorem, implies that it is only necessary to sum the first 10 powers of A to determine if a connection is possible.

b. Determine whether it is possible to get from every state to every other state. (You may choose to use the `Sum` command.)

c. If it is possible to get from every state to every other state, determine the largest number of flights required to get between two states.

Coding Theory

Coding theory, as you may well know, is used for a variety of purposes relating to the security of information. We are interested in a scheme that encodes information so that only someone knowing the code can decipher a message.

Let us begin by assigning a number from 1 to 26 to the letters of the alphabet. No fancy scheme is necessary here: We can just use 1 for a, 2 for b, and so on. So our code is suitable for transmitting somewhat literate messages, we will also assign 0 to the space character, 27 to the period, and 28 to the question mark. We could add more punctuation marks, but the space, period, and question mark will suffice for our example.

Here is the entire translation table.

Translation Table

0	1	2	3	4	5	6	7	8	9
` `	a	b	c	d	e	f	g	h	i
10	11	12	13	14	15	16	17	18	19
j	k	l	m	n	o	p	q	r	s
20	21	22	23	24	25	26	27	28	
t	u	v	w	x	y	z	.	?	

---

[22]Note that the calculation described in *In[2]* requires the computation of 45 matrix products. This calculation can be done more efficiently by using Horner form, as follows.
```
In[3]:=  S = A; Id=IdentityMatrix[10];
Do[S=(S+Id).A,{i,1,9}]
```

Let's agree to use a 5×5 encoding matrix `codeMtx` for the problem. The matrix `codeMtx` must be invertible because `codeMtx`$^{-1}$ will be used to decode the message.

Since `codeMtx` is 5×5, the message matrix `msgMtx` will have to be $5 \times n$ so that the product `codeMtx` x `msgMtx` can be formed. This requires that the number of characters in the message be a multiple of 5. The message can be padded with spaces, so this is not a problem.

For example, consider the message "what is the opening line of moby dick?" For this message you get the 5×8 "message matrix"

$$
\text{msgMtx} = \begin{bmatrix} w & h & a & t & & i & s & \\ t & h & e & & o & p & e & n \\ i & n & g & & l & i & n & e \\ & o & f & & m & o & b & y \\ & d & i & c & k & ? & & \end{bmatrix}
$$

When translated to numeric form using the translation table, you get the following numeric message matrix.

$$
\text{nMsgMtx} = \begin{bmatrix} 23 & 8 & 1 & 20 & 0 & 9 & 19 & 0 \\ 20 & 8 & 5 & 0 & 15 & 16 & 5 & 14 \\ 9 & 14 & 7 & 0 & 12 & 9 & 14 & 5 \\ 0 & 15 & 6 & 0 & 13 & 15 & 2 & 25 \\ 0 & 4 & 9 & 3 & 11 & 28 & 0 & 0 \end{bmatrix}
$$

The coded numerical message matrix is now given by

```
cnMsgMtx = codeMtx X nMsgMtx
```

The recipient can decode the message by computing `codeMtx`$^{-1}$ x `cnMsgMtx` to obtain `nMsgMtx`, then using the translation table to obtain `msgMtx`.

In *Mathematica*, the message matrix can be defined easily as follows. (This will not work if any of the lowercase letters of the alphabet are assigned. You may want to begin a fresh session or use `Clear[a, b, c, . . ., z]`.)

Assign names to the punctuation marks.

```
In[1]:= S:=" "; P:="."; Q="?"
```

The quotes (`"`) are required to define the space, period, and question marks; be sure to put a space between the quotation marks in the definition of S.

Make a list of the characters that will be used.

```
In[2]:= charLst =
   {S,a,b,c,d,e,f,g,h,i,j,k,l,m,n,o,
   p,q,r,s,t,u,v,w,x,y,z,P,Q};
```

For this to work, none of the names in charLst—other than S, P, and Q—can have an assigned value.

Make a list of the message, padded out to 40 characters. Check Mathematica's output to be sure you got what you wanted. "S" should print as a space, and so on.

```
In[3]:= msgLst =
   {w,h,a,t,S,i,s,S,
   t,h,e,S,o,p,e,n,
   i,n,g,S,l,i,n,e,
   S,o,f,S,m,o,b,y,
   S,d,i,c,k,Q,S,S};
```

Define the message matrix.

```
In[4]:= msgMtx = Partition[msgLst,8];
```

The Partition command converts the list to a 5×8 matrix.

The translation of the message from alphabetic to numeric form or numeric to alphabetic form can be automated as follows.

Define a function alpha *that converts numeric data to alphabetic data.*

```
In[5]:= Do[alpha[ii] =
   charLst[[ii+1]],{ii,0,28}];
```

The counter ii is used to avoid a naming problem. If i were used, for example, alpha[i] would not be correct.

This defines the function numeric, *which converts alphabetic data to numeric data.*

```
In[6]:= Do[numeric[alpha[ii]] = ii,{ii,0,28}];
```

Observe that numeric is the functional inverse of alpha.

You can obtain nMsgMtx *by mapping* numeric *onto* msgMtx. *The third argument to* Map—*that is,* {2}—*tells* Map *to work at the second level, on the entries.*

```
In[7]:= nMsgMtx = Map[numeric,msgMtx,{2}];
   {{23,  8,   1,  20,   0,   9,   19,   0},
   {20,   8,   5,   0,   15,  16,   5,   14},
   {9,    14,  7,   0,   12,  9,    14,   5},
   {0,    15,  6,   0,   13,  15,   2,    25},
   {0,    4,   9,   3,   11,  28,   0,    0}}
```

Conversely, the recipient can recapture msgMtx *by applying* alpha *to* nMsgMtx.

```
In[8]:= Map[alpha,nMsgMtx,{2}]//MatrixForm
```

```
Out[8]//MatrixForm=
    w  h  a  t     i  s
    t  h  e     o  p  e  n
    i  n  g     l  i  n  e
    o  f     m  o  b  y
    d  i  c  k  ?
```

Problems on Coding Theory

In the following, assume codeMtx is the 5×5 matrix $[c_{ij}]$ with $c_{ij} = \min(i, j)$.

1. Use the matrix codeMtx defined above to encode the message treated in the example of the section.
2. Decode the message contained in the following coded numeric message matrix. Assume that the code matrix is the matrix codeMtx given above.

$$
\text{cnMsgMtx} = \begin{bmatrix}
24 & 29 & 54 & 38 & 6 & 27 & 36 \\
48 & 58 & 88 & 68 & 7 & 54 & 72 \\
60 & 78 & 108 & 93 & 8 & 72 & 89 \\
72 & 98 & 128 & 118 & 9 & 90 & 106 \\
81 & 117 & 136 & 131 & 10 & 95 & 118
\end{bmatrix}
$$

3. Use the Numeric function and the matrix codeMtx to encode the following message:

    this is the end of the chapter. keep going, it
    gets even better.

2 The Algebra of Vectors

In *Mathematica*, all matrices—including $n \times 1$ and $1 \times n$ matrices—require two indices to address their entries.

You use two subscripts to address any matrix entry— even if the matrix appears one-dimensional.

```
In[1]:= B = {{1,2,3,4}}
In[2]:= B[[1]]
Out[2]= {1, 2, 3, 4}
```

2.1 Introduction to Vectors in *Mathematica*

In *Mathematica*, vectors act like matrices, except they require only a single index to address their entries. A vector is a list, whereas a matrix is a list of lists.

2.1.1 Defining Vectors in *Mathematica*

You can define a vector in the same ways you can define a list. The most common methods for defining n-vectors are given in the following.

Vectors in *Mathematica*

- v = {a$_1$, a$_2$, . . . , a$_n$}
- v = Array[*fcn*, {n}][1]
- v = Table[*expr*, {i,1,n}][2]

This defines the vector **u** = *(a, b, c) directly as a list.*

```
In[3]:= u = {a, b, c}
Out[3]= {a, b, c}
```

[1]The braces around the length (n) are optional for a vector.
[2]The specification of 1 as the starting point is optional. Other starting points can be used as well.

This uses a generating function to define the 3-vector

$$\mathbf{v} = (v_i) \text{ with } v_i = \frac{2^i}{i}.^3$$

```
In[4]:= v = Array[Function[i, 2^i/i], 3]
```

$$Out[4]= \{2, 2, \frac{8}{3}\}$$

The first argument to `Array` is the generating function; the second is the length of the vector. Note that the expression `2^i/i` does not evaluate to 2^1.

You can also use built-in or your own functions to define vectors.

```
In[5]:= Array[Exp,3]
```
$$Out[5]= \{E, E^2, E^3\}$$

In this case, the first argument is the function defined by $\exp(x) = \mathbf{e}^x$. (Recall that $\mathbf{e}$ is denoted E in *Mathematica*.)

Here an expression is used to define a 3-vector with the `Table` *command.*

```
In[6]:= w := Table[2^i/i, {i,3,5}]
```

Note that *Mathematica* does not echo the definition because the delayed assignment operator (:=) is used. This has consequences for $\mathbf{w}$, as we will see shortly.

Editing Vectors

The ith entry of a vector $\mathbf{v}$ *is denoted* `v[[i]]` *in Mathematica.*

```
In[7]:= v[[1]]
Out[7]= 2
```

To modify an entry, simply reassign it. This changes the first component of $\mathbf{v}$ *to* 1.

```
In[8]:= v[[1]] = 1
Out[8]= 1

In[9]:= v
```
$$Out[9]= \{1, 2, \frac{8}{3}\}$$

Note that if a vector is originally defined using ":=" you cannot reassign its entries.

```
In[10]:= w[[1]] = 1
Part::noval:
   Symbol w in part assignment does not have an
immediate value.
Out[10]= 1
```

The definition of $\mathbf{w}$ *in* %6 *used ":=" and has not changed.*

```
In[11]:= w
```
$$Out[11]= \{\frac{8}{3}, 4, \frac{32}{5}\}$$

---

[3]Alternatively, the generating function can be given in the form `2^#/#&`.

2.1.2 Vector Arithmetic

```
[+, -, *, /, Dot, ., Length,
norm⁴, Cross⁵, Subscripted]
```

Mathematica uses the same notation for addition, subtraction, and scalar multiplication of vectors as it does for matrices. This notation is summarized in the following table.

Vector Arithmetic

Operation	Standard Notation	*Mathematica* Notation
addition	$\mathbf{u} + \mathbf{v}$	u + v
subtraction	$\mathbf{u} - \mathbf{v}$	u - v
scalar multiplication	$k\,\mathbf{u}$	k u
		k * u
	$\dfrac{1}{k}\mathbf{u}$	1/k * u
		u/k
dot product	$\mathbf{u} \cdot \mathbf{v}$	u . v
		Dot[u,v]
cross product	$\mathbf{u} \times \mathbf{v}$	Cross[u,v]

Although vectors are printed horizontally in *Mathematica*, vectors are inherently neither rows nor columns—perhaps they are best thought of as *n*-tuples written horizontally to conserve screen space.

*Define vectors **u** and **v** to use as examples. Notice the effect of the* Subscripted *command.*

```
In[1]:= u = Table[Subscripted["u"[i]], {i,3}]
Out[1]= {u₁, u₂, u₃}
```

```
In[2]:= v = Table[Subscripted["v"[i]],{i,3}]
Out[2]= {v₁, v₂, v₃}
```

*This computes the sum of **u** and **v**.*

```
In[3]:= u + v
Out[3]= {u₁ + v₁, u₂ + v₂, u₃ + v₃}
```

*This computes the scalar product k**u**.*

```
In[4]:= k u
Out[4]= {k u₁, k u₂, k u₃}
```

Recall that the Euclidean inner product $\langle \mathbf{u}, \mathbf{v} \rangle$ is often called the dot product and denoted $\mathbf{u} \cdot \mathbf{v}$.

---

[4]This is not a built-in function.

[5]The Cross command is in the LinearAlgebra package.

This computes the Euclidean inner product $\langle \mathbf{u}, \mathbf{v} \rangle$ of $\mathbf{u}$ and $\mathbf{v}$.[6]

```
In[5]:= u . v
Out[5]= u1 v1 + u2 v2 + u3 v3
```

This demonstrates the standard definition $\langle \mathbf{u}, \mathbf{v} \rangle = \sum_{i=1}^{n} u_i v_i$ for $n = 3$.

The inner product $A\mathbf{v}$ of a matrix A and a vector $\mathbf{v}$ is the vector of inner products of the rows of A with $\mathbf{v}$.

```
In[6]:= A = Table[Subscripted[a[10 i + j]], {i,1,3},
        {j,1,3}]
Out[6]=
  {{a11,  a12,  a13},

   {a21,  a22,  a23},

   {a31,  a32,  a33}}
```

```
In[7]:= A . u
Out[7]=
{u1 a11 + u2 a12 + u3 a13,
 u1 a21 + u2 a22 + u3 a23,
 u1 a31 + u2 a32 + u3 a33}
```

Note that the ith entry uses the ith row of A.

The inner product of a vector $\mathbf{u}$ and a matrix A is the vector of inner products of $\mathbf{u}$ with the columns of A.

```
In[8]:= u . A
Out[8]=
{u1 a11 + u2 a21 + u3 a31,
 u1 a12 + u2 a22 + u3 a32,
 u1 a13 + u2 a23 + u3 a33}
```

Note that the ith entry uses the ith column of A.
In general, $\langle A, \mathbf{u} \rangle$ and $\langle \mathbf{u}, A \rangle$ are not the same.

Use Length to get the number of components of a vector.

```
In[9]:= Length[u]
Out[9]= 3
```

You can define a norm function to determine the length of the vector.

```
In[10]:= norm[x_]:= Sqrt[Sum[x[[i]]^2,
         {i,1,Length[x]}]]
```

```
In[11]:= norm[u]
Out[11]= Sqrt[u1^2 + u2^2 + u3^2]
```

---

[6]You can use the command Dot [u, v]. *Mathematica* translates $\mathbf{u} \cdot \mathbf{v}$ to Dot [u, v] before evaluating it.

Recall that, in general, the Euclidean norm is given by

$$\|\mathbf{u}\| = \sqrt{\sum_{i=1}^{n} u_i^2}$$

Use the `Cross` *command to compute the cross product* $\mathbf{c} = \mathbf{u} \times \mathbf{v}$ *of vectors.*[7,8]

```
In[12]:= c = Cross[u,v]
Out[12]= {-(u₃ v₂) + u₂ v₃, u₃ v₁ - u₁ v₃,
-(u₂ v₁) + u₁ v₂}
```

This is the standard definition of $\mathbf{u} \times \mathbf{v}$.
   Recall that for vectors in $\Re^n$, the cross product $\mathbf{c} = \mathbf{u} \times \mathbf{v}$ satisfies $\langle \mathbf{c}, \mathbf{u} \rangle = \langle \mathbf{c}, \mathbf{v} \rangle = 0$.

This verifies the identity
$\mathbf{u} \cdot (\mathbf{u} \times \mathbf{v}) = 0.$

```
In[13]:= Expand[u . Cross[u,v]]
Out[13]= 0
```

`Expand` is required here to simplify the result to 0.
   Of course, *Mathematica*'s vector commands work with numerical vectors as well.

2.1.3 Working with Parts of Vectors and Matrices
`[List, $Post, Partition]`

Beginning with this section, we assume the assignment `$Post := If[MatrixQ[#],MatrixForm[#],#]&` has been made. This means that some sets of sets will be displayed as matrices. Overall, this assignment will make the output easier to interpret.

```
$Post := If[MatrixQ[#], MatrixForm[#], #]&
```

Throughout the remainder of the text we assume that `MatrixForm` is used to display matrices.

Define the matrix A for use as an example. The `Subscripted` *command is used to make the later results easier to interpret.*

```
In[1]:= $Post := If[MatrixQ[#],MatrixForm[#],#]&

In[2]:= A = Table[Subscripted[a[10i+j]],
    {i,5}, {j,5}]
```

---

[7]The `Cross` command is in the `LinearAlgebra` package.
[8]You can use the operator notation u ~ `Cross` ~ v if you prefer.

Out[2]//MatrixForm=

$$\begin{array}{ccccc} a_{11} & a_{12} & a_{13} & a_{14} & a_{15} \\ a_{21} & a_{22} & a_{23} & a_{24} & a_{25} \\ a_{31} & a_{32} & a_{33} & a_{34} & a_{35} \\ a_{41} & a_{42} & a_{43} & a_{44} & a_{45} \\ a_{51} & a_{52} & a_{53} & a_{54} & a_{55} \end{array}$$

Taking Things Apart

The rows and columns of any matrix *A* are naturally associated with vectors—the row and column vectors of *A*.

Use A[[i]] *to extract the ith row vector.*

In[3]:= A[[1]]
Out[3]= {a_{11}, a_{12}, a_{13}, a_{14}, a_{15}}

This gives the first row vector of *A*. The column vectors can similarly be obtained using the Transpose command. As vectors, both the row and column vectors print in horizontal form.

Use A[[{n_1,...,n_k}]] *to pick out the n_1st, ..., n_kth row vectors from a matrix.*

In[4]:= A[[{1,3,5}]]
Out[4]//MatrixForm=

$$\begin{array}{ccccc} a_{11} & a_{12} & a_{13} & a_{14} & a_{15} \\ a_{31} & a_{32} & a_{33} & a_{34} & a_{35} \\ a_{51} & a_{52} & a_{53} & a_{54} & a_{55} \end{array}$$

The output prints as a matrix because it is a list of equal-length vectors.

Use Transpose[A][[i]] *to extract the ith column vector.*

In[5]:= Transpose[A][[1]]
Out[5]= {a_{11}, a_{21}, a_{31}, a_{41}, a_{51}}

This picks out the 1st, 3rd, *and* 5th *columns of A.*

In[6]:= Transpose[A][[{1,3,5}]]
Out[6]//MatrixForm=

$$\begin{array}{ccccc} a_{11} & a_{21} & a_{31} & a_{41} & a_{51} \\ a_{13} & a_{23} & a_{33} & a_{43} & a_{53} \\ a_{15} & a_{25} & a_{35} & a_{45} & a_{55} \end{array}$$

Putting Things Together

Vectors can be assembled into matrices, as either columns or rows. The following demonstrates some useful ways of doing this.

You can use {} *to build a matrix using a given sequence of row vectors.*

In[7]:= M = {A[[1]],A[[3]]}
Out[7]//MatrixForm=

$$\begin{array}{ccccc} a_{11} & a_{12} & a_{13} & a_{14} & a_{15} \\ a_{31} & a_{32} & a_{33} & a_{34} & a_{35} \end{array}$$

Notice that the result is labeled *M*.

Use Transpose *and* {} *to build a matrix using specified column vectors.*

```
In[8]:= T = Transpose[{A[[3]],A[[5]]}]
Out[8]//MatrixForm=
```

$$\begin{array}{cc} a_{31} & a_{51} \\ a_{32} & a_{52} \\ a_{33} & a_{53} \\ a_{34} & a_{54} \\ a_{35} & a_{55} \end{array}$$

Notice that the result is named *T*.

You can use Append *to append a row to a matrix.*

```
In[9]:= v = {a,b,c,d,e};

In[10]:= Append[M,v]
Out[10]//MatrixForm=
```

$$\begin{array}{ccccc} a_{11} & a_{12} & a_{13} & a_{14} & a_{15} \\ a_{31} & a_{32} & a_{33} & a_{34} & a_{35} \\ a & b & c & d & e \end{array}$$

In general, Append is used to append an entry to the end of a list. In this case, M is a list of vectors, and v is a vector.

You can use Table *and* Append *to append a vector to a matrix as a column.*

```
In[11]:= Table[Append[T[[i]], v[[i]]], {i,5}]
Out[11]//MatrixForm=
```

$$\begin{array}{ccc} a_{31} & a_{51} & a \\ a_{32} & a_{42} & b \\ a_{33} & a_{43} & c \\ a_{34} & a_{54} & d \\ a_{35} & a_{55} & e \end{array}$$

Here, the entry v[[i]] is appended to vector T[[i]] for $i = 1, \ldots, 5$.

For the following, we redefine *A* as a 3×3 matrix, and define a new 3×3 matrix *B*.

Define A and B as subscripted 3×3 symbolic matrices.

```
In[12]:= A = Table[Subscripted[a[10 i + j]],
{i,3},{j,3}]
Out[12]//MatrixForm=
```

$$\begin{array}{ccc} a_{11} & a_{12} & a_{13} \\ a_{21} & a_{22} & a_{23} \\ a_{31} & a_{32} & a_{33} \end{array}$$

```
In[13]:= B = Table[Subscripted[b[10 i + j]],
{i,3},{j,3}]
Out[13]//MatrixForm=
```

$$\begin{array}{ccc} b_{11} & b_{12} & b_{13} \\ b_{21} & b_{22} & b_{23} \\ b_{31} & b_{32} & b_{33} \end{array}$$

You can use Table *and* Join *to augment a matrix by a matrix. This makes it unnecessary to use* AppendRows, *which otherwise requires that you load the* LinearAlgebra *package.*

```
In[14]:= Table[Join[A[[i]], B[[i]]], {i,1,3}]
Out[14]//MatrixForm=
```

$$\begin{matrix} a_{11} & a_{12} & a_{13} & b_{11} & b_{12} & b_{13} \\ a_{21} & a_{22} & a_{23} & b_{21} & b_{22} & b_{23} \\ a_{31} & a_{32} & a_{33} & b_{31} & b_{32} & b_{33} \end{matrix}$$

Join *also gives you an easy way to "stack" matrices.*

In this regard, note that if **v** *is a vector, then* {**v**} *is a matrix; thus* Join *also can be used to append a vector as a row.*

```
In[15]:= Join[A,B]
Out[15]//MatrixForm=
```

$$\begin{matrix} a_{11} & a_{12} & a_{13} \\ a_{21} & a_{22} & a_{23} \\ a_{31} & a_{32} & a_{33} \\ b_{11} & b_{12} & b_{13} \\ b_{21} & b_{22} & b_{23} \\ b_{31} & b_{32} & b_{33} \end{matrix}$$

2.1.4 Solving Linear Matrix/Vector Equations
[LinearSolve]

If A is an $m \times n$ matrix and **b** is an m-vector, then there may exist vectors **x** for which $A\mathbf{x} = \mathbf{b}$. The solutions can be found by applying Gaussian elimination and back-substitution to the augmented matrix $[A,\mathbf{b}]$.

Define A and **b** *for use as an example.*

```
In[1]:= A = Table[i+j, {i,5}, {j,5}]
Out[1]//MatrixForm=
```

$$\begin{matrix} 2 & 3 & 4 & 5 & 6 \\ 3 & 4 & 5 & 6 & 7 \\ 4 & 5 & 6 & 7 & 8 \\ 5 & 6 & 7 & 8 & 9 \\ 6 & 7 & 8 & 9 & 10 \end{matrix}$$

```
In[2]:= b = Table[i,{i,5}]
Out[2]= {1, 2, 3, 4, 5}
```

*You can solve the matrix/ vector equation A***x** = **b** *by applying Gaussian elimination and back-substitution to the augmented matrix* [A,**b**].

```
In[3]:= R = Table[Append[A[[i]], b[[i]]], {i,5}]
Out[3]//MatrixForm=
```

$$\begin{matrix} 2 & 3 & 4 & 5 & 6 & 1 \\ 3 & 4 & 5 & 6 & 7 & 2 \\ 4 & 5 & 6 & 7 & 8 & 3 \\ 5 & 6 & 7 & 8 & 9 & 4 \\ 6 & 7 & 8 & 9 & 10 & 5 \end{matrix}$$

```
In[4]:= F = RowReduce[R]
Out[4]//MatrixForm=
    1    0   -1   -2   -3    2
    0    1    2    3    4   -1
    0    0    0    0    0    0
    0    0    0    0    0    0
    0    0    0    0    0    0
```

Solve the system using back-substitution.[9]

```
In[5]:= Clear[x,t];
    Do[x[i]=t[i],{i,3,5}];
    Solve[Sum[F[[2,j]]x[j],{j,1,5}]==
     F[[2,6]],x[2]]
Out[5]//MatrixForm=
  x[2] -> -1 - 2 t[3] - 3 t[4] - 4 t[5]

In[6]:= x[2] = %[[1,1,2]]
Out[6]= -1 - 2 t[3] - 3 t[4] - 4 t[5]

In[7]:= Solve[Sum[F[[1,j]]x[j], {j,1,5}] ==
   F[[1,6]], x[1]]
Out[7]//MatrixForm=
  x[1] -> 2 + t[3] + 2 t[4] + 3 t[5]

In[8]:= x[1] = %[[1,1,2]]
Out[8]= 2 + t[3] + 2 t[4] + 3 t[5]
```

*The vector **g** is the most general solution of the equation $A\mathbf{x} = \mathbf{b}$. Here it is displayed as a column.*

```
In[9]:= g = Table[x[i], {i,5}]; g//ColumnForm
Out[9]=
  2 + t[3] + 2 t[4] + 3 t[5]
  -1 - 2 t[3] - 3 t[4] - 4 t[5]
  t[3]
  t[4]
  t[5]
```

*You can check that **g** is a solution of $A\mathbf{x} = \mathbf{b}$ by evaluating $A \cdot \mathbf{g} - \mathbf{b}$.*

```
In[10]:= A . g - b;
In[11]:= Simplify[%]
Out[11]=
  {0, 0, 0, 0, 0}
```

Mathematica's response `Out[10]` was suppressed because of its length. The `Simplify` command shortened it.[10]

---

[9]It is not necessary to clear the variables in a new session like this one. In a long session, however, it is a good precaution. It is all too easy to assign a variable, then later use it with the assumption that it is not assigned.

[10]The `Expand` command would work here just as well.

A matrix/vector equation of the form $\mathbf{x}A = \mathbf{b}$ can be solved using the transpose function. Since vectors are orientation independent in *Mathematica*, $\mathbf{x}A = \mathbf{b}$ is equivalent to $A^T\mathbf{x} = \mathbf{b}$.

A matrix equation of the form $AX = B$ can be solved by separately solving each of the equations $A\mathbf{x} = \mathbf{b}_i$, where $\mathbf{b}_i$ is the *i*th column vector of B. If $\mathbf{s}_i$ is the solution of $A\mathbf{x} = \mathbf{b}_i$, then $S = [\mathbf{s}_1, \ldots, \mathbf{s}_n]$ is the solution of $AX = B$, where n is the number of columns in B.

The sequence of steps

- Augment a matrix by a vector
- Row-reduce the augmented matrix
- Back-solve for the variables

occurs with such frequency in linear algebra that *Mathematica* has the special command `LinearSolve` that finds a solution, although it alone does not give the most general solution. We demonstrate its use.

LinearSolve returns a particular solution of a matrix/vector equation of the form $A\mathbf{x} = \mathbf{b}$.

```
In[10]:= LinearSolve[A,b]
Out[10]= {2, -1, 0, 0, 0}
```

Note that this is the particular solution obtained by setting `t[3] = t[4] = t[5] = 0` in the general solution obtained in %9.

Note the response returned by `LinearSolve` if Mathematica finds no solution of the equation $A\mathbf{x} = \mathbf{b}$.

```
In[11]:= LinearSolve[A,b]
LinearSolve::nosol:
  Linear equation encountered which has no solution.
Out[11]=
LinearSolve[{{2, 3, 4, 5, 6}, {3, 4, 5, 6, 7},
    {4, 5, 6, 7, 8}, {5, 6, 7, 8, 9},
    {6, 7, 8, 9, 10}}, {1, 2, 4, 4, 5}]
```

EXERCISES 2.1 _____

1. Enter the following vectors in your *Mathematica* session.
    a. The 5-vector $\mathbf{u} = (u_i)$ defined by $u_i = i!$.
    b. The 5-vector $\mathbf{v} = (v_i)$ defined by $v_i = i^i$.
    c. The 5-vector $\mathbf{w} = (w_i)$ defined by $w_i = (-1)^i$.
2. Using the vectors of Exercise 1,
    a. Compute the inner product of $\mathbf{u}$ and $\mathbf{v}$.
    b. Compute the norm, $\|\mathbf{u}\|$, of $\mathbf{u}$.
    c. Verify the triangle inequality $\|\mathbf{u} - \mathbf{w}\| \le \|\mathbf{u} - \mathbf{v}\| + \|\mathbf{v} - \mathbf{w}\|$.
    d. Verify the Cauchy-Schwarz inequality $|\langle\mathbf{u},\mathbf{v}\rangle| \le \|\mathbf{u}\| \, \|\mathbf{v}\|$.
3. Let $A = [a_{ij}]$ be the 3×5 matrix defined by the equation $a_{ij} = \max(i, j)$. Let $\mathbf{u} = (u_i)$ be the 3-vector defined by $u_i = i!$, and let $\mathbf{v}$ be the 5-vector

defined by $v_i = (-1)^i$. Determine which of the following are defined and evaluate those that are.

    a. **u**A b. A**u**   c. **v**A d. A**v**

4. Let A and **u** be as in Exercise 3. Find the general solution of the equation $A\mathbf{x} = \mathbf{u}$.

5. Let A and **u** be as in Exercise 3. Use Transpose and Append to append **u** to the matrix A as a column.

6. Let **u** be the 5-vector $\mathbf{u} = (1, 2, 3, 4, 5)$, and let A be as in Exercise 3. Find all solutions of the equation $\mathbf{x}A = \mathbf{u}$.

7. Give an example in which A and B are square matrices and **u** a vector for which $(A \cdot \mathbf{u}) \cdot B \neq A \cdot (\mathbf{u} \cdot B)$.

8. If A is a nonsingular matrix, the unique solution of the equation $AX = I$ is A^{-1}. Use row-reduction to find the inverse of the 5×5 matrix A with (i, j) entry $a_{ij} = \max(i, j)$. Multiply A and your answer to verify your solution.

9. For any vector $\mathbf{a} = (a_1, \ldots, a_n)$, denote by A the one-row matrix $A = [a_1, \ldots, a_n]$. Then two vectors

$$\mathbf{a} = (a_1, a_2, \ldots, a_n) \qquad \text{and} \qquad \mathbf{x} = (x_1, x_2, \ldots, x_n)$$

are orthogonal (have inner product zero) if and only if the product of the row matrix $A = [a_1 \ a_2 \ \ldots \ a_n]$ and the vector **x** is zero. It follows that the set of all vectors orthogonal to a given vector **a** is the solution set of the homogeneous linear system $A\mathbf{x} = \mathbf{0}$. Obtain a parametric description of all vectors **x** orthogonal to the vector $\mathbf{a} = (1, 2, 3, 4, 5)$. This set is known as the *orthogonal complement* of **a**.

10. If M is any matrix, the set of vectors **x** that satisfies $M\mathbf{x} = \mathbf{0}$ is the set of vectors orthogonal to *all* rows of M. Find a parametric description of all vectors **x** orthogonal to all the rows of the 3×7 matrix $M = [m_{ij}]$, where $m_{ij} = i - j$. Note the relationship between the rank of M, the width of M, and the number of parameters in the solution. Experimentally determine if a similar relationship holds for other matrices. Can you explain this? (The rank of a matrix is the number of nonzero rows in its row-reduced form.)

11. It is sometimes desirable to define at one time a family of related vectors. In *Mathematica* this is conveniently done using a loop . The following demonstrates the technique.

Mathematica uses a default value of 1 if the start value is not specified.

```
In[1]:= Do[u[i] = Table[i+j,{j,5}];
Print[u[i]],{i,4}]
Out[1]=
    {2, 3, 4, 5, 6}
    {3, 4, 5, 6, 7}
    {4, 5, 6, 7, 8}
    {5, 6, 7, 8, 9}
```

Use a Do loop to define the collection $\{\mathbf{w}_i\}_{i=1}^{24}$ of 12-vectors where the jth component of $\mathbf{w}_i$ is i^j.

2.2 The Solutions of a Homogeneous Linear System
[NullSpace]

Enter the coefficient matrix.

A linear system of the form $Ax = 0$ is said to be homogeneous. The general solution s_g of any linear system $Ax = b$ can always be written in the form $s_g = s_p + s_h$, where s_h is the general solution of the homogeneous linear system $Ax = 0$ and s_p is any particular solution of the equation $Ax = b$ (verify). Consider the following example.

```
In[1]:= A = Table[i+j,{i,5},{j,7}]
Out[1]//MatrixForm=
    2   3   4   5   6    7    8
    3   4   5   6   7    8    9
    4   5   6   7   8    9   10
    5   6   7   8   9   10   11
    6   7   8   9  10   11   12
```

This is a matrix for which the system $Ax = 0$ has nontrivial solutions. You can use NullSpace to get the general solution of the equation $Ax = 0$.

Apply NullSpace.

```
In[2]:= NullSpace[A]
Out[2]//MatrixForm=
    5   -6   0   0   0   0   1
    4   -5   0   0   0   1   0
    3   -4   0   0   1   0   0
    2   -3   0   1   0   0   0
    1   -2   1   0   0   0   0
```

The result is a list of 7-vectors, which in *Mathematica* is an $n \times 7$ matrix.

Here is the general solution s_h *of the homogeneous equation* $Ax = 0$.[11]

```
In[3]:= s[h] = Sum[t[i]%[[i]],{i,Length[%2]}]
Out[3]=
{5 t[1] + 4 t[2] + 3 t[3] + 2 t[4] + t[5],
 -6 t[1] - 5 t[2] - 4 t[3] - 3 t[4] - 2 t[5],
 t[1], t[2], t[3], t[4], t[5]}
```

You can use NullSpace in combination with LinearSolve to obtain the general solution of any matrix/vector equation $Ax = b$.

Here is a vector **b** *for which the equation* $Ax = b$ *has a solution. We use* LinearSolve *to find a particular solution.*[12]

```
In[4]:= b = {35,42,49,56,63}
Out[4]= {35, 42, 49, 56, 63}

In[5]:= s[p] = LinearSolve[A,b]
Out[5]= {-14, 21, 0, 0, 0, 0, 0}
```

---

[11]Using Length gives a quick and accurate count of the number of terms in %2.
[12]LinearSolve was introduced in Section 2.1.4.

The general solution s_g of the system $Ax = b$ is given by $s_g = s_p + s_h$.

```
In[6]:= s[g] = s[p] + s[h]
Out[6]=
{-14 + 5 t[1] + 4 t[2] + 3 t[3] + 2 t[4] + t[5],
 21 - 6 t[1] - 5 t[2] - 4 t[3] - 3 t[4] - 2 t[5],
 t[5], t[4], t[3], t[2], t[1]}
```

Verify the calculation.

```
In[7]:= Expand[A . s[g] - b]
Out[7]= {0, 0, 0, 0, 0}
```

EXERCISES 2.2

1. Let $A = [a_{ij}]$ be the 5×11 matrix defined by $a_{ij} = \min(i, j)$. Find the general, parameterized solution s_g of the matrix/vector equation $Ax = b$ where $b = (1, 2, 3, 4, 5)$.
2. Let $A = [a_{ij}]$ be the 5×7 matrix defined by $a_{ij} = i/(i + j)$. Find the general, parameterized solution s_h of the matrix/vector equation $Ax = 0$. Write s_h as a sum of the form $k_1 v_1 + k_2 v_2$.
3. Let $A = [a_{ij}]$ be the 6×6 matrix defined by $a_{ij} = \max(i, j)$. Let $b = (1, 2, 3, 4, 5, 6)$. Find the general solution s_g of the equation $Ax = b$.
4. Let $A = [a_{ij}]$ be the 5×12 matrix defined by $a_{ij} = i + j - 1$. Let $b = (6, 6, 6, 6, 6)$. Find the general solution s_g of the equation $Ax = b$.
5. Let $A = [a_{ij}]$ be the 6×11 matrix defined by $a_{ij} = i - j + 1$. Let $b = (1, 2, 2, 3, 3, 3)$. Find the general solution s_g of the equation $Ax = b$.

2.3 Span and Linear Independence

One of the fundamental problems of vector spaces is the determination of the vectors u that are linear combinations of a given set $\{v_1, v_2, \ldots, v_s\}$ of vectors. The set $\{\sum_{i=1}^{s} k_i v_i\}$ of all such vectors is called the   *span*   or   *lin* of $\{v_1, v_2, \ldots, v_s\}$. In n-space you can determine if a given vector u lies in the span of vectors $v_1, v_2, \ldots, v_s$ by using the LinearSolve command. The key is that a vector b is a linear combination of vectors $v_1, v_2, \ldots, v_s$ if and only if the vector/matrix equation $[v_1, v_2, \ldots, v_s]x = b$ has a solution. The technique is easily applied by hand in smaller problems.

This defines a collection $\{v_i\}_{i=1}^{12}$ of 10-vectors using a Do *loop.*[13]

```
In[1]:= Do[v[i] =
  Table[i/1+Mod[i+j,5], {j,10}], {i,12}]
```

---

[13]m mod n is the remainder on dividing m by n. For example, 7 mod 5 is 2, 8 mod 5 is 3, 10 mod 5 is 0.

If you get an error message here, unassign the name v and reenter the command; if you are not in a new session, v may already have a conflicting definition.

Here is a vector that may lie in the span of the vectors $v_1, \ldots, v_{12}$.

```
In[2]:= u = Array[1&,10]
Out[2]= {1, 1, 1, 1, 1, 1, 1, 1, 1, 1}
```

Note that you cannot use $\mathbf{v}$ for the name of this vector without hiding the definitions of $v[1], \ldots, v[12]$.

This shows that $\mathbf{u}$ is a linear combination of the vectors $\{v_i\}_{i=1}^{12}$ and returns a vector of coefficients.

```
In[3]:= M = Transpose[{v[1],v[2],
  v[3],v[4],v[5],v[6],v[7],v[8],
  v[9],v[10],v[11],v[12]}];
```

```
In[4]:= a = LinearSolve[M,u]
Out[4]=
```

$$\{\frac{1}{25}, \frac{1}{25}, \frac{1}{25}, \frac{1}{25}, \frac{1}{25}, 0, 0, 0, 0, 0, 0, 0\}$$

If $\mathbf{a} = (a_i)$, then $\mathbf{u} = \sum_{i=1}^{12} a_i \mathbf{v}_i$.

You can easily check the solution.

```
In[5]:= Sum[a[[i]]v[i], {i,12}]
Out[5]= {1, 1, 1, 1, 1, 1, 1, 1, 1, 1}
```

Note that the expression evaluates to $\mathbf{u}$, as it should.

Here a second vector $\mathbf{w}$ is checked to determine whether it lies in the span of $\{v_i\}_{i=1}^{12}$.

```
In[6]:= w = Table[i^2,{i,10}];
```

```
In[7]:= a = LinearSolve[M,w];
LinearSolve::nosol:
    Linear equation encountered which has no solution.
```

Recall that a sequence $v_1, v_2, \ldots, v_s$ of vectors is linearly independent if the only solution of the homogeneous system $[v_1, v_2, \ldots, v_s]\mathbf{x} = \mathbf{0}$ is the trivial one, $\mathbf{x} = \mathbf{0}$. You can use NullSpace or RowReduce to determine this.

This gives the dimension of the solution space of the equation $[v_1, \ldots, v_{12}]\mathbf{x} = \mathbf{0}$.[14]

```
In[8]:= M = Table[v[j][[i]], {i,10}, {j,12}];
```

```
In[9]:= Length[NullSpace[M]]
Out[9]= 7
```

---

[14]This input gives the same matrix M as %3.

In this case the vectors are linearly dependent. The general solution of $[\mathbf{v}_1, \ldots, \mathbf{v}_{12}]\mathbf{x} = \mathbf{0}$ has 7 parameters.

You can check Mathematica's result by using row-reduction on M.

```
In[10]:= RowReduce[M]
Out[10]//MatrixForm=
```

$$
\begin{bmatrix}
1 & 0 & 0 & 0 & 0 & \frac{6}{5} & \frac{1}{5} & \frac{1}{5} & \frac{1}{5} & \frac{1}{5} & \frac{7}{5} & \frac{2}{5} \\
0 & 1 & 0 & 0 & 0 & \frac{1}{5} & \frac{6}{5} & \frac{1}{5} & \frac{1}{5} & \frac{1}{5} & \frac{2}{5} & \frac{7}{5} \\
0 & 0 & 1 & 0 & 0 & \frac{1}{5} & \frac{1}{5} & \frac{6}{5} & \frac{1}{5} & \frac{1}{5} & \frac{2}{5} & \frac{2}{5} \\
0 & 0 & 0 & 1 & 0 & \frac{1}{5} & \frac{1}{5} & \frac{1}{5} & \frac{6}{5} & \frac{1}{5} & \frac{2}{5} & \frac{2}{5} \\
0 & 0 & 0 & 0 & 1 & \frac{1}{5} & \frac{1}{5} & \frac{1}{5} & \frac{1}{5} & \frac{6}{5} & \frac{2}{5} & \frac{2}{5} \\
0 & 0 & 0 & 0 & 0 & 0 & 0 & 0 & 0 & 0 & 0 & 0 \\
0 & 0 & 0 & 0 & 0 & 0 & 0 & 0 & 0 & 0 & 0 & 0 \\
0 & 0 & 0 & 0 & 0 & 0 & 0 & 0 & 0 & 0 & 0 & 0 \\
0 & 0 & 0 & 0 & 0 & 0 & 0 & 0 & 0 & 0 & 0 & 0 \\
0 & 0 & 0 & 0 & 0 & 0 & 0 & 0 & 0 & 0 & 0 & 0
\end{bmatrix}
$$

It is clear from this that the equation $[\mathbf{v}_1, \ldots, \mathbf{v}_{12}]\mathbf{x} = \mathbf{0}$ has nontrivial solutions.

This checks the linear independence of the vectors $\mathbf{v}_1, \ldots, \mathbf{v}_5$.[15]

```
In[11]:= R:= Table[v[j][[i]], {i,10}, {j,5}]

In[12]:= Length[NullSpace[R]]
Out[12]= 0
```

This shows that the vectors $\mathbf{v}_1, \ldots, \mathbf{v}_5$ are linearly independent.

EXERCISES 2.3 _____

1. Determine if the vector $\mathbf{b} = (1, 2, 3, 4, 5)$ lies in the span of the following sets of vectors.
   a. $\mathbf{v}_1 = (5, 4, 3, 2, 1)$, $\mathbf{v}_2 = (4, 3, 2, 1, 5)$, $\mathbf{v}_3 = (3, 2, 1, 5, 4)$
   b. $\mathbf{v}_1 = (2, 3, 4, 5, 6)$, $\mathbf{v}_2 = (3, 4, 5, 6, 7)$
2. Determine if the vector $\mathbf{b} = (1,1,1,1,1)$ lies in the span of the following sets of vectors.
   a. $\mathbf{v}_1 = (5, 4, 3, 2, 1)$, $\mathbf{v}_2 = (1, 2, 3, 4, 5)$, $\mathbf{v}_3 = (3, 2, 1, 5, 4)$
   b. $\mathbf{v}_1 = (2, 3, 4, 5, 6)$, $\mathbf{v}_2 = (8, 7, 6, 5, 4)$, $\mathbf{v}_3 = (1, 0, 1, 0, 1)$

---

[15]The dimension of the null space of a matrix A is called the *nullity* of A.

3. Determine if the 15-vector $\mathbf{v} = (v_i)$ defined by $v_i = i$ lies in the span of the 15-vectors $\mathbf{w}_i$ for $i = 1, \ldots, 15$, where the jth component w_{ij} of $\mathbf{w}_i$ is given by $w_{ij} = i - j$. Do the same for the vector $\mathbf{v} = (v_i)$ defined by $v_i = i^2$.

In Exercises 4–7, use the 10-vectors $\mathbf{v}_i = (v_{ij})$ defined by $v_{ij} = 1/(1 + (i - j \bmod 5))$ for $i = 1, \ldots, 10$.

4. Determine if the vectors $\mathbf{v}_1, \mathbf{v}_2, \ldots, \mathbf{v}_{10}$ are linearly independent.
5. Determine if any of $\mathbf{v}_1, \mathbf{v}_2, \ldots, \mathbf{v}_{10}$ are linear combinations of preceding vectors.
6. Repeat Exercise 4 for $\mathbf{v}_1, \mathbf{v}_2, \ldots, \mathbf{v}_5$.
7. Determine if any of $\mathbf{v}_1, \mathbf{v}_2, \ldots, \mathbf{v}_5$ are linear combinations of preceding vectors.

2.4 Bases, Dimension, and Coordinates

Recall that a linearly independent spanning set for a vector space V is called a *basis*. You can obtain a basis for a subspace of n-space from a spanning set using row-reduction. The set of linear combinations of the rows of an $m \times n$ matrix A is a subspace of $\Re^n$ and is called the *row space* of A. The key to the following is that the row space is not changed by elementary row operations (verify).

This generates the vectors $\{\mathbf{v}_i\}_{i=1}^{12}$ *used in the previous section.*

```
In[1]:= Do[v[i]=
Table[i/1+Mod[i+j,5], {j,10}], {i,12}]
```

This forms the vectors $\{\mathbf{v}_i\}_{i=1}^{12}$ *into a matrix M in which the vectors* $\mathbf{v}_i$ *are the rows.*

```
In[2]:= M = Table[v[i], {i,12}]
Out[2]//MatrixForm=
```

3	4	5	1	2	3	4	5	1	2
5	6	2	3	4	5	6	2	3	4
7	3	4	5	6	7	3	4	5	6
4	5	6	7	8	4	5	6	7	8
6	7	8	9	5	6	7	8	9	5
8	9	10	6	7	8	9	10	6	7
10	11	7	8	9	10	11	7	8	9
12	8	9	10	11	12	8	9	10	11
9	10	11	12	13	9	10	11	12	13
11	12	13	14	10	11	12	13	14	10
13	14	15	11	12	13	14	15	11	12
15	16	12	13	14	15	16	12	13	14

The nonzero rows of any echelon form of the matrix M form a basis for the row space of M.

```
In[3]:= G = RowReduce[M]
Out[3]//MatrixForm=
    1   0   0   0   0   1   0   0   0   0
    0   1   0   0   0   0   1   0   0   0
    0   0   1   0   0   0   0   1   0   0
    0   0   0   1   0   0   0   0   1   0
    0   0   0   0   1   0   0   0   0   1
    0   0   0   0   0   0   0   0   0   0
    0   0   0   0   0   0   0   0   0   0
    0   0   0   0   0   0   0   0   0   0
    0   0   0   0   0   0   0   0   0   0
    0   0   0   0   0   0   0   0   0   0
    0   0   0   0   0   0   0   0   0   0
    0   0   0   0   0   0   0   0   0   0
```

The five nonzero rows of G form a basis for the subspace spanned by $\{v_i\}_{i=1}^{12}$, but they do not form a subset of $\{v_1, v_2, \ldots, v_{12}\}$.

The following extracts a basis from the row-reduced matrix.

Recall that the number of nonzero rows of the matrix is its rank.

```
In[4]:= B = Table[G[[i]], {i,5}]
Out[4]//MatrixForm=
    1   0   0   0   0   1   0   0   0   0
    0   1   0   0   0   0   1   0   0   0
    0   0   1   0   0   0   0   1   0   0
    0   0   0   1   0   0   0   0   1   0
    0   0   0   0   1   0   0   0   0   1
```

A sequence $v_1, v_2, \ldots, v_n$ of vectors is linearly independent if and only if $v_1 \neq 0$ and no v_i is a linear combination of $v_1, \ldots, v_{i-1}$ (or, equivalently, none is a linear combination of those after it). It is obvious by this criterion that the rows in B are linearly independent: No element is a linear combination of following elements (that is, if the order is reversed, no element is a linear combination of preceding elements).

You can easily tell which of a sequence $v_1, v_2, \ldots, v_n$ of vectors is a linear combination of preceding terms of the sequence by row-reducing the matrix $[v_1, v_2, \ldots, v_n]$. A vector v_i is *not* a linear combination of vectors $v_1, v_2, \ldots, v_{i-1}$ if and only if the reduced row-echelon form G of the matrix $[v_1, v_2, \ldots, v_n]$ has a first nonzero entry (in some row) in the ith column. It follows that if the first nonzero entries of the rows of G appear in columns $i_1, \ldots, i_s$, then $v_{i_1}, \ldots, v_{i_s}$ are a basis for the subspace spanned by $v_1, v_2, \ldots, v_n$.

Consider the previous example with $v_1, v_2, \ldots, v_{12}$ once again.

Place the vectors in a
matrix as columns.

```
In[5]:= Transpose[Table[v[i], {i,12}]]
Out[5]//MatrixForm=
```

3	5	7	4	6	8	10	12	9	11	13	15
4	6	3	5	7	9	11	8	10	12	14	16
5	2	4	6	8	10	7	9	11	13	15	12
1	3	5	7	9	6	8	10	12	14	11	13
2	4	6	8	5	7	9	11	13	10	12	14
3	5	7	4	6	8	10	12	9	11	13	15
4	6	3	5	7	9	11	8	10	12	14	16
5	2	4	6	8	10	7	9	11	13	15	12
1	3	5	7	9	6	8	10	12	14	11	13
2	4	6	8	5	7	9	11	13	10	12	14

Now, row-reduce the matrix.

```
In[6]:= RowReduce[%]
Out[6]//MatrixForm=
```

1	0	0	0	0	$\frac{6}{5}$	$\frac{1}{5}$	$\frac{1}{5}$	$\frac{1}{5}$	$\frac{1}{5}$	$\frac{7}{5}$	$\frac{2}{5}$
0	1	0	0	0	$\frac{1}{5}$	$\frac{6}{5}$	$\frac{1}{5}$	$\frac{1}{5}$	$\frac{1}{5}$	$\frac{2}{5}$	$\frac{7}{5}$
0	0	1	0	0	$\frac{1}{5}$	$\frac{1}{5}$	$\frac{6}{5}$	$\frac{1}{5}$	$\frac{1}{5}$	$\frac{2}{5}$	$\frac{2}{5}$
0	0	0	1	0	$\frac{1}{5}$	$\frac{1}{5}$	$\frac{1}{5}$	$\frac{6}{5}$	$\frac{1}{5}$	$\frac{2}{5}$	$\frac{2}{5}$
0	0	0	0	1	$\frac{1}{5}$	$\frac{1}{5}$	$\frac{1}{5}$	$\frac{1}{5}$	$\frac{6}{5}$	$\frac{2}{5}$	$\frac{2}{5}$
0	0	0	0	0	0	0	0	0	0	0	0
0	0	0	0	0	0	0	0	0	0	0	0
0	0	0	0	0	0	0	0	0	0	0	0
0	0	0	0	0	0	0	0	0	0	0	0
0	0	0	0	0	0	0	0	0	0	0	0

By inspection, each of $v_6, \ldots, v_{12}$ is a linear combination of preceding vectors, and none of $v_1, \ldots, v_5$ is a linear combination of preceding vectors. It follows that $v_1, \ldots, v_5$ is a basis for the subspace spanned by $v_1, \ldots, v_{12}$.

Coordinatization

Bases are used to "coordinatize" vector spaces, making it possible to do anything in any n-dimensional vector space that you would do in $\Re^n$. For example, the standard basis $S = \{1, x, x^2, \ldots, x^5\}$ for the vector space P_5 of polynomials of degree five or less associates the "coordinate vector" $(a_0, a_1, a_2, a_3, a_4, a_5)$ with the polynomial $p = a_0 + a_1 x + a_2 x^2 + a_3 x^3 + a_4 x^4 + a_5 x^5$. The polynomials $p_i = x^i$ themselves correspond to the 6-tuples $e_1 = (1, 0, 0, 0, 0, 0), \ldots, e_6 = (0, 0, 0, 0, 0, 1)$. If we let $(p)_S$ denote the coordinate vector of a polynomial p, then $p = \sum_{i=1}^{k} c_i q_i$ if and only if $(p)_S = \sum_{i=1}^{k} c_i (q_i)_S$. This reduces questions about P_5 to questions about $\Re^6$. The same technique can be used in general.

Change of Coordinates

The coordinatization that one gets from a particular basis **B** is peculiar to **B**. If it is desirable to work with a different basis, one gets a different coordinate system as well.

The key relationship between a basis $\mathbf{B} = \{\mathbf{b}_1, \mathbf{b}_2, \ldots, \mathbf{b}_n\}$ and the coordinates of other vectors is given by the simple identity $B(\mathbf{v})_{\mathbf{B}} = \mathbf{v}$, where $B = [\mathbf{b}_1, \mathbf{b}_2, \ldots, \mathbf{b}_n]$. If $\mathbf{C} = \{\mathbf{c}_1, \mathbf{c}_2, \ldots, \mathbf{c}_n\}$ is a second basis, and if $C = [\mathbf{c}_1, \mathbf{c}_2, \ldots, \mathbf{c}_n]$, then $C(\mathbf{v})_{\mathbf{C}} = \mathbf{v}$ and hence $B(\mathbf{v})_{\mathbf{B}} = C(\mathbf{v})_{\mathbf{C}}$. If **B** and **C** are in $\Re^n$, it follows that $(\mathbf{v})_{\mathbf{C}} = C^{-1}B(\mathbf{v})_{\mathbf{B}}$. The matrix $C^{-1}B$ is called the **B-to-C change of coordinate matrix** or *transition matrix*. In general, the **B**-to-**C** change of coordinate matrix has an ith column vector $(\mathbf{b}_i)_{\mathbf{C}}$.

Note that the reduced row-echelon form of the matrix $[C, B]$ is $[I, C^{-1}B]$. This gives another procedure for finding the transition matrix.

EXERCISES 2.4

1. Find bases for each of the following vector spaces.

   a. The subspace of $\Re^5$ spanned by the vectors $\{\mathbf{v}_i\}_{i=1}^{4}$, where $\mathbf{v}_i$ is the 5-vector defined by $\mathbf{v}_i = (i, i+1, i+2, i+3, i+4)$.

   b. The subspace of $\Re^6$ spanned by the vectors $\{\mathbf{v}_i\}_{i=1}^{7}$ where $\mathbf{v}_i = (v_{ij})$ is the 6-vector defined by $v_{ij} = 1/(i+j)$.

   c. The solution space of the linear system $A\mathbf{x} = \mathbf{0}$, where $A = [a_{ij}]$ is the 7×9 matrix defined by $a_{ij} = 1/(i+j-1)$.

2. Determine if the polynomial $p = \sum_{j=0}^{12} x^j$ is a linear combination of the polynomials $q_i = \sum_{j=0}^{12} (x-i)^j$ for $i = 1, \ldots, 13$. Note: You may wish to use Expand on the q_i. The coefficient of x^i in a polynomial $q = \sum_{i=0}^{12} c_i x^i$ in *expanded form* is returned by the *Mathematica* command Coefficient[q,x,i] (for example, the coefficient of x^3 in q is given by Coefficient[q,x,3]).

3. Determine if the polynomials q_i in Exercise 2 are a basis for P_{12}. Note: The polynomials q_i are a basis for P_{12} if and only if the associated coordinate vectors $(q_i)_{\mathbf{B}}$ of the q_i, with respect to a basis **B**, are a basis for $\Re^{13}$. For example, you might use the coordinates with respect to the basis $\mathbf{B} = \{1, x, x^2, \ldots, x^{12}\}$.

4. Let $B = [b_{ij}]$ be the 5×5 matrix given by $b_{ij} = \max(i, j)$. Let $C = [c_{ij}]$ be the 5×5 matrix given by $c_{ij} = \min(i, j)$. Denote the columns of B by $\mathbf{b}_1, \ldots, \mathbf{b}_5$, and denote the columns of C by $\mathbf{c}_1, \ldots, \mathbf{c}_5$. Let $\mathbf{B} = \{\mathbf{b}_1, \ldots, \mathbf{b}_5\}$ and $\mathbf{C} = \{\mathbf{c}_1, \ldots, \mathbf{c}_5\}$. Let $\mathbf{v} = (5, 4, 3, 2, 1)$.

   a. Find the **B**-coordinates of $\mathbf{v}$ by direct calculation.
   b. Find the **C**-coordinates of $\mathbf{v}$ by direct calculation.
   c. Find the **B**-to-**C** change of coordinate matrix P.
   d. Find the **C**-to-**B** change of coordinate matrix Q.
   e. Verify that $P(\mathbf{v})_\mathbf{B} = (\mathbf{v})_\mathbf{C}$.
   f. Verify that $Q(\mathbf{v})_\mathbf{C} = (\mathbf{v})_\mathbf{B}$.
   g. Verify that $PQ = I$.

2.5 Subspaces Associated with a Matrix

If A is an $m \times n$ matrix with real entries, the set of linear combinations of the row vectors is a subspace of $\mathfrak{R}^n$ called the *row space of A*. In Section 2.4 the row space was used to find a basis for a subspace of $\mathfrak{R}^n$ given a finite spanning set.

Other subspaces associated with a matrix are:

- Its column space—the collection of linear combinations of its column vectors.
- Its null space—the set of solutions of the equation $A\mathbf{x} = \mathbf{0}$.
- Its kernel—the kernel is the same as the null space.
- Its range space—the collection of vectors $\mathbf{b}$ of the form $\mathbf{b} = A\mathbf{x}$, for some $\mathbf{x}$. The range space is equal to the column space.

One of the most useful ways of describing a subspace is by giving a basis for it. In Section 2.4 you found a basis from a spanning set using row-reduction. You can use the same techniques to find bases for the row space or column space of any matrix. A basis for the null space is a bit more involved and is most easily found using *Mathematica*'s NullSpace command (though it can be found directly by row-reduction and back-substitution).

Define the matrix A.

```
In[1]:= A = Table[i+j, {i,5}, {j,7}]
Out[1]//MatrixForm=
    2   3   4   5   6    7    8
    3   4   5   6   7    8    9
    4   5   6   7   8    9   10
    5   6   7   8   9   10   11
    6   7   8   9  10   11   12
```

Solve the matrix/vector
*equation A**x** = **0**.*

```
In[2]:= B = NullSpace[A]
Out[2]//MatrixForm=
    5   -6   0   0   0   0   1
    4   -5   0   0   0   1   0
    3   -3   0   0   1   0   0
    2   -3   0   1   0   0   0
    1   -2   1   0   0   0   0
```

The five vectors displayed as rows are a basis for the null space of the matrix *A*.

EXERCISES 2.5 _____

1. For a pseudorandom 5×7 matrix *A* of integers, verify that the dimension of the row space of *A* is equal to the dimension of the column space of *A*. This result is true in general, and is commonly stated in the form

   row rank = column rank

   (Use the `Random[Integer,{-100,100}]` command to generate the matrix.)

2. Let $f(i, j) = i + j$. For each of the following matrices find bases for the null space, the row space, and the column space.
   a. The 5×13 matrix $A = [a_{ij}]$ defined by $a_{ij} = f(i, j)$.
   b. The 11×7 matrix $A = [a_{ij}]$ defined by $a_{ij} = f(i, j)$.
   c. The 16×8 matrix $A = [a_{ij}]$ defined by $a_{ij} = f(i, j)$.

3. Each $m \times n$ matrix in Exercise 2 has a row-space basis with two vectors and a null-space basis with $n - 2$ vectors. Can this be generalized?

4. Let $h(i, j) = 1/(i + j - 1)$. Find bases for the null space, row space, and column space of the $m \times n$ matrix $A = [h(i, j)]$ for each of the following cases.
   a. $m = 13, n = 15$
   b. $m = 14, n = 3$
   c. $m = 27, n = 5$

2.6 The Gram-Schmidt Procedure

Given a (finite) basis $\mathbf{B} = \{\mathbf{v}_1, \mathbf{v}_2, \ldots, \mathbf{v}_s\}$ for a vector space with an inner product, it is always possible to find an orthogonal basis $\mathbf{C} = \{\mathbf{w}_1, \mathbf{w}_2, \ldots, \mathbf{w}_s\}$. The technique is called the *Gram-Schmidt procedure*. (A set $\{\mathbf{w}_1, \mathbf{w}_2, \ldots, \mathbf{w}_s\}$ of vectors is said to be orthogonal if $\langle \mathbf{w}_i, \mathbf{w}_j \rangle = 0$ whenever $i \neq j$.)

Recall that the orthogonal projection of a vector **u** onto a vector **v** is given by $\text{proj}_v(\mathbf{u}) = \dfrac{\langle \mathbf{u}, \mathbf{v} \rangle}{\langle \mathbf{v}, \mathbf{v} \rangle} \mathbf{v}$, where $\langle \mathbf{u}, \mathbf{v} \rangle$ denotes the inner product of **u** and **v**.

The Gram-Schmidt procedure is stated inductively as follows. Given a sequence $\mathbf{v}_1, \mathbf{v}_2, \ldots, \mathbf{v}_s$ of vectors,

$$\mathbf{w}_1 = \mathbf{v}_1$$

$$\mathbf{w}_{i+1} = \mathbf{v}_{i+1} - \sum_{j=1}^{i} \text{proj}_{\mathbf{w}_j}(\mathbf{v}_{i+1}).$$

Gram-Schmidt with normalization then "normalizes" each vector by dividing it by its norm.

Assume, for example, you are given the collection $\{\mathbf{v}_i\}_{i=1}^{5}$ of vectors in real 7-space, where the jth component of $\mathbf{v}_i$ is $v_{ij} = \max(i, j)$. The following produces an orthogonal basis $\mathbf{C} = \{\mathbf{w}_i\}_{i=1}^{5}$ for the subspace V spanned by the vectors $\{\mathbf{v}_i\}_{i=1}^{5}$.

This defines the vectors $\{\mathbf{v}_i\}_{i=1}^{5}$ in the session.

```
In[1]:= Do[v[i]= Table[Max[i,j], {j,7}], {i,5}]
```

This verifies that $\{\mathbf{v}_i\}_{i=1}^{5}$ is a basis for the subspace V they span.

```
In[2]:= B ={v[1],v[2],v[3],v[4],v[5]}
Out[2]//MatrixForm=
```

1	2	3	4	5	6	7
2	2	3	4	5	6	7
3	3	3	4	5	6	7
4	4	4	4	5	6	7
5	5	5	5	5	6	7

```
In[3]:= RowReduce[%]
Out[3]//MatrixForm=
```

1	0	0	0	0	0	0
0	1	0	0	0	0	0
0	0	1	0	0	0	0
0	0	0	1	0	0	0
0	0	0	0	1	$\frac{6}{5}$	$\frac{7}{5}$

The result shows that $\mathbf{v}_1, \ldots, \mathbf{v}_5$ are linearly independent—each row has a nonzero entry. It follows that $\mathbf{v}_1, \ldots, \mathbf{v}_5$ are a basis for V.

This defines iprod(**u**, **v**) *as the Euclidean inner product of* **u** *and* **v**.	`In[4]:= iprod[u_,v_] := u . v`

This defines the orthogonal projection proj$_v$(**u**) = $\dfrac{\langle \mathbf{v}, \mathbf{u} \rangle}{\langle \mathbf{v}, \mathbf{v} \rangle}$ **v**; *that is, of* **u** *onto* **v**.	`In[5]:= proj[v_][u_] := iprod[v,u]/iprod[v,v] v`

You can reuse this code later with a different inner product.

This defines the vectors $\mathbf{w}_i =$ $\mathbf{v}_i - \displaystyle\sum_{j=1}^{i-1} \mathrm{proj}_{\mathbf{w}_j}(\mathbf{v}_i).$	`In[6]:= Do[w[i] = v[i] - Sum[proj[w[j]][v[i]],` `{j,1,i-1}], {i,1,5}]`

You can easily check that the procedure works as claimed.

This verifies that the vectors $\{\mathbf{w}_i\}_{i=1}^{5}$ *are mutually orthogonal.*	`In[7]:= Table[w[i] . w[j], {i,1,5}, {j,1,5}]` `Out[7]//MatrixForm=`

$$
\begin{array}{ccccc}
140 & 0 & 0 & 0 & 0 \\[2mm]
0 & \dfrac{139}{140} & 0 & 0 & 0 \\[3mm]
0 & 0 & \dfrac{135}{139} & 0 & 0 \\[3mm]
0 & 0 & 0 & \dfrac{14}{15} & 0 \\[3mm]
0 & 0 & 0 & 0 & \dfrac{55}{63}
\end{array}
$$

The (i, j) entry is $\langle \mathbf{w}_i, \mathbf{w}_j \rangle$, and the diagonal entries are the squares of the norms of $\mathbf{w}_1, \ldots, \mathbf{w}_5$. This procedure did not normalize the vectors. Normalization can be achieved by dividing each $\mathbf{w}_i$ by its norm, which is `Sqrt[w[i] . w[i]]` in *Mathematica* notation.[16]

This normalizes the vectors $\mathbf{w}_1, \ldots, \mathbf{w}_5$.	`In[8]:= norm[x_] := Sqrt[x . x]` `In[9]:= Do[w[i] = w[i]/norm[w[i]], {i,1,5}]`

---

[16]Alternatively, you could use the `Normalize` command in the `LinearAlgebra` package.

This verifies the normali-
zation.

```
In[10]:= Table[Simplify[w[i] . w[j]], {i,1,5},
         {j,1,5}]
Out[10]//MatrixForm=
    1   0   0   0   0
    0   1   0   0   0
    0   0   1   0   0
    0   0   0   1   0
    0   0   0   0   1
```

If, as in this case, you are using the standard Euclidean inner product, you can also use *Mathematica*'s GramSchmidt command.

This uses Mathematica's
built-in GramSchmidt[17]
command to obtain an
orthogonal basis.

```
In[11]:= G = GramSchmidt[B];
```

B was assigned the value {v[1],...,v[5]} earlier in %2.

This compares the vectors
produced by the
GramSchmidt command
to the vectors $\{w[i]\}_{i=1}^{5}$.

```
In[12]:= Table[G[[i]] - w[i], {i,1,5}]
Out[12]//MatrixForm=
    0   0   0   0   0   0   0
    0   0   0   0   0   0   0
    0   0   0   0   0   0   0
    0   0   0   0   0   0   0
    0   0   0   0   0   0   0
```

The results of the two calculations are the same.

EXERCISES 2.6 _____

1. Let $\{v_i\}_{i=1}^{3}$ be the collection of 3-vectors defined by $v_i = (v_{ij})$, where $v_{ij} = 1/(i + j)$. Verify that the vectors v_i are linearly independent and apply the Gram-Schmidt procedure to obtain an orthogonal basis for Euclidean 3-space. Verify your answer.

2. Let $\{v_i\}_{i=1}^{6}$ be the collection of 8-vectors defined by $v_i = (v_{ij})$, where $v_{ij} = i/(i + j)$, and let V be the subspace spanned by $\{v_i\}_{i=1}^{6}$. Verify that the vectors v_i are linearly independent and apply the Gram-Schmidt procedure to

[17]GramSchmidt is in the LinearAlgebra package and thus will not work unless the package is first loaded. GramSchmidt can be used with more than one argument. For example, you can use a second argument of Normalized -> False, or you can change the inner product using a command like InnerProduct -> myfunction. However, if you use GramSchmidt before loading LinearAlgebra`Master`, you may "shadow" the definition. If this happens, use the command Remove[GramSchmidt], and then use GramSchmidt.

obtain a set of vectors that is orthogonal with respect to the Euclidean inner product. Verify your answer.

3. Use the solution from Exercise 2 to obtain a basis for V that consists of mutually orthogonal vectors, each of norm one—that is, an orthonormal basis for V.

4. Let $\{v_i\}_{i=1}^{6}$ be the collection of 8-vectors defined by $v_i = (v_{ij})$, where $v_{ij} = 1/(i + j)$. Define the inner product of the 8-vectors $\mathbf{x} = (x_i)$ and $\mathbf{y} = (y_i)$ by

$$\langle \mathbf{x}, \mathbf{y} \rangle = \sum_{i=1}^{8} i x_i y_i .$$

Apply the Gram-Schmidt procedure to the vectors $\{v_i\}_{i=1}^{6}$ to obtain an orthonormal spanning set relative to the given inner product.

2.7 Applications

Stability and Steady-State Vectors

Many physical situations are nicely described by a vector of values. For example, a vector could be used to record the fraction of the customers buying each of a collection of competing brands.

   A situation in which a number of companies are competing for the same customers can be thought of as a dynamic system: Customers can change from brand to brand depending on price, advertising, or other factors. A vector can be used to record a state of the system.

   In many cases, the forces acting on a dynamic system can be summarized in a matrix M so that the $(n + 1)$st state vector of the system can be determined from the nth state vector by the simple formula $\mathbf{s}_{n+1} = M\mathbf{s}_n$. In some particularly important cases, the system tends toward a steady state $\mathbf{s}$ that satisfies $M\mathbf{s} = \mathbf{s}$. The matrix M is known as the *transition matrix* and the vector $\mathbf{s}$ (if it exists) is known as a *steady-state vector*.

   For example, assume two high-quality ice cream stores, The Freezer and The Creamery, open next door to each other in River City. Assume that year after year, $\frac{2}{3}$ of The Freezer's customers are repeat customers from the previous year, whereas $\frac{1}{3}$ of them are converts from The Creamery. At the same time, assume that $\frac{5}{9}$ of The Creamery's customers are faithful repeaters and $\frac{4}{9}$ are adventurous experimenters from The Freezer. Then The Freezer gets $\frac{2}{3}$ of their own customers back plus $\frac{4}{9}$ of The Creamery's customers, while The Creamery gets $\frac{5}{9}$ of their own customers and $\frac{1}{3}$ of The Freezer's customers. If $\mathbf{s}_n$ is the 2-vector with $\mathbf{s}_n[1]$ being the fraction of all customers patronizing The Freezer in the nth year and $\mathbf{s}_n[2]$ being the fraction of all customers patronizing The Creamery in the nth year, then the matrix that gives $\mathbf{s}_{n+1}$ from $\mathbf{s}_n$ is simply

$$M = \begin{bmatrix} \dfrac{2}{3} & \dfrac{4}{9} \\[2mm] \dfrac{1}{3} & \dfrac{5}{9} \end{bmatrix}$$

If $\mathbf{s} = (f, c)$, then

$$M\mathbf{s} = \left(\frac{2}{3} f + \frac{4}{9} c, \ \frac{1}{3} f + \frac{5}{9} c \right)$$

Note that the sum of the entries in any column of M is 1 and that all entries are nonnegative. If the rows and columns of M are labeled F and C (for Freezer and Creamery) in that order, then the (i, j) entry is the fraction of j's customers that move to i's establishment: The (F, F) entry is the fraction of The Freezer's customers who continue to patronize The Freezer, the (F, C) entry is the fraction of The Creamery's customers who move to The Freezer, the (C, F) entry is the fraction of The Freezer's customers who move to The Creamery, and the (C, C) entry is the fraction of The Creamery's customers who stay on at The Creamery.

Assume that both establishments have a good fair start, with (say) each having $\dfrac{1}{2}$ of the potential clientele. The "initial-state vector" is $\mathbf{s}_0 = \left(\dfrac{1}{2}, \dfrac{1}{2} \right)$, where the first coordinate gives the fraction of the local ice cream eaters who patronize The Freezer in the first year, and the second coordinate gives the fraction of the ice cream eaters who patronize The Creamery in the first year.

At the end of the first year, after everybody has reevaluated his or her choice, the vector $\mathbf{s}_1$, which gives the current state, is given by $\mathbf{s}_1 = M\mathbf{s}_0$, and so on.

This defines the initial-state vector $\mathbf{s}_0$ and the transition matrix M.	`In[1]:= s[0] = {1/2,1/2};` `In[2]:= M = {{2/3,4/9},{1/3,5/9}};`

This gives the state of affairs at the end of the first year.

`In[3]:= s[1] = M . s[0]`

$$Out[3] = \{ \frac{5}{9}, \ \frac{4}{9} \}$$

This does not appear to bode well for The Creamery—it lost $\left(\dfrac{1}{2} - \dfrac{4}{9} \right) \Big/ \left(\dfrac{1}{2} \right)$

$\approx 11\%$ of its business to The Freezer.

This gives the state of affairs after two years.

`In[4]:= s[2] = M . s[1]`

$$Out[4] = \{ \frac{46}{81}, \ \frac{35}{81} \}$$

This gives a bit rosier picture for The Creamery; it lost only $\left(\frac{4}{9} - \frac{35}{81}\right)\Big/\left(\frac{4}{9}\right) \approx 2.8\%$ of its business to The Freezer this time—certainly much better than the first year.

This gives the state of affairs for the next five years.

```
In[5]:= Do[s[i+1]= M . s[i]; Print[s[i+1]],
        {i,2,6}]
Out[5]=
```
$$\{\frac{416}{729}, \frac{313}{729}\}$$
$$\{\frac{3748}{6561}, \frac{2813}{6561}\}$$
$$\{\frac{33740}{59049}, \frac{25309}{59049}\}$$
$$\{\frac{303676}{531441}, \frac{227765}{531441}\}$$
$$\{\frac{2733116}{4782969}, \frac{2049853}{4782969}\}$$

Sometimes exact answers may not be the easiest to interpret. You can easily change the answers to decimal percents.

This gives the same data in decimal percent form. The percent sign (%) must be enclosed in quotes for this to work.

```
In[6]:= Do[Print[N[100s[i],3]"%"],{i,1,7}]
Out[6]=
{55.6 %, 44.4 %}
{56.8 %, 43.2 %}
{57.1 %, 42.9 %}
{57.1 %, 42.9 %}
{57.1 %, 42.9 %}
{57.1 %, 42.9 %}
{57.1 %, 42.9 %}
```

The Creamery might be happier with a larger share of the market, but it looks as if its future is secure; the system stabilizes at about (57%, 43%). An interesting aspect of this problem is that the outcome is virtually independent of the initial-state vector s_0. Even if one of the businesses starts with all of the customers, after three or four years the distribution is still about (57%, 43%).

Although the ice cream parlor example may appear somewhat simplistic, it demonstrates a property common to such systems: they tend toward a state of equilibrium. There exists a "steady-state vector" s satisfying $Ms = s$ to which the s_n converge.

Mathematica provides the tools for finding the steady-state vectors. Note that the equation $Ms = s$ is equivalent to the equation $(Id - M)s = 0$, where Id is the identity matrix. Hence, the steady-state vectors form the null space of the matrix $Id - M$.

This gives a basis for the space of all steady-state vectors.

```
In[7]:= Id[2]  := IdentityMatrix[2]
```

```
In[8]:= NullSpace[Id[2] - M]
```
$$Out[8]= \{\{\frac{4}{3},\ 1\}\}$$

This scales the single basis vector so that the sum of its coordinates is one.

```
In[9]:= s = %/(%[[1,1]] + %[[1,2]])
```
$$Out[9]= \{\{\frac{4}{7},\ \frac{3}{7}\}\}$$

Note that $s \approx (57\%, 43\%)$ and that, because of the physical constraints on the problem, it is the only possible steady-state vector of the system.

Problems on Steady-State Vectors

1. Verify that The Freezer/Creamery example tends toward (57%, 43%) even if
   a. The Freezer starts with all the customers
   b. The Creamery starts with all the customers

2. Assume that five paint stores open in River City, all competing for the same customers. Due to price fluctuations of differing brands, customer satisfaction, and other variables, some customers try different stores, while others do not. Assume that in year $n + 1$, the fraction of store i's customers who were customers of store j in year n is given by the transition matrix

$$M = \frac{1}{10} \begin{bmatrix} 2 & 3 & 2 & 4 & 2 \\ 3 & 2 & 1 & 1 & 2 \\ 1 & 1 & 3 & 1 & 2 \\ 3 & 2 & 3 & 1 & 3 \\ 1 & 2 & 1 & 3 & 1 \end{bmatrix}$$

Find the steady-state vector s and investigate how quickly the annual state vectors s_n converge to it, given

$$s_0 = (\frac{1}{5}, \frac{1}{5}, \frac{1}{5}, \frac{1}{5}, \frac{1}{5}).$$

3. Let $A = [a_{ij}]$ be the 10×10 matrix given by $a_{ij} = \max(i, j)$. Let $d = (d_i)$ be the 10-vector given by $d_i = \sum_{j=1}^{10} a_{ij}$. Let $M = [m_{ij}]$ be the matrix given by $m_{ij} = a_{ij}/d_j$. Note that the entries of M are all positive and that the column sums are all one. Find the steady-state vectors of M.

Orthogonal Projection

Given a subspace W of a real inner product space V and a vector $\mathbf{v}$ in V, there is one vector $\mathbf{u}$ in W that is closer to $\mathbf{v}$ (as measured by the norm $\| \mathbf{u} - \mathbf{v} \| = \sqrt{\langle \mathbf{u} - \mathbf{v}, \mathbf{u} - \mathbf{v} \rangle}$) than any other vector of W. The vector $\mathbf{u}$ is chosen so that $\mathbf{v} - \mathbf{u}$ is orthogonal to W (that is, to every vector in W), and it is called the *orthogonal projection* of $\mathbf{v}$ onto W.

Recall that the orthogonal projection $\mathbf{u} = \mathrm{proj}_{\mathbf{w}}(\mathbf{v})$ of a vector $\mathbf{v}$ onto a vector $\mathbf{w}$ is given by the formula $\mathbf{u} = \left(\dfrac{\langle \mathbf{v}, \mathbf{w} \rangle}{\langle \mathbf{w}, \mathbf{w} \rangle} \right) \mathbf{w}$. In this case, the vector $\mathbf{v} - \mathbf{u}$ is orthogonal to both $\mathbf{w}$ and $\mathbf{u}$, and $\mathbf{v}$ is the sum of the vectors $\mathbf{u}$ and $\mathbf{v} - \mathbf{u}$. Hence, $\mathbf{u}$ is in the subspace spanned by $\mathbf{w}$ and $\mathbf{v} - \mathbf{u}$ is orthogonal to the subspace spanned by $\mathbf{w}$. If $\{\mathbf{w}_i\}_{i=1}^{s}$ is an orthogonal basis for W, then the orthogonal projection $\mathbf{u}$ of $\mathbf{v}$ onto W is the sum of the orthogonal projections of $\mathbf{v}$ onto the $\mathbf{w}_i$; that is, $\mathbf{u} = \sum_{i=1}^{s} \mathrm{proj}_{\mathbf{w}_i}(\mathbf{v})$. In this case, the vector $\mathbf{v}$ is the sum of the vectors $\mathbf{u}$ and $\mathbf{v} - \mathbf{u}$, with $\mathbf{u}$ in the subspace spanned by the $\mathbf{w}_i$ and $\mathbf{v} - \mathbf{u}$ orthogonal to the subspace spanned by the $\mathbf{w}_i$.

Note that if $a_i = \dfrac{\langle \mathbf{v}, \mathbf{w}_i \rangle}{\langle \mathbf{w}_i, \mathbf{w}_i \rangle}$ for $i = 1, \ldots, s$, and if $\mathbf{a} = (a_i)$, then $[\mathbf{w}_1, \mathbf{w}_2, \ldots, \mathbf{w}_s]\mathbf{a} = \mathbf{u}$. Because $\mathbf{u}$ is the vector in W closest to $\mathbf{v}$, the vector $\mathbf{a}$ is considered an approximate solution of the matrix/vector equation $[\mathbf{w}_1, \mathbf{w}_2, \ldots, \mathbf{w}_s]\mathbf{x} = \mathbf{v}$.

Given any $m \times n$ matrix A and m-vector $\mathbf{v}$, it is possible to compute the orthogonal projection $\mathbf{u}$ of $\mathbf{v}$ onto the column space of A and then solve the equation $A\mathbf{x} = \mathbf{u}$. If A has rank n, then the solution is necessarily unique; otherwise it is not. (Verify.) In either case, solutions of the equation $A\mathbf{x} = \mathbf{u}$ are called *least-squares solutions* of the equation $A\mathbf{x} = \mathbf{v}$.

Consider the 7×5 matrix $A = [a_{ij}]$ defined by $a_{ij} = \min(i, j)$. Let $\mathbf{v}$ be the 7-vector $\mathbf{v} = (1, 2, 3, 4, 5, 6, 7)$.

Define A and $\mathbf{v}$.

```
In[1]:= A = Array[Min, {7,5}];
In[2]:= v = Table[i, {i,7}];
```

The matrix A has rank 5, as is easily verified by checking its nullity.[18]

```
In[3]:= Length[NullSpace[A]]
Out[3]= 0
```

It follows that the columns of A are a basis for its column space.

---

[18]Recall that for an $m \times n$ matrix A, rank(A) + nullity$(A) = n$.

You can obtain an orthogonal basis for the column space of *A* using the `Transpose` and `GramSchmidt` commands.

Apply `GramSchmidt` *to the transpose of A.*[19] *Normalization is turned off.*

```
In[4]:= B = GramSchmidt[Transpose[A],
        Normalized->False];
```

The vectors of the orthogonal basis can now be addressed as `B[[i]]` for *i* = 1, ..., 5.

This defines the orthogonal projection of any vector **u** *onto* **w** *(relative to the Euclidean inner product).*[20]

```
In[5]:= proj[w_][u_]:=(w . u/w . w)w
```

$$Out[5] = \frac{w \; w \; . \; u}{w \; . \; w}$$

You can now obtain the orthogonal projection of **v** *onto the column space of A.*

```
In[6]:= p = Sum[proj[B[[i]]][v], {i,1,5}]
Out[6]= {1, 2, 3, 4, 6, 6, 6}
```

This gives a least-squares solution **a** *of the equation Ax = v.*

```
In[7]:= a = LinearSolve[A,p]
Out[7]= {0, 0, 0, -1, 2}
```

Problems on Orthogonal Projection

1. Let $A = [a_{ij}]$ be the 7×5 matrix defined by $a_{ij} = 1/(i + j)$. Let $\mathbf{v} = (v_i)$ be the 7-vector defined by $v_i = i - 1$. Compute the orthogonal projection **u** of **v** onto the column space of *A* and use it to find the least-squares solution of the equation *A***x** = **v** by solving the equation *A***x** = **u**.

2. Let $A = [a_{ij}]$ be the 5×7 matrix defined by $a_{ij} = \min(i, j)$. Let $\mathbf{v} = (v_i)$ be the 5-vector defined by $v_i = i$. Find the least-squares solution of the equation *A***x** = **v** and use it to compute the orthogonal projection **u** of **v** onto the column space of *A*.

3. Let $A = [a_{ij}]$ be the 5×5 matrix defined by $a_{ij} = i + j$. Let $\mathbf{v} = (v_i)$ be the 5-vector defined by $v_i = i$.
   a. Find the orthogonal projection **c** of **v** onto the column space of *A* and use it to find the least-squares solution **u** of the equation *A***x** = **v**.
   b. Find the orthogonal projection **r** of **u** onto the row space of *A* and use it to compute the least-squares solution of the equation $A^T\mathbf{x} = \mathbf{u}$.
   c. Verify that the vector **r** of part b is a solution of the equation *A***x** = **c**.
   d. Verify that the vector **r** of part b is the solution of the least norm of the equation *A***x** = **c**. [Hint: Any vector **w** can be written in one and

[19]Recall that `GramSchmidt` is in the `LinearAlgebra` package.
[20]*Mathematica* has a `Projection` command in the `LinearAlgebra` package. `Projection[u,v]` returns the projection of **u** onto **v**.

only one way as the sum $\mathbf{w} = \mathbf{w}_1 + \mathbf{w}_2$ with $\mathbf{w}_1$ in the row space of A and $\mathbf{w}_2$ orthogonal to the row space of A. Consider the inequality $\|\mathbf{w}_1 + \mathbf{w}_2\| \leq \|\mathbf{w}_1\| + \|\mathbf{w}_2\|$.]

4. Let $A = [a_{ij}]$ be an $m \times n$ matrix of rank n, so that the columns of A are linearly independent. Then A^TA is an invertible $n \times n$ matrix (verify). If $\mathbf{w}$ is the orthogonal projection of a vector $\mathbf{b}$ onto the column space C of A, then $\mathbf{w}$ is a linear combination of the columns of A, say, $\mathbf{w} = A\mathbf{x}_0$. Then $\mathbf{x}_0$ is a least-squares solution of the equation $A\mathbf{x} = \mathbf{b}$, and $\mathbf{b} - A\mathbf{x}_0$ is orthogonal to each of the columns of A. Because the columns of A are the rows of A^T, it follows that $A^T(\mathbf{b} - A\mathbf{x}_0) = \mathbf{0}$, and hence that $A^T\mathbf{b} = A^TA\mathbf{x}_0$. Because A^TA is invertible, you can find $\mathbf{x}_0$ by multiplying $A^T\mathbf{b}$ by its inverse. Hence, in this case, the least-squares solution $\mathbf{x}_0$ of the equation $A\mathbf{x} = \mathbf{b}$ is given by $\mathbf{x}_0 = (A^TA)^{-1}A^T\mathbf{b}$. Use this formula to find the least-squares solution of the equation $A\mathbf{x} = \mathbf{b}$, where $A = [a_{ij}]$ is the 5×4 matrix with $a_{ij} = \min(i, j)$ for $1 \leq i \leq 5$ and $1 \leq j \leq 4$, and $\mathbf{b} = [b_i]$, with $b_i = i^2$ for $1 \leq i \leq 5$.

Curve Fitting with Too Many Points

In Chapter 1 polynomials were fit exactly to data—a polynomial of degree n (or less) to $n + 1$ data points. If you have more than $n + 1$ points through which the graph of a polynomial of degree n must fit, it may not be possible to do the job exactly, but it is possible to obtain a least-squares approximation.

Assume that by one means or another you have obtained the five data points $P_i(x_i, y_i) = \left(\dfrac{2\pi i}{6}, \dfrac{\sin 2\pi i}{6} \right)$ for $i = 1, \ldots, 6$, and that you need to fit a polynomial of degree three or less to them. This requires that you determine the vector $\mathbf{a} = (a_1, a_2, a_3, a_4)$ of coefficients for which the 6-vector $\mathbf{w} = (w_i)$ defined by $w_i = \displaystyle\sum_{j=1}^{4} a_j x_i^{j-1}$ for $i = 1, \ldots, 6$ is as close as possible to the vector $\mathbf{y} = (y_1, \ldots, y_6)$. If you form the 6×4 matrix $M = [x_i^{j-1}]$, then the problem is to find the least-squares solution $\mathbf{a}$ of the equation $M\mathbf{x} = \mathbf{y}$.

This defines the vector $\mathbf{x}$ *of x coordinates.*

```
In[1]:= x = Table[2 Pi i/6, {i,1,6}]
```
$Out[1]= \{ \dfrac{Pi}{3}, \dfrac{2\ Pi}{3}, Pi, \dfrac{4\ Pi}{3}, \dfrac{5\ Pi}{3}, 2\ Pi \}$

This defines the vector $\mathbf{y}$ *of y coordinates.*

```
In[2]:= y = Table[Sin[x[[i]]], {i,1,6}]
```
$Out[2]=$
$\{ \dfrac{Sqrt[3]}{2}, \dfrac{Sqrt[3]}{2}, 0, \dfrac{-Sqrt[3]}{2}, \dfrac{-Sqrt[3]}{2}, 0 \}$

This defines the 6×4 matrix
$M = [\, x_i^{j-1}\,]$. Matrices of this
form are called
Vandermonde matrices.

```
In[3]:= M = Table[x[[i]]^(j-1),
   {i,1,6}, {j,1,4}]
Out[3]//MatrixForm=
```

$$
\begin{matrix}
1 & \dfrac{Pi}{3} & \dfrac{Pi^2}{9} & \dfrac{Pi^3}{27} \\[2mm]
1 & \dfrac{2\ Pi}{3} & \dfrac{4\ Pi^2}{9} & \dfrac{8\ Pi^3}{27} \\[2mm]
1 & Pi & Pi^2 & Pi^3 \\[2mm]
1 & \dfrac{4\ Pi}{3} & \dfrac{16\ Pi^2}{9} & \dfrac{64\ Pi^3}{27} \\[2mm]
1 & \dfrac{5\ Pi}{3} & \dfrac{25\ Pi^2}{9} & \dfrac{125\ Pi^3}{27} \\[2mm]
1 & 2\ Pi & 4\ Pi^2 & 8\ Pi^3
\end{matrix}
$$

The following command sequence assigns **a** the value of a least-squares solution.

```
In[4]:= <<LinearAlgebra`Master`
```

Obtain an orthogonal basis
for the column space of M.[21]

```
In[5]:= B = GramSchmidt[Transpose[M],
   Normalized->False]
Out[5]//MatrixForm=
```

$$
\begin{matrix}
1 & 1 & 1 & 1 & 1 & 1 \\[2mm]
\dfrac{-5\ Pi}{6} & \dfrac{Pi}{2} & \dfrac{-Pi}{6} & \dfrac{Pi}{6} & \dfrac{Pi}{2} & \dfrac{5\ Pi}{6} \\[2mm]
\dfrac{10\ Pi^2}{27} & \dfrac{-2\ Pi^2}{27} & \dfrac{-8\ Pi^2}{27} & \dfrac{-8\ Pi^2}{27} & \dfrac{-2\ Pi^2}{27} & \dfrac{10\ Pi^2}{27} \\[2mm]
\dfrac{-Pi^3}{9} & \dfrac{7\ Pi^3}{45} & \dfrac{4\ Pi^3}{45} & \dfrac{-4\ Pi^3}{45} & \dfrac{-7\ Pi^3}{45} & \dfrac{Pi^3}{9}
\end{matrix}
$$

*Compute the projection **b** of*
***y** onto the column space of*
M, and solve the equation
$M\mathbf{x} = \mathbf{b}$.

```
In[6]:= proj[v_,u_] := (u . v/v . v)v

In[7]:= b = Sum[proj[B[[i]], y], {i,1,4}];

In[8]:= a = LinearSolve[M,b]
```

[21]Load the LinearAlgebra package before you enter this command, if you have not already done so.

$$Out[8] = \{ \frac{-1}{2 \; Sqrt[3]}, \; \frac{1775}{56 \; 3^{3/2} \; Pi},$$

$$\frac{-139 \; Sqrt[3]}{28 \; Pi^2}, \; \frac{13 \; Sqrt[3]}{8 \; Pi^3} \}$$

Now use **a** to define the polynomial *p* that best fits the data.

You can now define the "least-squares" polynomial p.

```
In[9]:= p = Sum[a[[i]]t^(i-1), {i,1,4}]
```

In situations involving approximations, as this one does, it is interesting to see just how well the approximate answer works. In this case, you can either compare the values $p(x_i)$ to the y_i or plot the points (x_i, y_i) and the graph of $y = p(x)$ together.

This plots all the points (x_i, y_i).

```
In[10]:= lp = ListPlot[Table[{x[[i]], y[[i]]},
   {i,1,6}]]
```

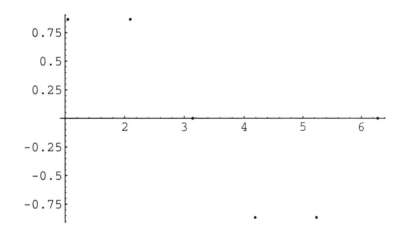

-Graphics-

This plots $y = p(x)$ on the interval $[1, 2\pi]$.

$In[11]:=$ graph = Plot[p, {t,1,2 Pi}]

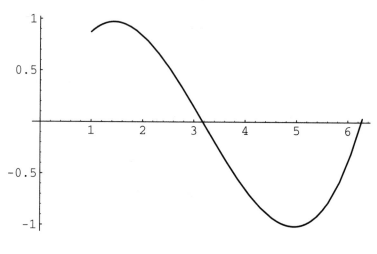

-Graphics-

You can use the Show *command to see the two graphs plotted together.*[22]

$In[12]:=$ Show[graph,lp]

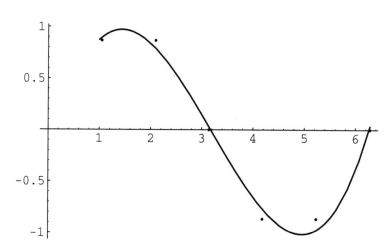

Note that it is possible that a polynomial of degree less than three (or even the zero polynomial) might better fit the data in some cases. For example, if all the points happened to lie in a line, the coefficients a_2 and a_3 would both turn out to be zero.

---

[22] The Show command requires that the plot of p be used. It will not accept the *command* to generate the plot (or a delayed computation of the plot).

Problems on Curve Fitting

1. Let $x_i = \dfrac{2\pi i}{20}$ and $y_i = \sin(x_i)$ for $i = 1, \ldots, 20$. Find the polynomial of degree five or less that best fits the data. Compare the result to that obtained in the text example for polynomials of degree three or less.

2. Fitting a polynomial by least squares gives the best possible answer, but it may not always be close. For example, let $q = \displaystyle\prod_{i=1}^{5} i(x - 3)$. You can enter q using *Mathematica*'s Product command—which has the same form as the Sum command—and use Expand to put it into standard form. Generate ten data points (x_i, y_i) from the graph of q using $x = 1, \ldots, 10$, and compute the polynomial p of degree three or less that gives the best least-squares fit. Plot the points (x_i, y_i) together with p. Note that the shape of p is a good fit to the points. Now compute the minimum difference $y_i - p(x_i)$. (You can partially automate this by applying *Mathematica*'s Min function to the table of differences.)

Curve Fitting with Other Inner Products

When working with functions, it makes good sense to measure the distance between two functions using the integral. You can do this by defining the inner product $\langle f, g \rangle$ of functions f and g to be the integral $\displaystyle\int_a^b f(x)g(x)dx$ on some predetermined interval $[a, b]$. The associated norm is given by $\|f - g\| = \sqrt{\displaystyle\int_{x=a}^{b} (f(x) - g(x))^2 dx}$, which is clearly related to the area between the graphs.

Assume, for example, that you want to find the polynomial expression of degree five or less for which the graph best fits the graph of $\sin(x)$ on the interval $[0, 2\pi]$. This has practical applications since polynomials are much easier to evaluate than transcendental functions like sine. You proceed as with the Euclidean inner product: Orthogonally project $\sin(x)$ onto the space P_5 of all polynomials of degree five or less.

This defines the inner product.

```
In[1]:= iprod[v_,u_]:=
Integrate[v u, {x,0,2 Pi}]
```

This gives `iprod[f[x],g[x]]` $= \displaystyle\int_0^{2\pi} f(x)\,g(x)\,dx$.

Define the projection of a function f onto a function g.

```
In[2]:=
proj[v_][u_]:=(iprod[v,u]/iprod[v,v])v
```

The parentheses are not necessary because of *Mathematica*'s evaluation rules.

This defines the standard basis for P_5.

```
In[3]:= Do[v[i] = x^(i-1),{i,1,6}]
```

With the exception of the bounds on i, this uses the same code that was used in Section 2.6 to apply Gram-Schmidt with the Euclidean inner product.

```
In[4]:= Do[w[i] = v[i]-
Sum[proj[w[j]][v[i]], {j,1,i-1}], {i,1,6}]
```

This gives the orthogonal projection of polysinx onto P_5.

```
In[5]:= polysinx = Sum[proj[w[i],Sin[x]],
  {i,1,6}]
```

You may find it of interest to plot *polysinx* and sin(x) together.

Note that polysinx is an expression, so you do not use polysinx[x] *in the* Plot *command.*

```
In[6]:= Plot[{polysinx, Sin[x]}, {x,0,2 Pi}]
```

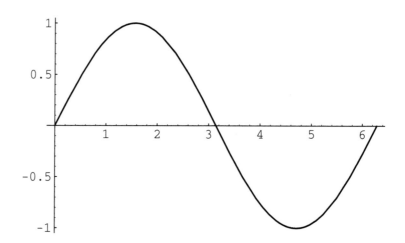

```
Out[6]= -Graphics-
```

Note that the two graphs are nearly identical.

Problems on Curve Fitting with Other Inner Products
1. Find the polynomial of degree seven or less that best approximates the cosine function on the interval [0, π].

2. The polynomials obtained from the Gram-Schmidt procedure from the standard basis $1, x, x^2, \ldots$ with the inner product $\langle f, g \rangle = \int_{-1}^{1} f(x) g(x) \, dx$ are called the *Legendre polynomials*. In particular, the nth term is called the nth Legendre polynomial. Generate the first seven Legendre polynomials and find the polynomial p in P_6 that best approximates the function $f(x) = \sin(x) + \cos(x)$ on the interval $[-1, 1]$ relative to the given inner product.

3 Eigenspaces

Eigenvalues and eigenvectors, also known as characteristic values and characteristic vectors, are among the most frequently applied topics commonly studied in undergraduate mathematics.

Recall that λ is an eigenvalue and $\mathbf{v} \neq \mathbf{0}$ is an associated eigenvector for A if $A\mathbf{v} = \lambda\mathbf{v}$. If, for example, multiplication by A represents the action of forces on a physical system with components represented by the vector $\mathbf{v}$, and if $A\mathbf{v} = \lambda\mathbf{v}$, then the components of the system are all changing at the same rate. If $\lambda = 1$, then the system is static.

For a given eigenvalue λ of A, the set of vectors $\mathbf{v}$ for which $A\mathbf{v} = \lambda\mathbf{v}$ is the null space of the matrix $A - \lambda I$. This is commonly called the λ-eigenspace of A.

3.1 Eigenvalues and Eigenvectors
[OutputForm]

Within the limits imposed by the time and resources available to it, *Mathematica* is capable of describing the eigenvalues and eigenvectors of any rational matrix. However, the case is simplest when the eigenvalues are either rational or roots of quadratic polynomials with rational coefficients. The case in which the eigenvalues are not roots of a rational polynomial of degree four or less is the most difficult and gives the least satisfying solution. (*Mathematica* is not limited strictly to matrices with rational entries, but we will use only rational examples.)

Here is a 4 × 4 matrix A that is typical of those used to study eigenvalue/eigenvector problems.

```
In[1]:= f[i_,j_] := If[i==j, i+j-1, i+j+1]

In[2]:= A = Array[f, {4,4}]
Out[2]//MatrixForm=
     1   4   5   6
     4   3   6   7
     5   6   5   8
     6   7   8   7
```

You can compute the characteristic matrix from the definition.

```
In[3]:= x IdentityMatrix[4] - A
Out[3]//MatrixForm=
    -1 + x    -4       -5       -6
    -4        -3 + x   -6       -7
    -5        -6       -5 + x   -8
    -6        -7       -8       -7 + x
```

Det *gives the characteristic polynomial, one of the most important applications of the determinant.*

```
In[4]:= p = Det[%]
Out[4]= -256 - 336 x - 140 x^2 - 16 x^3 + x^4
```

Use Solve *to find the eigenvalues.*

```
In[5]:= Solve[p==0, x]
Out[5]//MatrixForm=
x -> -2
x -> -2
```

$$x \rightarrow \frac{20 + 4\ Sqrt[41]}{2}$$

$$x \rightarrow \frac{20 - 4\ Sqrt[41]}{2}$$

Solve returns a list of four lists of the form {x -> root}. *Mathematica* interprets this as a 4 × 1 matrix, so it does not show the list braces.

You can temporarily override the MatrixForm setting of $Post by requesting the OutputForm.

The eigenvalues in OutputForm.

```
In[6]:= %//OutputForm
Out[6]//OutputForm=
```

$${\{x \rightarrow -2\},\ \{x \rightarrow -2\},\ \{x \rightarrow \frac{20 + 4\ Sqrt[41]}{2}\},}$$

$${\{x \rightarrow \frac{20 - Sqrt[41]}{2}\}}$$

As it stands, the *i*th eigenvalue is now addressed as %5[[i,1,2]], and the identity matrix by IdentityMatrix[4]. You can make the notation less cumbersome.

This sets up easy access to the identity matrix and the eigenvalues.[1]

```
In[7]:= lambda = x/. %;
In[8]:= Id[4] = IdentityMatrix[4];
```

The *i*th eigenvalue is now addressed simply as lambda[[i]], and the 4 × 4 identity matrix by Id[4].

[1]Entering the command lambda will not show you the definition of lambda. Use ??lambda to see the definition.

The λ_i-eigenspace of A is the null space of the matrix $\lambda_i I - A$. You can use *Mathematica*'s `NullSpace` command to find bases for the null spaces of the matrices $\lambda_i I - A$.

`NullSpace` gives the λ_1-eigenspace A.

```
In[9]:= NullSpace[lambda[[1]] Id[4] - A]
Out[9]//MatrixForm=
    2   -3   0   1
    1   -2   1   0
```

This is a list of vectors. The two vectors in the list form a basis for the λ_1-eigenspace.

We repeat the process for λ_3.

```
In[10]:= NullSpace[lambda[[3]] Id[4] - A]
Out[10]//MatrixForm=
```

$$\frac{-7 + 3\,\text{Sqrt}[41]}{20} \quad \frac{1 + \text{Sqrt}[41]}{10} \quad \frac{11 + \text{Sqrt}[41]}{10} \quad 1$$

The matrix A is special in that its characteristic polynomial has no factors of degree greater than two, as demonstrated in the following.

The factorization of the characteristic polynomial of A.

```
In[11]:= Factor[p]
```
$$Out[11]= (2 + x)^2 \,(-64 - 20\,x + x^2)$$

The `factor` command returns a factorization of the form $r p_1^{e_1} p_2^{e_2} \dots p_k^{e_k}$, where r is a rational number and each p_i is a polynomial with integer coefficients. The p_i cannot be further factored as a product of polynomials with integer coefficients.

The approach demonstrated for A will work for any rational matrix as long as none of the factors p_i of its characteristic polynomial has degree three or greater.[2] In general, however, characteristic polynomials can have irreducible factors of any degree.

Here is a matrix with an irreducible[3] characteristic polynomial of degree three.[4]

```
In[12]:= A = Array[Max, {3,3}];
   Id[3]=IdentityMatrix[3];
   p = Det[x Id[3] - A]
```
$$Out[12]= -3 - 11\,x - 6\,x^2 + x^3$$

```
In[13]:= Factor[p]
```
$$Out[13]= -3 - 11\,x - 6\,x^2 + x^3$$

---

[2]Strictly speaking, it will work as long as the descriptions or the roots are not too complicated. It will fail for many, but not all, matrices with characteristic polynomials that have irreducible factors of degree three or greater.

[3]Throughout, *irreducible* is used to mean irreducible over the rational numbers.

[4]It appears that all matrices of the form [max(i, j)] have irreducible characteristic polynomials.

According to *Out [13]*, the matrix *A* has an irreducible characteristic polynomial of degree three.

In this case, the descriptions of the eigenvalues are too complicated for the equation $(\lambda I - A_3)\mathbf{x} = \mathbf{0}$ to be solved by NullSpace.

```
In[14]:= Solve[p == 0, x];
```

```
In[15]:= lambda = x /. %;
```

Here is λ_1.

```
In[16]:= lambda[[1]]
```

$$Out[16]= 2 \; + \; \frac{23 \; (\frac{2}{3})^{1/3}}{(369 \; + \; I \; \mathrm{Sqrt}[9843])^{1/3}} \; +$$

$$\frac{(369 \; + \; I \; \mathrm{Sqrt}[9843])^{1/3}}{18^{1/3}}$$

NullSpace *returns an incorrect answer. It should give a basis for the λ_1-eigenspace.*

```
In[17]:= NullSpace[lambda[[1]] Id[3] - A[3]]
Out[17]= {}
```

The answer is necessarily incorrect—an eigenvalue cannot have an associated zero-dimensional eigenspace. The description of the eigenvalue is too complicated to be handled by NullSpace. The problem is related to the difficulty of simplifying the radical expressions that arise in the calculation.

The complexity of the description by radicals of a root of a cubic or quartic factor is a barrier that potentially complicates the computation of the eigenvectors of matrices larger than 2×2. All symbolic computation programs suffer from this difficulty. Also troublesome is the fact that there is no analog of the quadratic, cubic, and quartic formulas for polynomials of degree five or greater.

In Section 3.3 we will show you how to solve this and similar problems involving matrices with characteristic polynomials that have irreducible factors of degree ≥ 3. Until then, we will choose examples for which this does not happen.

EXERCISES 3.1 _____

1. Find the eigenvalues and eigenvectors of the 2×2 matrix $B = [b_{ij}]$ where, for each *i* and *j*, b_{ij} is the minimum of *i* and *j*.
2. Find all the eigenvalues and eigenvectors of the 9×9 matrix $A = [a_{ij}]$ with $a_{ij} = 1$ for all *i* and *j*.
3. Find the eigenvalues and eigenvectors of the 3×3 matrix $Q = [q_{ij}]$ where, for each *i* and *j*, $q_{ij} = i/j$. Determine which of the eigenvalues are real and which are complex.

4. If $p = a_0 + a_1x + \cdots + a_{n-1}x^{n-1} + x^n$, the matrix

$$\begin{bmatrix} 0 & 0 & \cdots & 0 & -a_0 \\ 1 & 0 & \cdots & 0 & -a_1 \\ 0 & 1 & \cdots & 0 & -a_2 \\ & & \cdots & & \\ 0 & 0 & \cdots & 1 & -a_{n-1} \end{bmatrix}$$

is called the *companion matrix* of p. Verify for the following polynomials p that p is the characteristic polynomial of the companion matrix C of p.

a. $x + x^2 + x^3$
b. $1 - 2x + x^2$
c. $3 - 4x^2 + x^4$
d. $-1 + 3x - 3x^2 + x^3$

3.2 Similarity and Diagonalization

Eigenvalues and eigenvectors have a broad spectrum of applications, due in no small part to the role they play in *similarity theory*. Two square matrices A and B are said to be *similar* if B satisfies an equation of the form $B = P^{-1}AP$ for some nonsingular matrix P. The collection of all matrices similar to a given matrix A is called the *similarity class* of A.

It is often possible to simplify the solution of a matrix or matrix/vector equation by substitution of a similar matrix for the original.

For example, given a matrix equation $\mathbf{y} = A\mathbf{x}$ and a matrix $B = P^{-1}AP$, substituting $\mathbf{x} = P\overline{\mathbf{x}}$ and $\mathbf{y} = P\overline{\mathbf{y}}$ into the equation and then left-multiplying by P^{-1} yields the equivalent equation $P^{-1}P\overline{\mathbf{y}} = P^{-1}AP\overline{\mathbf{x}}$, which simplifies to $\overline{\mathbf{y}} = B\overline{\mathbf{x}}$. If B has a particularly simple form, the new equation may be much easier to solve than the original. If so, $\mathbf{x}$ and $\mathbf{y}$ are easily obtained from $\overline{\mathbf{x}}$ and $\overline{\mathbf{y}}$. In practice, substitution using similar matrices is particularly important when $\mathbf{x}$ and $\mathbf{y}$ are known only through an equation $\mathbf{y} = A\mathbf{x}$ and an additional relation, as when $\mathbf{x} = (x_i(t))$ is a vector of functions and $\mathbf{y}$ is the vector of derivatives $(x_i'(t))$. In matrix notation this is written $\mathbf{x}' = A\mathbf{x}$.

The simplest representative of the similarity class of a matrix A is a scalar matrix λI. However, the similarity class of λI consists only of λI itself; hence, for nonscalar matrices, the simplest representative would be a "block scalar" matrix—a diagonal matrix.

A matrix A that is similar to a diagonal matrix Dg is said to be *diagonalizable*; the process of finding a diagonal matrix Dg similar to A is called the *diagonalization of A*. Recall that an $n \times n$ matrix A is diagonalizable if and only if it has n linearly independent eigenvectors. This in turn is equivalent to the condition that for each eigenvalue λ of A, the dimension of the null space of $\lambda I - A$ is equal to the multiplicity of the eigenvalue λ as a root of the characteristic polynomial $C_A(x) = |xI - A|$ of A.

The restriction to rational matrices remains in effect.

The matrix A is a good first example.

```
In[1]:= f[i_,j_] := If[i == j, 0, 1]

In[2]:= A = Array[f, {5,5}]
Out[2]//MatrixForm=
    0  1  1  1  1
    1  0  1  1  1
    1  1  0  1  1
    1  1  1  0  1
    1  1  1  1  0
```

All entries of A are real numbers, and A is symmetric. Such matrices are always diagonalizable, and they always have real eigenvalues.

```
In[3]:= Id[5] = IdentityMatrix[5];

In[4]:= p = Det[x Id[5] - A]
Out[4]= -4 -15 x -20 x^2 -10 x^3 + x^5

In[5]:= lambda = x /. Solve[% == 0, x]
Out[5]= {-1, -1, -1, -1, 4}
```

A has just the two eigenvalues –1 and 4. You could use `Union[%]` to remove the duplicate terms.

You can use the bases of the eigenspaces to form a diagonalizing matrix. The notation Es[1||4] is chosen to suggest that the vectors correspond to $\lambda_1, \ldots, \lambda_4$.

```
In[6]:=
ES[1||4] = NullSpace[lambda[[1]] Id[5] - A]
Out[6]//MatrixForm=
   -1  0  0  0  1
   -1  0  0  1  0
   -1  0  1  0  0
   -1  1  0  0  0

In[7]:=
ES[5] = NullSpace[lambda[[5]] Id[5] - A]
Out[7]//MatrixForm=
    1  1  1  1  1
```

In each case, the number of basis vectors is the same as the multiplicity of λ_i as a root of *p*.

The desired diagonalizing matrix *P* has the four vectors of %6 and the one vector of %7 as its columns. In this case, $P = \{ES[1||4] \cup ES[5]\}^T$. You can use `Transpose` and one of `Join`, `Append`, or `AppendColumns`[5] to obtain *P*.

---

[5]If you use `Append`, use `ES[5][[1]]` in place of `ES[5]`, because you need to append the vector `ES[5][[1]]` to `ES[1|||5]`. However, before you use `AppendColumns`, you need to load `LinearAlgebra`Master``.

Use Transpose *and* Join *to construct the diagonalizing matrix.*

```
In[8]:= P = Transpose[Join[ES[1||4], ES[5]]]
Out[8]//MatrixForm=
    -1   -1   -1   -1   1
     0    0    0    1   1
     0    0    1    0   1
     0    1    0    0   1
     1    0    0    0   1
```

Mathematica can verify that $P^{-1}AP$ is diagonal. The eigenvalues appear on the diagonal according to the ordering of the vectors in P.

```
In[9]:= Inverse[P] . A . P
Out[9]//MatrixForm=
    -1    0    0    0    0
     0   -1    0    0    0
     0    0   -1    0    0
     0    0    0   -1    0
     0    0    0    0    4
```

In some cases, the descriptions of the eigenvalues and eigenvectors are more complicated, as seen in the following.

The matrix B defined here has more complicated eigenvalues.

```
In[1]:= g[i_,j_] := If[i == j, i+j-1, i+j]

In[2]:= B = Array[g, {3,3}]
Out[2]//MatrixForm=
    1    3    4
    3    3    5
    4    5    5
```

Find the eigenvalues.

```
In[3]:= Id[3] = IdentityMatrix[3];

In[4]:= p = Det[x Id[3] - B]
Out[4]= -17 -27 x -9 x² + x³

In[5]:= lambda = x /. Solve[p == 0, x]
Out[5]= {-1, (10 + Sqrt[168])/2, (10 - Sqrt[168])/2}
```

At this point you can be sure *B* is theoretically diagonalizable. There is always at least one eigenvector for each eigenvalue, and in this case there are three distinct eigenvalues. *Mathematica* can do the diagonalization because the roots are not too complicated.

Find the eigenspace bases.

```
In[6]:=
ES[1] = NullSpace[lambda[[1]] Id[3] - B]
Out[6]//MatrixForm=
    1   -2   1
```

```
In[7]:=
ES[2] = NullSpace[lambda[[2]] Id[3] - B]
Out[7]//MatrixForm=
```

$$\frac{-5 + Sqrt[168]}{13} \quad \frac{4 + Sqrt[42]}{13} \quad 1$$

```
In[8]:=
ES[3] = NullSpace[lambda[[3]] Id[3] - B]
Out[8]//MatrixForm=
```

$$\frac{-5 - Sqrt[168]}{13} \quad \frac{4 - Sqrt[42]}{13} \quad 1$$

You could save typing by using a Do loop.

```
In[9]:= Do[ES[i] =
NullSpace[lambda[[i]] Id[3] - B], {i,1,3}]
```

You can now build the diagonalizing matrix in the same manner you used earlier for A.

```
In[10]:= P =
Transpose[Join[ES[1],ES[2],ES[3]]]
Out[10]//MatrixForm=
```

$$\begin{matrix} 1 & \frac{-5 + Sqrt[168]}{13} & \frac{-5 - Sqrt[168]}{13} \\ -2 & \frac{4 + Sqrt[42]}{13} & \frac{4 - Sqrt[42]}{13} \\ 1 & 1 & 1 \end{matrix}$$

The result checks.[6]

```
In[11]:= Together[Inverse[P] . B . P]
Out[11]//MatrixForm=
-1        0                0
0         5 + Sqrt[42]     0
0         0                5 - Sqrt[42]
```

Without the `Together` command, the author's system crashed with the message

```
Format::lcont:
  Line continuation print object too wide.
```

This shows the difficulty of working with radical expressions.

---

[6]The `Together` command is used here to simplify the output.

Here is an example that involves complex eigenvalues.

Note that the matrix M is
not symmetric.

```
In[1]:= M = {{0,1,0,0},
             {-1,0,0,0},
             {0,0,0,2},
             {0,0,-2,0}};

In[2]:= Id[4] = IdentityMatrix[4];
```

Calculate the characteristic
polynomial.

```
In[3]:= p = Det[x Id[4] - M]]
Out[3]= 4 + 5 x² + x⁴
```

Find the eigenvalues.

```
In[4]:= lambda = x /. Solve[p == 0, x]
Out[4]= {I, -I, 2 I, -2 I}
```

There are four distinct eigenvalues, all purely imaginary.

Compute the eigenspace
bases.

```
In[5]:= Do[ES[i]=
    NullSpace[lambda[[i]] Id[4] - M], {i,1,4}]
```

Form the transition matrix.

```
In[6]:= P =
Transpose[Join[ES[1],ES[2],ES[3],ES[4]]]
Out[6]//MatrixForm=
    -I   I    0    0
     1   1    0    0
     0   0   -I    I
     0   0    1    1
```

Check your result.

```
In[7]:= Together[Inverse[P] . M . P]
Out[7]//MatrixForm=
     I    0     0     0
     0   -I     0     0
     0    0    2 I     0
     0    0     0   -2 I
```

EXERCISES 3.2 _____

1. Let $A = [a_{ij}]$ be the 5×5 matrix with

$$a_{ij} = \begin{cases} i+j-1 & \text{if } i = j \\ i+j+1 & \text{if } i \neq j \end{cases}$$

   Determine if A is diagonalizable and, if so, find a diagonalizing matrix P.

2. Let $A = [a_{ij}]$ be the 4×4 matrix with

$$a_{ij} = \begin{cases} 1 & \text{if } i > j \\ 0 & \text{otherwise} \end{cases}$$

   Determine if A is diagonalizable and, if so, find a diagonalizing matrix P.

3. Let $A = [a_{ij}]$ be the 5×5 matrix with

$$a_{ij} = \begin{cases} 2 & \text{if } i = j \\ 1 & \text{if } i \neq j \end{cases}$$

Determine if A is diagonalizable and, if so, find a diagonalizing matrix P.

4. Let $A = [a_{ij}]$ be the 4×4 matrix defined by $a_{ij} = i + j - 1$. Determine if A is diagonalizable and, if so, find a diagonalizing matrix.

5. Let $A = [a_{ij}]$ be the 4×4 matrix defined by $a_{ij} = \min(i, j) + \max(i, j)$. Determine if A is diagonalizable and, if so, find a diagonalizing matrix.

3.3 Dealing with Difficult Radicals

If M is a matrix with rational entries, the characteristic polynomial $p(x) = |xI - A|$ has rational coefficients. *Mathematica* is capable of factoring such a polynomial as a product of polynomials that have rational coefficients and cannot be further factored with polynomials having rational coefficients. We call such a polynomial *irreducible*. (Actually, we should say irreducible over the rational numbers.) *Mathematica*'s ability to do this faithfully leads to a technique for finding the eigenvalues of (rational) matrices that have characteristic polynomials with factors of degree three or greater.

Consider the 3×3 matrix

$$A = \begin{bmatrix} 1 & 2 & 3 \\ 2 & 2 & 3 \\ 3 & 3 & 3 \end{bmatrix}$$

The (i, j) entry of this matrix is the maximum of i and j. The matrix was used earlier in Section 3.1 as an example of a matrix for which *Mathematica* could not find the eigenvectors using the `NullSpace` command. One of its eigenvalues (found by `Solve`) is

$$r = 2 + \frac{23 \sqrt[3]{\frac{2}{3}}}{\sqrt[3]{369 + i\sqrt{9843}}} + \frac{\sqrt[3]{369 + i\sqrt{9843}}}{\sqrt[3]{18}}$$

In finding the solutions of a system of linear equations using row-reduction, you cannot multiply or divide a row by zero. The problem `NullSpace` has in finding the associated eigenvectors is that it cannot simplify the expressions that develop in the solution process, to the point that it can determine whether they are nonzero.

Consider the following *Mathematica* session.

Define the matrix M. $In[1]:=$ `A = Array[Max, {3,3}]`

```
Out[1]//MatrixForm=
    1    2    3
    2    2    3
    3    3    3
```

Define I₃.

$$In[2]:= Id[3] = IdentityMatrix[3];$$

Define p.

```
In[3]:= p = Det[x Id[3] - A]
Out[3]= -3 -11 x - 6 x^2 + x^3
```

Now let *r* denote a root of *p*. Form the characteristic matrix *rI – A* but with *r* left as a symbol, and row-reduce *rI – A,* being sure not to multiply (or divide) a row by zero. The key is that the only way a polynomial in *r* can be zero is if it is a multiple of $q = p(r)$. This is a matter dealt with in the branch of algebra known as *field theory.*

Define $q = p(r)$ and CM = rI – A.

```
In[4]:= q = p /.{x -> r}
Out[4]= -3 -11 r - 6 r^2 + r^3
```

```
In[5]:= CM = r Id[3] - A
Out[5]//MatrixForm=
    -1 + r   -2        -3
    -2       -2 + r  -3
    -3       -3        -3 + r
```

Begin the row-reduction.

```
In[6]:= CM[[1]] = CM[[1]]/CM[[1,1]]; CM
Out[6]//MatrixForm=
```

$$
\begin{array}{ccc}
1 & \dfrac{-2}{-1 + r} & \dfrac{-3}{-1 + r} \\
-2 & -2 + r & -3 \\
-3 & -3 & -3 + r
\end{array}
$$

Zero the entries below the leading one in the (1,1) position.

```
In[7]:= CM[[2]] = CM[[2]] + 2 CM[[1]];
In[8]:= CM[[3]] = CM[[3]] + 3 CM[[1]];
In[9]:= CM = CM//Together
Out[9]//MatrixForm=
```

$$
\begin{array}{ccc}
1 & \dfrac{-2}{-1 + r} & \dfrac{-3}{-1 + r} \\
0 & \dfrac{-2 - 3 r + r^2}{-1 + r} & \dfrac{-3 (1 + r)}{-1 + r} \\
0 & \dfrac{-3 (1 + r)}{-1 + r} & \dfrac{-6 - 4 r + r^2}{-1 + r}
\end{array}
$$

None of the terms is zero because none of the numerators is a multiple of $-3 - 11r - 6r^2 + r^3$. Continue to divide the second row by the (2,2) entry.

```
In[10]:= CM[[2]] = CM[[2]]/CM[2,2];
In[11]:= CM = CM//Together
Out[11]//MatrixForm=
```

$$
\begin{array}{ccc}
1 & \dfrac{-2}{-1 + r} & \dfrac{-3}{-1 + r} \\[2ex]
0 & 1 & \dfrac{-3\ (1 + r)}{-2 - 3\ r + r^2} \\[2ex]
0 & \dfrac{-3\ (1 + r)}{-1 + r} & \dfrac{-6 - 4\ r + r^2}{-1 + r}
\end{array}
$$

Continue the reduction, checking at each step to be sure you do not multiply (or divide) a row by zero. Note that the (3,3) entry is ultimately zero because $q = p(r)$ is a root of its numerator.

```
In[12]:=
 CM[[1]] = CM[[1]] - CM[[1,2]] CM[[2]];

In[13]:=
 CM[[3]] = CM[[3]] - CM[[3,2]] CM[[2]];

In[14]:= CM = CM//Together
Out[14]//MatrixForm=
```

$$
\begin{array}{ccc}
1 & 0 & \dfrac{-3r}{-2 - 3\ r + r^2} \\[2ex]
0 & 1 & \dfrac{-3\ (1 + r)}{-2 - 3\ r + r^2} \\[2ex]
0 & 0 & \dfrac{-3 - 11\ r - 6\ r^2 + r^3}{-2 - 3\ r + r^2}
\end{array}
$$

The numerator of the (3,3) entry is p(r), so it is zero. Zero the (3,3) entry. The result is now in echelon form.

```
In[15]:= CM[[3,3]] = 0; CM
Out[15]//MatrixForm=
```

$$
\begin{array}{ccc}
1 & 0 & \dfrac{-3r}{-2 - 3\ r + r^2} \\[2ex]
0 & 1 & \dfrac{-3\ (1 + r)}{-2 - 3\ r + r^2} \\[2ex]
0 & 0 & 0
\end{array}
$$

Apply NullSpace to get the general eigenvector associated with r. A set with one vector is returned.

```
In[16]:= NullSpace[CM]//Together
Out[16]//MatrixForm=
```

$$
\begin{array}{ccc}
\dfrac{3r}{-2 - 3\ r + r^2} & \dfrac{3\ (1 + r)}{-2 - 3\ r + r^2} & 1
\end{array}
$$

Extract the vector.

$In[17]:= $[[1]]$

$$Out[17]= \{ \frac{3\ r}{-2\ -\ 3\ r\ +\ r^2}, \frac{3\ (1\ +\ r)}{-2\ -\ 3\ r\ +\ r^2}, 1\}$$

If you like, you can clear the denominators from the vector and still have the entries be polynomials of degree two or less, as follows.

Clear the denominators.

```
In[18]:=
%17 Denominator[%17[[1]]]
Out[18]=
{3 r, 3(1 + r), -2 - 3 r + r^2}
```

For each value of the root *r*, the vector %18 is an associated eigenvector. Each substitution produces a corresponding eigenvector.

The following demonstrates the procedure.

Compute all the eigen-values.

$In[19]:= Solve[q == 0, r];$

*Following this command, the i*th *eigenvalue is* lambda[[i]].

$In[20]:= lambda = r /. %;$

Now define the eigenspaces.

$In[21]:= Do[ES[i] = %18 /. \{r -> r[i]\}, \{i,1,3\}]$

Form the diagonalizing matrix. We suppress the output because of its length.

$In[22]:= P =$
$\quad$ Transpose[Join[{ES[1]},{ES[2]},{ES[3]}]];

This shows the (1,1) *entry. The remainder is suppressed because of its length.*

$Out[22]=$

$$3\ (2\ +\ \frac{23\ 2^{1/3}}{(1107\ +\ 3\ I\ Sqrt[9843])^{1/3}}\ +$$

$$\frac{(1107\ +\ 3\ I\ Sqrt[9843])^{1/3}}{3\ 2^{1/3}}$$

The procedure just outlined is rather lengthy. Alternatively, it is also possible to use NullSpace directly on $rI - A$ and force it to test that it is not multiplying or dividing by a multiple of $q = p(r)$. This is done as follows.

This makes NullSpace *check that it is not multiply-ing or dividing by a multiple of p(r).*

$In[23]:= NullSpace[r\ Id[3]\ -\ A,$
$\quad$ ZeroTest -> (PolynomialMod[#,q] == 0&)]

*The result is somewhat
different in appearance from
%18, but it is equally good.*

Out[23]//MatrixForm=

$$\frac{-3+r}{3} \quad -\frac{9+2(-3+r)}{3r} \quad \frac{9+2(-3+r)}{3r} \quad 1$$

From this point, the solution proceeds as in %19 through %22. However, the resulting quantities are too complicated for *Mathematica* to verify that $P^{-1}AP$ is the appropriate diagonal matrix unless you settle for decimal form.

If the characteristic polynomial p of a matrix A has more than one irreducible factor, then the technique of this section should be applied to the factors of degree greater than two, and the technique of the earlier sections should be applied to the factors of degree two or less.

EXERCISES 3.3

1. Work through the calculations of this section in a *Mathematica* session and verify that %18 and %23 are equivalent. (Clear the denominators from %23 and apply `PolynomialMod` as with %18.)
2. Define M and P as in this section. Set `P = N[P]` and verify that the product $P^{-1}MP$ is "approximately diagonal."
3. Find a diagonalizing matrix P for the 4×4 matrix $M = [\max(i, j)]$.
4. Find a diagonalizing matrix P for the 4×4 matrix $M = [\min(i, j)]$. Note that the characteristic polynomial is not irreducible in this case.
5. Give a formal description of a diagonalizing matrix for the 5×5 matrix $M = [\max(i, j)]$.
6. Let M_{11} be the 2×2 matrix $M_{11} = [\max(i, j)]$. Let $M_{12} = M_{21}$ be the 2×2 zero matrix, and let M_{22} be the 2×2 matrix $M_{22} = [\min(i, j)]$. Find a diagonalizing matrix for the matrix $M = \begin{bmatrix} M_{11} & M_{12} \\ M_{21} & M_{22} \end{bmatrix}$.

3.4 Triangularization
[SubMatrix]

Not all square matrices are diagonalizable, even in theory. For example, the matrix $\begin{bmatrix} 1 & 1 \\ 0 & 1 \end{bmatrix}$ is not diagonalizable. However, if a factorization $C_A(x) = \prod_{i=1}^{n}(x - \lambda_i)$ of the characteristic polynomial of a matrix A can be found, then it is always possible to find an upper-triangular matrix $T = [t_{ij}]$ with $t_{ii} = \lambda_i$, which is similar to A. Note that if $P^{-1}AP = T$, then substituting $\mathbf{y} = P\overline{\mathbf{y}}$ and $\mathbf{x} = P\overline{\mathbf{x}}$ into the equation $\mathbf{y} = A\mathbf{x}$ and left-multiplying by P^{-1} yields the equivalent upper-triangular system $\overline{\mathbf{y}} = T\overline{\mathbf{x}}$. In applications, this equivalent system can often be solved using back-substitution.

One technique of triangularizing an $n \times n$ matrix A is based on the following four observations.

1. If $\lambda_1, \lambda_2, \ldots, \lambda_s$ are eigenvalues of A with associated linearly independent eigenvectors $\mathbf{v}_1, \mathbf{v}_2, \ldots, \mathbf{v}_s$, respectively, and if $\mathbf{v}_1, \mathbf{v}_2, \ldots, \mathbf{v}_n$ is a basis for $\Re^n$, then the matrix $P_1 = [\mathbf{v}_1, \mathbf{v}_2, \ldots, \mathbf{v}_n]$ satisfies

$$
P_1^{-1}AP_1 = \begin{bmatrix} \lambda_1 & * & \cdots & * & * \\ 0 & \lambda_2 & & * & * \\ & & \cdots & & \\ 0 & 0 & \cdots & \lambda_s & * \\ 0 & 0 & \cdots & 0 & B \end{bmatrix}
$$

   where B is an $(n - s) \times (n - s)$ matrix.
2. The eigenvalues of B are a subset of the eigenvalues of A.
3. If $P_1^{-1}AP_1$ is as in 1), and if the matrix Q triangularizes B, then the matrix

$$
P_2 = \begin{bmatrix} I_2 & 0_{s \times (n-s)} \\ 0_{(n-s) \times (n-s)} & Q \end{bmatrix}
$$

   triangularizes the matrix $P_1^{-1}AP_1$.
4. If P_1 and P_2 are as in 1) and 3), respectively, then the matrix $P_0 = P_1P_2$ triangularizes A.

The following example demonstrates this technique for triangularization.

Consider the 4×4 matrix M. It is not diagonalizable, as you will see.

```
In[1]:= M = {{4, 4, 4, 4},
             {-3, -4, -8, -9},
             {3, 6, 11, 10},
             {-1, -2, -3, -1}};
        Id[4] = IdentityMatrix[4];
```

Find the eigenvalues of the matrix M.

```
In[2]:= p = Det[x Id[4] - M]
Out[2]= 36 - 60 x + 37 x^2 - 10 x^3 + x^4

In[3]:= lambda = x /. Solve[p == 0, x]
Out[3]= {3, 2, 3, 2}
```

M has two distinct eigenvalues: 2 and 3.

Find the eigenspaces.

```
In[4]:= ES[1] =
NullSpace[lambda[[1]] Id[4] - M]
Out[4]//MatrixForm=
  0   1   -2   1
```

```
In[5]:= ES[2] =
 NullSpace[lambda[[2]] Id[4] - M]
Out[5]//MatrixForm=
 -2  1  0  0
```

Call the two basis vectors $\mathbf{v}_1$ and $\mathbf{v}_2$, respectively.

Both eigenspaces are one-dimensional, whereas each λ_i has multiplicity two as a root of p. The matrix M is not diagonalizable.

Extend the eigenvectors $\mathbf{v}_1$, $\mathbf{v}_2$ to a basis $\mathbf{v}_1, \mathbf{v}_2, \mathbf{v}_3, \mathbf{v}_4$ for $\mathfrak{R}^4$. You can get $\mathbf{v}_3, \mathbf{v}_4$ as a basis for the null space of the matrix S.

```
In[6]:= S = Join[ES[1],ES[2]]
Out[6]//MatrixForm=
  0  1  -2  1
 -2  1   0  0
```

```
In[7]:= A = NullSpace[S]
Out[7]//MatrixForm=
```

$$-(\frac{1}{2}) \quad -1 \quad 0 \quad 1$$
$$1 \quad\quad 2 \quad 1 \quad 0$$

Thinking of S and A as sets, the set $S \cup A$ forms a basis for $\mathfrak{R}^4$. (Why?)

Set up the matrix $P_1 = [\mathbf{v}_1, \mathbf{v}_2, \mathbf{v}_3, \mathbf{v}_4]$ and use it to get a partially triangularized matrix T_1.

```
In[8]:= P[1] = Transpose[Join[S,A]];
```

```
In[9]:= T[1] = Inverse[P[1]] . M . P[1]
Out[9]//MatrixForm=
```

$$3 \quad 0 \quad -(\frac{71}{58}) \quad -(\frac{344}{29})$$
$$0 \quad 2 \quad \frac{10}{29} \quad -(\frac{227}{29})$$
$$0 \quad 0 \quad \frac{79}{29} \quad \frac{112}{29}$$
$$0 \quad 0 \quad \frac{3}{58} \quad \frac{66}{29}$$

The matrix P_1 partially triangularizes the matrix A, leaving a 2×2 submatrix B in the lower right-hand corner to be dealt with.

Extract the untriangularized lower right-hand submatrix B.

```
In[10]:= B = SubMatrix[%, {3,3}, {2,2}]
Out[10]//MatrixForm=
```

$$\frac{79}{29} \quad\quad \frac{112}{29}$$
$$\frac{3}{58} \quad\quad \frac{66}{29}$$

The second argument to Submatrix indicates that the submatrix begins at the (3,3) entry. The third argument indicates that B is 2×2.

Now find a triangularizing matrix for B.

Find the eigenvalues of the matrix B.

```
In[11]:= Det[x[Id[2] - B]];

In[12]:= x /. Solve[% == 0, x]
Out[12]= {3, 2}
```

Notice that the eigenvalues of B are eigenvalues of M. This will always be the case. (Verify.)

Find bases for the eigenspaces of B. Call them ES[3] and ES[4].

```
In[13]:= Do[ES[i] =
NullSpace[%[[i-2]] Id[2] - B], {i,3,4}]
```

When i is 3, $i - 2$ is 1, so `ES[3] = NullSpace[3 Id[2] - B]`. Similarly, `ES[4] = NullSpace[2 Id[2] - B]`.

Set up the matrices Q with columns from $\mathrm{ES}_3 \cup \mathrm{ES}_4$ and $P_2 = \begin{bmatrix} I_2 & 0 \\ 0 & Q \end{bmatrix}$. P_2 can be defined using BlockMatrix.

```
In[14]:= Q = Transpose[Join[ES[3],ES[4]]]
Out[14]//MatrixForm=
```

$$14 \qquad -(\frac{16}{3})$$
$$1 \qquad 1$$

```
In[15]:= Z[2] = Array[0 &, {2,2}]
Out[15]//MatrixForm=
    0   0
    0   0

In[16]:= P[2] = BlockMatrix[Id[2], Z[2], Z[2], Q]
Out[16]//MatrixForm=
    1   0   0   0
    0   1   0   0
```
$$0 \qquad 0 \qquad 14 \qquad -(\frac{16}{3})$$
```
    0   0   1   1
```

The matrix P_2 is invertible and triangularizes the matrix T_1. Can you see why? You may wish to check it.

The matrix $P_0 = P_1P_2$ now triangularizes M.[7,8]

```
In[17]:= P[0] = P[1] . P[2];

In[18]:= Inverse[P[0]] . M . P[0]
Out[18]//MatrixForm=
```

$$\begin{bmatrix} 3 & 0 & -29 & -(\frac{16}{3}) \\ 0 & 2 & -3 & -(\frac{29}{3}) \\ 0 & 0 & 3 & 0 \\ 0 & 0 & 0 & 2 \end{bmatrix}$$

Can you explain why the product $P_0 = P_1P_2$ triangularizes A?

EXERCISES 3.4

Triangularize the following matrices.

1. The 4×4 matrix $A = [a_{ij}]$, where $a_{ij} = \begin{cases} 1 & \text{if } i > j \\ 0 & \text{otherwise} \end{cases}$.

2. The 4×4 matrix $A = [a_{ij}]$, where $a_{ij} = \begin{cases} 1 & \text{if } i + j \text{ is odd} \\ 0 & \text{if } i + j \text{ is even} \end{cases}$.

3. The 4×4 matrix $A = [a_{ij}]$, where $a_{ij} = \begin{cases} 2 & \text{if } i \leq 2 \\ 0 & \text{otherwise} \end{cases}$.

4. The 4×4 matrix $A = [a_{ij}]$, where $a_{ij} = \begin{cases} 0 & \text{if } i = j \\ 1 & \text{if } i \neq j \end{cases}$.

3.5 Automating the Processes
```
[Eigensystem]
```

The procedure for diagonalizing or triangularizing a matrix is not conceptually difficult, and *Mathematica* certainly speeds up its execution. However, in applications involving diagonalization or triangularization, the method is no longer of central interest. Instead, these processes take on the mechanical nature of row-reduction—they become a means to an end.

---

[7]It would be natural to call the product P. This works in *Mathematica*, but it would shadow the definitions of the matrices $P[1]$ and $P[2]$.

[8]*Mathematica* has a built-in command that can be used to triangularize matrices. You may want to investigate it. Enter ?Jordan* for information on your system; the commands are version dependent. In Version 2.2, the command is JordanDecomposition.

Mathematica has an `Eigensystem` command that returns both the eigenvalues and the associated eigenvectors in a list. The `Eigensystem` command allows you to determine at a glance whether a matrix is diagonalizable. It also provides easy access to the eigenvectors for you to use in constructing a diagonalizing or triangularizing matrix. The following demonstrates.

Consider the matrix A.

```
In[1]:= A = Array[1 &, {5,5}]
Out[1]//MatrixForm=
    1    1    1    1    1
    1    1    1    1    1
    1    1    1    1    1
    1    1    1    1    1
    1    1    1    1    1
```

Apply the `Eigensystem` *command.*

```
In[2]:= ES[A]  = Eigensystem[A]
Out[2]=
{{0, 0, 0, 0, 5}, {{-1, 0, 0, 0, 1},
    {-1, 0, 0, 1, 0}, {-1, 0, 1, 0, 0},
    {-1, 1, 0, 0, 0}, {1, 1, 1, 1, 1}}}
```

The first entry of the response list is a list of the eigenvalues of *A*. The second entry of the response list is a list of vectors—one for each entry in the list of eigenvalues. If λ_i is the *i*th entry of the eigenvalue list, and if $\mathbf{v}_i$ is the *i*th entry of the vector list, then necessarily $A\mathbf{v}_i = \lambda_i \mathbf{v}_i$. However, $\mathbf{v}_i$ may be **0**. The number of *nonzero* eigenvectors corresponding to a repeated eigenvalue will be the dimension of the corresponding eigenspace.

The ith eigenvalue is `lambda[[i]]`.

```
In[3]:= lambda = %[[1]]
Out[3]= {0, 0, 0, 0, 5}
```

The ith vector is `Q[[i]]`. *The matrix Q^T is a diagonalizing matrix.*

```
In[4]:= Q = [%%[[2]]]
Out[4]//MatrixForm=
    -1    -1    -1    -1    1
     0     0     0     1    1
     0     0     1     0    1
     0     1     0     0    1
     1     0     0     0    1
```

Verify the result.[9]

```
In[5]:= P = Transpose[Q];
```

---

[9]The verification can be very time-consuming and may, on occasion, overload the resources of *Mathematica*. However, when the eigenvalues are rational this will not occur.

```
In[6]:= Inverse[P] . A . P
Out[6]//MatrixForm=
    0    0    0    0    0
    0    0    0    0    0
    0    0    0    0    0
    0    0    0    0    0
    0    0    0    0    5
```

Here is a matrix that is not diagonalizable; it served earlier as an example for triangularization. We triangularize it again using `Eigensystem`.

Consider the matrix M.

```
In[1]:= M = {{4,   4,   4,    4},
             {-3,  -4,  -8,  -9},
             {3,   6,   11,  10},
             {-1,  -2,  -3,  -1}};
```

Find the eigensystem.

```
In[2]:= ES[M] = Eigensystem[M]
Out[2]=
{{2,  2,  3,  3}, {{-2,  1,  0,  0}, {0,  0,  0,  0},
     {0,  1,  -2,  1}, {0,  0,  0,  0}}}
```

There are two distinct eigenvalues and only two nonzero vectors.

Name the eigenvalues and the nonzero vectors.

```
In[3]:= lambda = %[[1]]
Out[3]= {2,  2,  3,  3}
```

```
In[4]:= Q = %%[[2,{1,3}]]
Out[4]= -2    1    0    0
         0    1    -2   1
```

Extend the row vectors of Q to a basis for 4-space.

```
In[5]:= A = NullSpace[Q]
Out[5]//MatrixForm=
```

$$-(\frac{1}{2}) \quad -1 \quad 0 \quad 1$$

$$1 \quad\quad 2 \quad 1 \quad 0$$

The transpose of this array will partially diagonalize A.

```
In[6]:= Join[Q,A]
Out[6]//MatrixForm=
-2    1    0    0
0     1    -2   1
```

$$-(\frac{1}{2}) \quad -1 \quad 0 \quad 1$$

$$1 \quad\quad 2 \quad 1 \quad 0$$

```
In[7]:= P[1] = Transpose[%];
```

Partially triangularize M
with P_1.

$In[8]:= T[1] = Inverse[P[1]] . M . P[1]$
$Out[8]//MatrixForm=$

$$\begin{array}{cccc} 2 & 0 & \dfrac{10}{29} & -(\dfrac{227}{29}) \\[2mm] 0 & 3 & -(\dfrac{71}{58}) & -(\dfrac{344}{29}) \\[2mm] 0 & 0 & \dfrac{79}{29} & \dfrac{112}{29} \\[2mm] 0 & 0 & \dfrac{3}{58} & \dfrac{66}{29} \end{array}$$

Extract the untriangularized
lower right-hand submatrix.

$In[9]:= B = SubMatrix[\%, \{3,3\}, \{2,2\}]$
$Out[9]//MatrixForm=$

$$\begin{array}{cc} \dfrac{79}{29} & \dfrac{112}{29} \\[2mm] \dfrac{3}{58} & \dfrac{66}{29} \end{array}$$

Apply Eigensystem.

$In[10]:= Eigensystem[\%]$

$Out[10]= \{\{2, 3\}, \{\{-(\dfrac{16}{3}), 1\}, \{14, 1\}\}\}$

Set up a diagonalizing
matrix Q for the submatrix
and form the block matrix

$$P_2 = \begin{bmatrix} I_2 & 0 \\ 0 & Q \end{bmatrix}.$$

$In[11]:= Q = Transpose[\%[[2]]];$
$Z[2] = Array[0 \&, \{2,2\}];$
$Id[2] = IdentityMatrix[2];$
$P[2] = BlockMatrix[Id[2], Z[2], Z[2], Q]$

$Out[11]//MatrixForm=$

$$\begin{array}{cccc} 1 & 0 & 0 & 0 \\ 0 & 1 & 0 & 0 \\[2mm] 0 & 0 & -(\dfrac{16}{3}) & 14 \\[2mm] 0 & 0 & 1 & 1 \end{array}$$

The matrix $P_0 = P_1 P_2$
triangularizes M.[10]

$In[12]:= P[0] = P1 . P2;$
$Inverse[P[0]] . M . P[0]$

---

[10]There is no need to use Together or Simplify if the eigenvalues are rational, as in this case.

Out[12]//MatrixForm=

$$\begin{matrix} 2 & 0 & -(\dfrac{29}{3}) & -3 \\ 0 & 3 & -(\dfrac{16}{3}) & -29 \\ 0 & 0 & 2 & 0 \\ 0 & 0 & 0 & 3 \end{matrix}$$

The `Eigensystem` command makes for much faster diagonalization and somewhat faster triangularization.[11] Note, however, that `Eigensystem` can fail when the characteristic polynomial $p(x) = |xI - A|$ has an irreducible factor of degree three or higher.

EXERCISES 3.5 _____

In Exercises 1–5, use `Eigensystem` to determine if the given matrix is diagonalizable and, if so, give a diagonalizing matrix P and the associated diagonalized form of A.

1. Let $A = [a_{ij}]$ be the 5×5 matrix with $a_{ij} = \begin{cases} i+j-1 & \text{if } i = j \\ i+j+1 & \text{if } i \neq j \end{cases}$.

2. Let $A = [a_{ij}]$ be the 4×4 matrix with $a_{ij} = \begin{cases} 1 & \text{if } i > j \\ 0 & \text{otherwise} \end{cases}$.

3. Let $A = [a_{ij}]$ be the 5×5 matrix with $a_{ij} = \begin{cases} 2 & \text{if } i = j \\ 1 & \text{if } i \neq j \end{cases}$.

4. Let $A = [a_{ij}]$ be the 4×4 matrix defined by $a_{ij} = i + j - 1$.

5. Let $A = [a_{ij}]$ be the 4×4 matrix defined by $a_{ij} = \min(i, j) + \max(i, j)$.

Triangularize the following matrices using `Eigensystem`.

6. The 4×4 matrix $A = [a_{ij}]$, where $a_{ij} = \begin{cases} 1 & \text{if } i > j \\ 0 & \text{otherwise} \end{cases}$.

7. The 4×4 matrix $A = [a_{ij}]$, where $a_{ij} = \begin{cases} 1 & \text{if } i + j \text{ is odd} \\ 0 & \text{if } i + j \text{ is even} \end{cases}$.

8. The 4×4 matrix $A = [a_{ij}]$, where $a_{ij} = \begin{cases} 2 & \text{if } i \leq 2 \\ 0 & \text{otherwise} \end{cases}$.

9. The 4×4 matrix $A = [a_{ij}]$, where $a_{ij} = \begin{cases} 0 & \text{if } i = j \\ 1 & \text{if } i \neq j \end{cases}$.

---

[11]In Version 2.2, the command `JordanDecomposition[M]` produces an upper-triangular matrix similar to A and a triangularizing matrix.

3.6 Orthogonal Diagonalization

Assume that A is a square real matrix and that all the eigenvalues of A are real. Shur's theorem says that A is similar to an upper-triangular matrix and that the triangularizing matrix P can be chosen so that $P^T = P^{-1}$, that is, so that P is orthogonal.[12] If A is symmetric, P is orthogonal and $P^{-1}AP = U$ is upper triangular, then the relation $P^{-1} = P^T$ yields $U^T = (P^TAP)^T = P^TAP = U$.

If A is symmetric, an orthogonal diagonalizing matrix Q can be computed from any diagonalizing matrix P, using Gram-Schmidt with normalization on the columns of P.

For example, consider the matrix $A = \begin{bmatrix} 1 & 1 & 1 \\ 1 & 1 & 1 \\ 1 & 1 & 1 \end{bmatrix}$. The matrix A is symmetric, and therefore orthogonally diagonalizable. (It is also true that a real matrix is orthogonally diagonalizable only if it is symmetric. Can you prove this?)

The pure function `1&` *generates the matrix A.*

```
In[1]:= A = Array[1 &, {3,3}]
Out[1]//MatrixForm=
    1    1    1
    1    1    1
    1    1    1
```

Apply `Eigensystem`.

```
In[2]:= ES[1] = Eigensystem[A]
Out[2]= {{0, 0, 3},
  {{-1, 0, 1}, {-1, 1, 0}, {1, 1, 1}}}
```

Use Gram-Schmidt with normalization.[13]

```
In[3]:= Q = [GramSchmidt[%[[2]]]
Out[3]//MatrixForm=
```

$$-\left(\frac{1}{Sqrt[2]}\right) \quad 0 \quad \frac{1}{Sqrt[2]}$$

$$-\left(\frac{1}{Sqrt[6]}\right) \quad Sqrt\left[\frac{2}{3}\right] \quad -\left(\frac{1}{Sqrt[6]}\right)$$

$$\frac{1}{Sqrt[3]} \quad \frac{1}{Sqrt[3]} \quad \frac{1}{Sqrt[3]}$$

$P = Q^T$ is the orthonormal diagonalizing matrix.

```
In[4]:= P = Transpose[%];
```

---

[12]Charles G. Cullen, *Linear Algebra and Differential Equations* (Boston: Prindle Weber & Schmidt, 1979).
[13]`GramSchmidt`, like `Eigensystem`, may stumble on sets of vectors involving complicated radicals.

```
In[5]:= Q . A . P
Out[5]//MatrixForm=
    0    0    0
    0    0    0
    0    0    3
```

EXERCISES 3.6

1. Prove that an orthogonally diagonalizable (real) matrix is symmetric.
2. Orthogonally diagonalize the 5×5 matrix $A = [a_{ij}]$ defined by $a_{ij} = 1$ for $i, j = 1, \ldots, 5$.
3. Orthogonally diagonalize the 6×6 matrix $A = [a_{ij}]$ defined by $a_{ij} = \begin{cases} 1 & \text{if } i + j \text{ is even} \\ 0 & \text{if } i + j \text{ is odd} \end{cases}$.
4. Orthogonally diagonalize the 4×4 matrix $A = [a_{ij}]$ defined by $a_{ij} = \begin{cases} 1 & \text{if } i > j \\ 0 & \text{otherwise} \end{cases}$.

3.7 Applications

Systems of Linear Differential Equations

It is often necessary to solve systems of differential equations that involve several functions. In matrix/vector form, a system of homogeneous first-order linear differential equations can be written $\mathbf{y}' = A\mathbf{y}$, where $\mathbf{y} = (y_1, y_2, \ldots, y_n)$ is the vector of unknown functions and the symbol $\mathbf{y}'$ is used for the vector of derivatives $\mathbf{y}' = (y_1', y_2', \ldots, y_n')$.

For example, the system

$$\begin{cases} y_1' = 2y_1 + 3y_2 \\ y_2' = -y_1 - 2y_2 \end{cases}$$

can be written in matrix form as $\mathbf{y}' = A\mathbf{y}$, where $A = \begin{bmatrix} 2 & 3 \\ -1 & -2 \end{bmatrix}$. If A is diagonalizable with $P^{-1}AP = \begin{bmatrix} \lambda_1 & 0 \\ 0 & \lambda_2 \end{bmatrix}$, then the original system is equivalent to the "diagonal system" $\mathbf{z}' = \begin{bmatrix} \lambda_1 & 0 \\ 0 & \lambda_2 \end{bmatrix} \mathbf{z}$, with $\mathbf{y} = P\mathbf{z}$, where $\mathbf{z} = (z_1, z_2)$. This matrix equation is equivalent to the system

$$\begin{cases} z_1' = \lambda_1 z_1 \\ z_2' = \lambda_2 z_2 \end{cases}$$

and hence the equations are said to be *unlinked*.

Define the matrix A.

```
In[1]:= A = {{2,3},{-1,-2}};
```

Check to see if A is diagonalizable.

```
In[2]:= ES = Eigensystem[A]
Out[2]= {{-1, 1},
     {{-1, 1}, {-3, 1}}}
```

The matrix A is diagonalizable with diagonalizing matrix $P = (\text{ES})^T_2$.

The original system is equivalent to the diagonal system $\mathbf{z}' = \begin{bmatrix} -1 & 0 \\ 0 & 1 \end{bmatrix} \mathbf{z}$,

with $\mathbf{y} = P\mathbf{z}$, where $\mathbf{z} = (z_1, z_2)$. The matrix equation is equivalent to the system

$$\begin{cases} z_1'(x) = -z_1(x) \\ z_2'(x) = z_2(x) \end{cases}$$

Once $\mathbf{z}$ is known the solutions of the original system are given by $\mathbf{y} = P\mathbf{z}$. In this case, the solutions are known to be $z_1 = K_1 e^{-x}$ and $z_2 = K_2 e^x$.

Define $\mathbf{z} = (z_1, z_2)$ and compute $\mathbf{y}$.

```
In[3]:= z = {K[1] E^(-x), K[2] E^x}
```
$$Out[3]= \{\frac{K[1]}{E^x}, \ E^x \ K[2]\}$$

```
In[4]:= y = P . z
Out[4]=
```
$$\{-(\frac{K[1]}{E^x}), \ -3 \ E^x \ K[2], \ \frac{K[1]}{E^x} + E^x \ K[2]\}$$

In some cases you might wish to use DSolve to solve the unlinked equations.

DSolve can be used to solve the unlinked equations. This solves for z_1.[14,15,16]

```
In[5]:= Clear[z];
   DSolve[z[1]'[x] == - z[1][x], z[1][x], x]
```
$$Out[5]= z[1][x] \ -> \ \frac{C[1]}{E^x}$$

Now consider the example $\mathbf{y}' = M\mathbf{y}$, where

$$M = \begin{bmatrix} 8 & 14 & 17 \\ 0 & 1 & 2 \\ -2 & -4 & -5 \end{bmatrix}$$

---

[14]DSolve can solve many systems of differential equations, but the technique demonstrated here is worth learning in its own right.

[15]It is necessary to clear $\mathbf{z}$ because it was assigned a value in %3.

[16]You can use D[y[x],x] in place of y'[x] if you prefer. It is sometimes more convenient.

Define the matrix M and check its eigensystem.

```
In[1]:= M = {{2,2,1},
             {1,3,4},
             {-1,-2,-2}};

In[2]:= Eigensystem[M]
Out[2]= {{1, 1, 2},
```

$$\{\{-2, 1, 0\}, \{0, 0, 0\}, \{-(\frac{15}{2}), 2, 1\}\}\}$$

The matrix is not diagonalizable, but it is triangularizable.

Extend the set of (nonzero) eigenvectors to a basis.[17] You can use NullSpace *for this.*

```
In[3]:= Q = %[[2]][[{1,3}]]
Out[3]//MatrixForm=
```

$$\begin{array}{ccc} -2 & 1 & 0 \\ -(\dfrac{15}{2}) & 2 & 1 \end{array}$$

```
In[4]:= A = NullSpace[Q]
Out[4]//MatrixForm=
```

$$\begin{array}{ccc} \dfrac{2}{7} & \dfrac{4}{7} & 1 \end{array}$$

Form a matrix with column vectors from %3 and %4.

```
In[5]:= P[1] = Transpose[Join[Q,A]]
Out[5]//MatrixForm=
```

$$\begin{array}{ccc} -2 & -(\dfrac{15}{2}) & \dfrac{2}{7} \\ 1 & 2 & \dfrac{4}{7} \\ 0 & 1 & 1 \end{array}$$

You can now use P_1 to begin the triangularization of *M*.

The matrix P_1 triangularizes M.

```
In[6]:= T[1] = Inverse[P[1]] . M . P[1]
Out[6]//MatrixForm=
```

$$\begin{array}{ccc} 1 & 0 & \dfrac{138}{7} \\ 0 & 2 & -(\dfrac{62}{7}) \\ 0 & 0 & 1 \end{array}$$

[17]Eigenvectors are always nonzero. Here you need to avoid the zero vector in the vector list.

In this case, the triangularization took only one step.

$In[7]:=$ T = T[1]; P = P[1];

The system $\mathbf{z}' = T\mathbf{z}$ is now equivalent to the original system $\mathbf{y}' = M\mathbf{y}$. This system is solved using back-substitution. In equation form, $\mathbf{z}' = T\mathbf{z}$ is given by

$$\begin{cases} z_1' = z_1 + \dfrac{138}{7} z_3 \\[2mm] z_2' = \qquad 2z_2 + \dfrac{62}{7} z_3 \\[2mm] z_3' = \qquad\qquad z_3 \end{cases}$$

Set up the required vectors.[18]

$In[8]:=$ z = {z1[x], z2[x], z3[x]};

$In[9]:=$ Tz = T . z;

Solve for z_3.[19]

$In[10]:=$ DSolve[z3'[x] == Tz[[3]], z[[3]], x]
$Out[10]//MatrixForm=$ z3[x] -> E^X C[1]

The *Mathematica* output indicates that the result is a 1×1 matrix. Hence, the value E^X C[1] is addressable as %[[1,1,2]].

Assign z_3 with C[1] *replaced by* K[1].

$In[11]:=$ z3[x] = %[[1,1,2]] /. {C[1] -> K[1]}
$Out[11]=$ E^X K[1]

The substitution of K[1] for C[1] is made because C[1] is a system variable. *Mathematica* will use it again in the solution for z_2, but then it will have a different meaning.

Solve for z_2 and assign it with C[1] *replaced by* K[2].

$In[12]:=$ DSolve[z2'[x] == Tz[[2]], z[[2]], x]
$Out[12]//MatrixForm=$

   z2[x] -> E^2 ^{X} C[1] + $\dfrac{62\ E^X\ K[1]}{7}$

$In[13]:=$ z2[x] = %[[1,1,2]] /. {C[1] -> K[2]};

Note that *Mathematica* did reuse C[1], and it would have even if K[1] were not used in z_1, yielding a less general solution.

---

[18]We use z1 for z_1, and so on. The definition z = {z[1][x], z[2][x], z[3][x]} is not usable in *Mathematica*.
[19]D[z[3][x],x] or D[z[[3]],x] could be used here in place of z3'[x].

Solve for z_1. Assign $z_1(x)$ the value of the solution with C[1] *replaced by* K[3]. *In this case, the introduction of* K[3] *is purely for aesthetic reasons.*

```
In[14]:= DSolve[z1'[x] == Tz[[1]], z[[1]], x]
Out[14]//MatrixForm=
```

$$z1[x] \; -> \; \frac{E^X \; (7 \; C[1] + 138 \; x \; K[1])}{7}$$

```
In[15]:= z1[x] = %[[1,1,2]] /. {C[1] -> K[3]}
```

The solutions of the original system **y′ = My** *are now given by* **y = Pz**.

```
In[16]:= y = P . z
Out[16]=
```

$$\{ \frac{2 \; E^X \; K[1]}{7} - \frac{15 \, (\frac{62 \; E^X \; K[1]}{7} + E^2 \; X \; K[2])}{2} - $$

$$\frac{2 \; E^X \; (138 \; x \; K[1] + 7 \; K[3])}{7} \; ,$$

$$\frac{4 \; E^X \; K[1]}{7} + 2 \; (\frac{62 \; E^X \; K[1]}{7}) \; + \; E^2 \; X \; K[2] + $$

$$\frac{E^X \; (138 \; x \; K[1] + 7 \; K[3])}{7} \; ,$$

$$\frac{69 \; E^X \; K[1]}{7} \; + \; E^2 \; X \; K[2] \}$$

You may wish to check the solutions. This is generally a good idea.

You can use D[y,x] *to compute* **y′**.[20]

```
In[17]:= Expand[D[y,x] - M . y]
Out[17]= {0, 0, 0}
```

Exercises on Systems of Differential Equations

1. Solve the system of linear differential equations **y′ = My**, where $M = [m_{ij}]$ is the 4×4 matrix given by $m_{ij} = i + j$.
2. Solve the system of liner differential equations

$$
\begin{aligned}
y_1' &= & & y_2 &+ & & y_4 \\
y_2' &= & y_1 &+ & & y_3 & \\
y_3' &= & & y_2 &+ & & y_4 \\
y_4' &= & y_1 &+ & & y_3 &
\end{aligned}
$$

---

[20]Expand is generally quicker than Simplify.

3. Solve the system of linear differential equations $\mathbf{y}' = M\mathbf{y}$, where

$$M = \begin{bmatrix} 1 & -2 & -2 & -2 & -2 \\ 2 & 6 & 4 & 4 & 4 \\ -3 & -6 & -6 & -10 & -10 \\ 1 & 2 & 3 & 6 & 1 \\ 1 & 2 & 3 & 4 & 9 \end{bmatrix}$$

4. Solve the system of linear differential equations $\mathbf{y}' = M\mathbf{y}$, where

$$M = \begin{bmatrix} 2 & 0 & -1 & -1 & -1 \\ 3 & 8 & 8 & 7 & 7 \\ -3 & -6 & -6 & -7 & -8 \\ 1 & 2 & 3 & 5 & 4 \\ 0 & 0 & 0 & 0 & 2 \end{bmatrix}$$

5. Solve the system of linear differential equations $\mathbf{y}' = M\,\mathbf{y}$, where

$$M = \begin{bmatrix} -205 & -409 & -613 & -817 & -1021 & -1225 \\ 494 & 986 & 1479 & 1972 & 2465 & 2958 \\ -662 & -1323 & -1986 & -2648 & -3310 & -3972 \\ 539 & 1078 & 1618 & 2156 & 2695 & 3234 \\ -272 & -544 & -816 & -1087 & -1360 & -1632 \\ 70 & 140 & 210 & 280 & 351 & 421 \end{bmatrix}$$

Problems on Differential Equations
1. A linear differential equation can be solved by setting up an equivalent system of first-order differential equations. The process is simple, but effective and important.

Consider the second-order differential equation

$$y''(x) + y'(x) + 2y(x) = e^x$$

The solution depends on the simple trick of introducing additional temporary variables $u_1 = y$ and $u_2 = y'$. With this substitution, the original equation is now equivalent to the system

$$\begin{aligned} u_1' &= & u_2 \\ u_2' &= -2u_1 & -u_2 & + e^x \end{aligned}$$

In matrix/vector form, this is simply $\mathbf{u}' = M\mathbf{u} + \mathbf{k}$, where

$$M = \begin{bmatrix} 0 & 1 \\ -2 & -1 \end{bmatrix}, \quad \mathbf{u} = (u_1, u_2), \quad \mathbf{u}' = (u_1', u_2'), \quad \mathbf{k} = (0, e^x)$$

The solution can be found by finding an upper-triangular matrix T similar to M. If $T = P^{-1}MP$, then the original equation is equivalent to the upper-triangular system $\mathbf{z}' = T\mathbf{z} + P^{-1}\mathbf{k}$. Solve the system $\mathbf{z}' = T\mathbf{z} + P^{-1}\mathbf{k}$ by back-substitution, using DSolve as required, and find $\mathbf{u} = P\mathbf{z}$. Then, with $\mathbf{u} = (u_1, u_2)$, $y = u_1$ is the general solution.

The general solution y can be written in the form $y = y_{Re} + y_{Im}\,i$ where y_{Re} and y_{Im} are real-valued functions. Then

$$y'' + y' + 2y = \mathbf{e}^x$$

and

$$(y''_{Re} + y'_{Re} + 2y_{Re}) + (y''_{Im} + y'_{Im} + 2y_{Im})i = \mathbf{e}^x$$

It follows that

$$y''_{Re} + y'_{Re} + 2y_{Re} = \mathbf{e}^x$$

The desired solution is most likely y_{Re}. Find y_{Re}.

2. Scientists in Elpmis have experimentally determined that the local populations $r(t)$ of rabbits and $f(t)$ of foxes are related by the differential equations

$$\begin{cases} r'(t) = \dfrac{r(t)}{75} - \dfrac{f(t)}{150} \\[2ex] f'(t) = \dfrac{r(t)}{75} - \dfrac{f(t)}{300} \end{cases}$$

a. Find the (real) approximate populations $r(t)$ and $f(t)$ in floating-point form at time $t = 10$, 20, and 100, assuming there are 1000 of each at time $t = 0$.

b. Repeat the problem assuming there are 2000 rabbits and 1000 foxes.

3. Engineers in Spring City are interested in the system shown. The springs are assumed to be linear and massless.

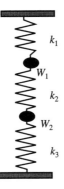

The weight W_2 is pulled down from its equilibrium position and released. The motion of the weights can be analyzed using Newton's second law of motion and Hooke's law. The equations governing the motion are

$$\frac{w_1 y_1''(t)}{g} = -k_1 y_1(t) + k_2 [y_2(t) - y_1(t)]$$

$$\frac{w_2 y_2''(t)}{g} = -k_2 [y_2(t) - y_1(t)] - k_3 y_2(t)$$

where

- w_1 is the weight of W_1 in pounds
- w_2 is the weight of W_2 in pounds
- k_1 is Hooke's constant for the upper spring, in pounds per foot
- k_2 is Hooke's constant for the middle spring, in pounds per foot
- k_3 is Hooke's constant for the lower spring, in pounds per foot
- $g = 32$ ft/sec^2
- $y_1(t)$ and $y_2(t)$ are the positions of W_1 and W_2 at time t relative to their equilibrium positions
- $y_1(0) = y_2(0) = 0$

Convert the second-order system to an equivalent first-order system and solve the latter for $y_1(t)$ and $y_2(t)$, given the following information: $y_1(0) = 10$, $y_2(0) = 12$, $w_1 = 32$, $w_2 = 32$, $k_1 = 12$, $k_2 = 10$, $k_3 = 12$.

The Matrix Exponential Function
[MatrixExp]

From the elementary theory of infinite series, the exponential function $\exp(x) = \mathbf{e}^x$ has the series expansion

$$\mathbf{e}^x = \sum_{i=0}^{\infty} \frac{1}{i!} x^i$$

As you know, the exponential function arises in solving the class of differential equations of the form $y' = ay$. The general solution of $y' = ay$ is given by $y = K\mathbf{e}^{ax}$.

Although it is a most interesting idea, there is no problem extending the definition of the exponential function—or many other functions that can be defined by convergent power series—to matrices: For a matrix A, the function $\mathbf{e}^{At}$ is defined by the series

$$\mathbf{e}^{At} = \sum_{i=0}^{\infty} \frac{I}{i!} (At)^i = I + At + \frac{(At)^2}{2!} + \frac{(At)^3}{3!} + \cdots$$

The interest in the matrix exponential function is motivated by the fact that if $\mathbf{y} = \mathbf{y}(t)$ is a vector of functions, if A is a square (scalar) matrix, and if $\mathbf{y}_0$ is a vector, then the matrix equation $\mathbf{y}' = A\mathbf{y}$ has $\mathbf{y} = \mathbf{e}^{At}\mathbf{y}_0$ as a solution.

If A is the diagonal matrix with $\lambda_1, \ldots, \lambda_n$ on the main diagonal, then it is easy to see that $\mathbf{e}^{At}$ is diagonal with $\mathbf{e}^{\lambda_1 t}, \ldots, \mathbf{e}^{\lambda_n t}$ on its main diagonal; that is,

$$\mathbf{e}^{At} = \begin{bmatrix} \mathbf{e}^{\lambda_1 t} & 0 & \cdots & 0 \\ 0 & \mathbf{e}^{\lambda_2 t} & \cdots & 0 \\ \vdots & & \vdots & \vdots \\ \vdots & & \vdots & 0 \\ 0 & 0 & \cdots & \mathbf{e}^{\lambda_n t} \end{bmatrix}$$

It turns out that if $P^{-1}AP = J = \mathrm{diag}(\lambda_1, \ldots, \lambda_n)$, then $A = PBP^{-1}$, $A^2 = PB^2P^{-1}, \ldots,$ and ultimately $\mathbf{e}^{At} = Pe^{Jt}P^{-1}$; that is,

$$\mathbf{e}^{At} = P\begin{bmatrix} \mathbf{e}^{\lambda_1 t} & 0 & \cdots & 0 \\ 0 & \mathbf{e}^{\lambda_2 t} & \cdots & 0 \\ \vdots & & \vdots & \vdots \\ \vdots & & \vdots & 0 \\ 0 & 0 & \cdots & \mathbf{e}^{\lambda_n t} \end{bmatrix}P^{-1}$$

Hence, if A is diagonalizable, the exponential function can be computed.

More generally, you can use *Mathematica*'s built-in `MatrixExp` command to compute $\mathbf{e}^{At}$.

Compute $\mathbf{e}^{At}$ using `MatrixExp`.

```
In[1]:= A = {{2,3},{-1,-2}};

In[2]:= MatrixExp[A t]
Out[2]//MatrixForm=
```

$$\frac{-1}{2\ \mathrm{E}^t} + \frac{3\ \mathrm{E}^t}{2} \qquad \frac{-3}{2\ \mathrm{E}^t} + \frac{3\ \mathrm{E}^t}{2}$$

$$\frac{1}{2\ \mathrm{E}^t} - \frac{\mathrm{E}^t}{2} \qquad \frac{3\ \mathrm{E}^t}{2} - \frac{\mathrm{E}^t}{2}$$

Mathematica is not limited to computing the exponential $\mathbf{e}^{At}$ for diagonalizable matrices. It can do the calculation for any matrix for which it can calculate the eigenvalues—if they are not overly complicated in terms of radicals.

Exercises on the Matrix Exponential Function

1. Compute the exponential $\mathbf{e}^{J_3 t}$ of the matrix

$$J_3 = \begin{bmatrix} 2 & 1 & 0 \\ 0 & 2 & 1 \\ 0 & 0 & 2 \end{bmatrix}$$

The matrix J_3 is called a *Jordan block*. It has a fixed value on the main diagonal, ones on the first super diagonal, and zeros elsewhere.

2. Compute the exponential $\mathbf{e}^{At}$ of the 4×4 matrix $A = [a_{ij}]$ defined by $a_{ij} = 1$.

3. Compute the exponential e^{At} for the 4×4 matrix $A = [a_{ij}]$, where $a_{ij} = \begin{cases} i & \text{if } i > j \\ 0 & \text{if } i \le j \end{cases}$.

4. Repeat Exercise 1 for the $n \times n$ analog J_n of the Jordan block matrix for $n = 4, \ldots, 6$.

Problems on the Matrix Exponential

1. It was noted in the discussion of the exponential that $e^{At}y_0$ is a solution of the matrix equation $y' = Ay$. Let $A = [a_{ij}]$ be the 4×4 matrix A defined by
$$a_{ij} = \begin{cases} i & \text{if } i < j \\ 0 & \text{if } i \ge j \end{cases}. \text{ Use the matrix exponential to solve } y' = Ay.$$

2. Find a system of first-order differential equations equivalent to the fourth-order equation $y'''' - 6y''' + 13y'' + 4I = 0$. Use the exponential function to solve the system.

3. Use the matrix exponential to solve Problem 2 (the rabbits and foxes problem) of the previous section, Systems of Linear Differential Equations.

4. Use the matrix exponential to solve Problem 3 (the springs and weights problem) of the previous section, Systems of Linear Differential Equations.

Systems of Recurrence Relations
`[RSolve]`

It is sometimes convenient to denote the nth derivative of a function f by $D^n(f)$. Then the mth-order differential equation

$$a_0 y + a_1 D(y) + \cdots + a_m D^m(y) = e^x$$

($a_m = 1$) can be rewritten in the form

$$D^m(y) = b_{m-1} D^{m-1}(y) + \cdots + b_0 y + e^x$$

where $b_j = -a_j$ for $j = 0, \ldots, m - 1$. Applying the differential operator D^i to both sides yields the relation

$$D^{m+i}(y) = b_{m-1} D^{m+i-1}(y) + \cdots + b_0 D^i(y) + e^x$$

which recurs for all integers $i \ge 0$. This is an example of a *linear recurrence relation* of length m, a fixed linear relation between the ith term of a sequence—in this case, the sequence of ith derivatives of the function $y(x)$—and the m terms immediately preceding it. Linear recurrence relations are also called *difference equations* or *linear recurrence equations*.

You can use the `RSolve` command in the `DiscreteMath` package to solve a recurrence relation. The syntax is similar to that for `DSolve`. (You must first load the package.)

Consider, for example, the recurrence relation

$$f(n + 1) = f(n) + n + 1$$

Load the DiscreteMath *package.*

In[1]:= <<DiscreteMath`Master`

Use RSolve *to solve the relation.*

In[2]:= RSolve[f[n + 1] == f[n] + n + 1, f[n], n]

Out[2]= {{f[n] -> $\frac{n(1 + n)}{2}$ + f[0]}}

The result indicates a dependence on $f(0)$. Do you see why? You can specify an initial value for f, either by replacing $f(0)$ in %2 or by specifying in the RSolve command the value of $f(0)$ as a second equation. In the latter case, the two equations must be put into a list.

This gives the particular solution with $f(0) = 0$ *by replacement.*

In[3]:= %2 /. {f[0] -> 0}

Out[3]= {{f[n] -> -1 - n + $\frac{(1 + n)(2 + n)}{2}$}}

This specifies the condition $f(0) = 0$ *in the command.*

In[4]:= RSolve[{f[n + 1] == f[n], f[0] == 0}, f[n], n]

Out[4]= f[n] -> -1 - n + $\frac{(1 + n)(2 + n)}{2}$

You can define f as a function. In this case, the defining expression is simplified.

In[5]:= f[n_] = Simplify[%[[1,1,2]]]

Out[5]= $\frac{n(1 + n)}{2}$

You may recognize $f(n)$ as the familiar formula for $\sum_{i=0}^{n} i$.

Diagonalization and triangularization also can be used to solve some systems of linear recurrence relations. Consider the system

$$\begin{cases} f_1(n + 1) = f_1(n) - 2f_2(n) \\ f_2(n + 1) = f_1(n) - 4f_2(n) \end{cases}$$

In matrix/vector form, this is simply $f(n + 1) = Mf(n)$, where $f(n) = (f_1(n), f_2(n))$ and $M = \begin{bmatrix} 1 & -2 \\ 1 & 4 \end{bmatrix}$. From this perspective, it is clear that if $f(0)$ is known, then $f(n) = M^n f(0)$ for all $n \geq 0$. However, this does not give the most useful solution. The following gives the coordinates $f_i(n)$ in closed form.

Enter the matrix M.

In[1]:= M = {{1,-2},
            {1,4}};

Check the eigensystem.

```
In[2]:= Eigensystem[M]
Out[2]= {{2, 3}, {{-2, 1}, {-1, 1}}}
```

In this case, M is diagonalized by the matrix $P = \begin{bmatrix} -2 & -1 \\ 1 & 1 \end{bmatrix}$.

Define the diagonalizing matrix P and the diagonalized matrix J.

```
In[3]:= P = Transpose[%[[2]]]
Out[3]//MatrixForm=
    -2    -1
     1     1
```

```
In[4]:= J = DiagonalMatrix[%%[[1]]]
Out[4]//MatrixForm=
     2     0
     0     3
```

The original system is now equivalent to the system $g(n + 1) = Jg(n)$, with $f(n) = Pg(n)$. In system form, g is given by the equations $g_1(n + 1) = 2g_1(n)$ and $g_2(n + 1) = 3g_2(n)$. It is clear that these equations are satisfied by $g_1(n) = k_1 2^n$ and $g_2(n) = k_2 3^n$. Here $g_1(0) = k_1$ and $g_2(0) = k_2$.

Solve the matrix system $g(n + 1) = Jg(n)$.

```
In[5]:= g[n_] := {k[1] 2^n, k[2] 3^n}
```

The vector-valued function g gives the general solution of the diagonal system: All particular solutions are obtained by varying the constants k_1 and k_2.

Find the solution of the original system.

```
In[6]:= f[n_] := P . g[n]
```

Note that f is a vector-valued function.

Check the solution by calculating the difference. In this case, simplification is required.

```
In[7]:= Simplify[f[n + 1] - M . f[n]]
Out[7]= {0,0}
```

The difference is **0**, so the solution is correct. However, in some cases involving radicals or other complicated expressions, *Mathematica* may be unable to simplify the difference to **0**. In these cases, you can check the value of the difference for several different integer values of n. You may also have to specify initial values.

Let M be an $n \times n$ matrix with real entries. Given a difference equation of the form $f(n + 1) = Mf(n)$, it is clear that there are vector-valued functions f that satisfy the relation with $f(n)$ in $\Re^n$. Simply choose $f(0)$ to be a vector with real entries, and define $f(n)$ inductively using the equation $f(n + 1) = Mf(n)$.

For the same reason, there exist solutions f for which the values $f(n)$ are complex. If a solution $f(n)$ contains complex entries, say $f(n) = f_{Re}(n) + if_{Im}(n)$, where $f_{Re}(n)$ and $f_{Im}(n)$ are real vectors, then the functions f_{Re} and f_{Im} are both solutions of the original equation, and both depend on their values at 0. If $f(0)$ has no imaginary part, $f(n)$ will also. However, the general solution over the complex numbers will differ from the general solution over the real numbers. In many cases, only real-valued solutions are of interest, but it is often not possible to obtain the general solution in closed form. If real initial values are specified, real-valued solutions f_1 and f_2 can be found in closed form, though the solutions may not obviously be real by their descriptions.

For example, consider the system $f(n +1) = Mf(n)$, where $M =$

$$\begin{bmatrix} -7 & -13 \\ 3 & 5 \end{bmatrix} \text{ and } f(0) = (2, 3).$$

Enter the matrix M.

```
In[1]:= M = {{-7,-13},
             {3,5}};
```

Compute the eigensystem. Here the expression is simplified.

```
In[2]:= Simplify[Eigensystem[M]]
Out[2]= {{-1 - I Sqrt[3], -1 + I Sqrt[3]},
```

$$\left\{\left\{-2 - \frac{I}{Sqrt[3]}, \ 1\right\}, \ \left\{-2 + \frac{I}{Sqrt[3]}, \ 1\right\}\right\}\right\}$$

The matrix is diagonalizable over the complex numbers.

Define the diagonalizing matrix P.

```
In[3]:= P = Transpose[%[[2]]];
```

Define the diagonalized matrix J.

```
In[4]:= J = DiagonalMatrix[%%[[1]]];
```

Let us denote the solution of the diagonalized system by h. Then $f(n) = Ph(n)$ for all integers $n \geq 0$, so $h(0) = P^{-1}f(0)$.

Compute the initial values of h(n).

```
In[5]:= Inverse[P] . {2,3}//Simplify
Out[5]=
```

$$\left\{\frac{3}{2} + 4 \ I \ Sqrt[3], \ \frac{3}{2} - 4 \ I \ Sqrt[3]\right\}$$

Solve the matrix system $h(n + 1) = Jh(n)$.[21] Parts of the output are suppressed because of its length.

```
In[6]:= h[n_] = (J^n) . %
Out[6]=
{0ⁿ (-I Sqrt[3] + · · ·) + · · · + · · · +
```

$$0^n \ \left(I \ Sqrt[3] - \frac{3I}{2} \ Sqrt[3] \ \left(2 - \frac{I}{Sqrt[3]}\right)\right)\right\}$$

---

[21] J^n does not return the *n*th power of a matrix, but it does in the case of a diagonal matrix.

The vector $h(n)$ gives the general solution of the diagonal system. But note the 0^n terms. Since *Mathematica* makes no assumption on the value of n this is reasonable. If n were negative, these terms would not simplify to 0. In this case, a little simplification seems in order.

Simplify h[n].

```
In[7]:= % /. {0^n -> 0};
```

Define f.

```
In[8]:= tempf[n_] = P . %;
  f[n_] := Simplify[tempf[n]]
```

This two-step definition of f will simplify the output every time f is applied.

Test f.

```
In[9]:= f[n]
Out[9]=
```

$$\{(-1 - I \; Sqrt[3])^n - \frac{17\,I}{2} \; Sqrt[3] \; (-1 - I \; Sqrt[3]^n +$$

$$(-1 + I \; Sqrt[3])^n + \frac{17\,I}{2} \; Sqrt[3] \; (-1 + I \; Sqrt[3]^n,$$

$$(-1 + I \; Sqrt[3])^n \; (\frac{3}{2} - 4 \; I \; Sqrt[3]) +$$

$$(-1 - I \; Sqrt[3])^n \; (\frac{3}{2} + 4 \; I \; Sqrt[3])\}$$

These are not obviously real numbers. Check a few particular values.

Compute some particular values of f.

```
In[10]:= f[0]
Out[10]= {2, 3}

In[11]:= f[5]
Out[11]= {784, -432}
```

Try f at a randomly chosen integer.

```
In[12]:= Random[Integer,{0,100}]
Out[12]= 43

In[13]:= f[43]
Out[13]= {-233096465088512, 92358976733184}
```

Apparently f is a real-valued vector function.

It is not necessary that the coefficient matrix of a system $f(n + 1) = Mf(n)$ of linear recurrence relations be diagonalizable in order to solve for $f_1(n)$ and $f_2(n)$ in closed form. This can be done from triangular form using back-substitution.

For example, consider the system $f(n +1) = Mf(n)$, where $f(n) = (f_1(n),$ $f_2(n))$ and $M = \begin{bmatrix} 2 & 1 \\ -1 & 4 \end{bmatrix}$.

Enter the matrix M.	`In[1]:= M = {{2,1},{-1,4}};`
Check the eigensystem of M.	`In[2]:= Eigensystem[M]` `Out[2]= {{3, 3}, {{1, 1}, {0, 0}}}`

The matrix *M* is not diagonalizable but it is triangularizable—in one step because of its size.

Define the triangularizing
matrix P.
	`In[3]:= Q = %[[2,{1}]]`
	`Out[3]//MatrixForm=`
	  1 1

`In[4]:= A = NullSpace[Q]`
`Out[4]//MatrixForm=`
 -1 1

`In[5]:= P = Transpose[Join[Q,A]]`
`Out[5]//MatrixForm=`
  1 -1
  1   1

Find an upper-triangular
matrix J similar to M.
	`In[6]:= J = Inverse[P] . M . P`
	`Out[6]//MatrixForm=`
	  3 2
	  0 3

Define h(n) and Jh(n).	`In[7]:= h[n_]:={h1[n],h2[n]}` `In[8]:= Jh[n_]:= J . h[n]`

The system $h(n + 1) = Jh(n)$ is now equivalent to the original system (with the addendum that $f = Ph$). In system form,

$$h_1(n + 1) = 3h_1(n) + 2h_2(n)$$
$$h_2(n + 1) = 3h_2(n)$$

Solve for $h_2(n)$.[22]	`In[9]:= RSolve[h[n + 1][[2]] == Jh[n][[2]],`
	 `h[n][[2]],n]`
	`Out[9]//MatrixForm=`
	 `h2[n] -> 3^n h2[0]`

Note that the solution involves the undetermined constant `h2[0]`. If the constant is left with this name, the solution cannot be called `h2[n]`.

---

[22]To use `RSolve`, you must first load the `DiscreteMath` package.

Assign $h_2(n)$, with h2[0] *replaced by* k[2].

```
In[10]:= % /. {h2[0] -> k[2]}
Out[10]//MatrixForm=
  h2[n] -> 3^n k[2]

In[11]:= h2[n_] = %[[1,1,2]]
Out[11]= 3^n k[2]
```

The function h2 is determined up to the arbitrary constant k[2] = h2[0].

Because $h_2(n)$ is known and the system is upper triangular, you can now determine $h_1(n)$.

```
In[12]:= RSolve[h[n + 1][[1]] == Jh[n][[1]],
  h[n][[1]],n]

Out[12]//MatrixForm=
  h1[n] -> 3^n h1[0] + 2 3^{-1 + n} n k[2]
```

Assign $h_1(n)$, with h1[0] *replaced by* k[1].

```
In[13]:= % /. {h1[0] -> k[1]}
Out[13]//MatrixForm=
  h1[n] -> 3^n k[1] + 2 3^{-1 + n} n k[2]

In[14]:= h1[n_] = %[[1,1,2]]
Out[14]= 3^n k[1] + 2 3^{-1 + n} n k[2]
```

The function h1 is now determined up to the arbitrary constants k[2] = h2[0] and k[1] = h1[0].

Now compute $f(n) = Ph(n)$.

```
In[15]:= f[n_] := P . h[n]
Out[15]=
  {3^n k[1] - 3^n k[2] + 2 3^{-1 + n} n k[2],
   3^n k[1] + 3^n k[2] + 2 3^{-1 + n} n k[2]}
```

See if the solution checks.

```
In[16]:= Expand[f[n + 1] - M . f[n]]
Out[16]= {0, 0}
```

Problems on Linear Recurrence Systems

1. A group of environmentalists in Elpmis are attempting to determine the stability of the populations of two species they are concerned may be endangered. Their research shows that the populations interact and change from year to year according to the recurrence relation $p(n + 1) = Mp(n)$,

    where $p(n) = (p_1(n), p_2(n))$ and $M = \dfrac{1}{600}\begin{bmatrix} 6 & -3 \\ 3 & -2 \end{bmatrix}$.

    a. If the current populations are given by $\mathbf{p}(0) = [1{,}000{,}000, 1{,}000{,}000]$, determine the approximate populations for each of the next ten years. Put the results in decimal form.

    b. No reliable estimates of current populations are available. Find the general solution of the system $p(n + 1) = Mp(n)$ and use it to investigate the possible future populations of the species depending on the current populations. What do you predict for the future?

2. The populations of three species in year n have been determined to be related by the recurrence relation $p(n + 1) = Mp(n)$, where $p(n) = (p_1(n),$ $p_2(n), p_3(n))$ and $M = \begin{bmatrix} 1 & 1 & 0 \\ -1 & 2 & 1 \\ -1 & -1 & 4 \end{bmatrix}$. Solve for $p(n)$ in general. Based on your solution (and the assumption that none of the populations is currently negative), is it possible to project the future of these species? What can you say if $\mathbf{p}(0) = (1, 5, 3)$? If $\mathbf{p}(0) = (3, 1, 5)$?

Quadratic Forms: The Principal Axis Theorem

In some geometric applications it is highly desirable to work in orthogonal coordinate systems. When this is the case, orthogonal diagonalization is preferred. In this section we consider one such application from analytic geometry, namely quadratic forms. Attempts to find a standardized form for quadratic forms in several variables provided some of the impetus for the initial work with eigenvalues and eigenvectors in the 18th and 19th centuries.

Consider the expression $ax^2 + 2bxy + cy^2$, called a *quadratic form* in x and y. This quadratic form can also be written as the matrix product $\mathbf{x}M\mathbf{x}$, where $M = \begin{bmatrix} a & b \\ b & c \end{bmatrix}$ and $\mathbf{x} = (x_1, x_2)$. In general, the expression $\sum\limits_{i=1}^{n} a_{ij}x_ix_j$ is a quadratic form in $x_1, x_2, \ldots, x_n$. It too can be written in the form $\mathbf{x}M\mathbf{x}$, and the coefficients can be chosen so that the matrix M is symmetric. (You can easily verify this with *Mathematica* for, say, $n = 3$.)

An equation of the form $\sum\limits_{i=1}^{n} a_{ij}x_ix_j = d$ is called a *quadratic equation*.

You have probably studied quadratic equations, at least in the case $n = 2$, with $a_{ij} = 0$ if $i \neq j$. Familiar examples include the ellipse $ax^2 + by^2 = 1$ and hyperbola $ax^2 - by^2 = 1$ $(a, b > 0)$. You may or may not have studied equations of the more general form $ax^2 + 2bxy + cy^2 = d$; however, this is easy to do in matrix form.

Consider the matrix equation $\mathbf{x}M\mathbf{x} = d$. If the coefficients are chosen so that the coefficient matrix M is symmetric—which is always possible by redefining the coefficients a_{ij} so that $a_{ij} = \dfrac{a_{ij} + a_{ji}}{2}$ —then M is orthogonally diagonalizable and there exists an orthogonal matrix P for which $P^{-1}MP$ is diagonal.

Because P is orthogonal, $P^{-1} = P^T$, and the equation $\mathbf{x}M\mathbf{x} = d$ can be rewritten as $(\mathbf{x}P)(P^TMP)(P^T\mathbf{x}) = d$. However, $P^T\mathbf{x} = \mathbf{x}P$ (verify), so with the substitution $\mathbf{y} = \mathbf{x}P$ this simplifies to $\mathbf{y}J\mathbf{y} = d$, where J is the diagonal matrix with

$\lambda_1, \lambda_2, \ldots, \lambda_n$ on its main diagonal. The associated quadratic equation is then

$$\sum_{i=1}^{n} \lambda_i y_i^2 = d.$$ We will refer to this as the *standard form* of the quadratic.

The graphs of quadratic equations in standard form are well known in 2-space and 3-space. The Principal Axis Theorem says that all quadratic equations in 2-space and 3-space have graphs of these known types.

Exercises on Quadratics

The following exercises call for plots of equations. You can `Solve` for one of the variables and plot the solution(s). If there is more than one part of the plot of a given equation, you can use `Show` to put the parts together.

1. Plot the following quadratics and find the standard form of the equations in y_1-y_2 coordinates.

    a. $3x_1^2 - 8x_1x_2 - 3x_2^2 = 1$

    b. $x_1x_2 = 1$

    c. $5x_1^2 + 6x_1x_2 + 3x_2^2 = 8$

    d. $x_2 - x_1^2 - 2x_1 = 1$ (*Hint:* Complete the square.)

2. Find the standard forms of the following quadratics. Use `Plot3D` to investigate their graphs.

    a. $x_1^2 + x_2^2 + x_3^2 - 2x_1x_2 - 2x_1x_3 - 2x_2x_3 = 3$

    b. $23x_1^2 + 50x_2^2 + 2x_3^2 - 72x_1x_3 = 50$

    c. $68x_1^2 + 50x_2^2 + 82x_3^2 + 48x_1x_3 = 500$

    d. $9x_1^2 + 6x_2^2 + 5x_3^2 - 4x_1x_2 = 500$

4 Linear Transformations

A function T from a vector space U to a vector space V is a *linear transformation* if $T(\mathbf{u}_1 + \mathbf{u}_2) = T(\mathbf{u}_1) + T(\mathbf{u}_2)$ and $T(k\mathbf{u}) = kT(\mathbf{u})$, for all vectors $\mathbf{u}$, $\mathbf{u}_1$, and $\mathbf{u}_2$ in U and all scalars k. Many of the most important functions between vector spaces are linear transformations. For example, if V is an n-dimensional vector space with basis $\mathbf{B}$, then the function $\mathbf{v} \mapsto (\mathbf{v})_\mathbf{B}$, which takes every vector $\mathbf{v}$ to its coordinate vector $(\mathbf{v})_\mathbf{B}$ with respect to the basis $\mathbf{B}$, is a linear transformation from V to $\mathfrak{R}^n$. If V is an inner product space and U is a subspace, then the function $\mathbf{v} \mapsto \text{proj}_U(\mathbf{v})$ is a linear transformation from V to U (or V to V). If A is an $m \times n$ matrix and U is a subspace of $\mathfrak{R}^n$, the function $\mathbf{v} \mapsto A\mathbf{v}$ is a linear transformation from U to $\mathfrak{R}^m$.

4.1 Linear Transformations in *Mathematica*

A linear transformation is a function and can be defined in *Mathematica* with any of the standard function definition styles.

This defines a linear transformation from $\mathfrak{R}^3$ to $\mathfrak{R}^4$.[1]

```
In[1]:= L[x_] :=
    {3 x[[1]] - 4 x[[2]],
     x[[2]] + 3 x[[3]],
     3 x[[1]] + x[[3]]/2,
     x[[3]]}
```

Define vectors $\mathbf{u}$ and $\mathbf{v}$ to use as examples.

```
In[2]:= u = {1,2,3}
Out[2]= {1, 2, 3}

In[3]:= v = Table[i!,{i,3}]
Out[3]= {1, 2, 6}
```

---

[1]Note that this definition of L does not really restrict the domain to $\mathfrak{R}^3$.

L can be applied to vector expressions as well as to vectors.

```
In[4]:= L[u]
```

$$Out[4]= \{-5, 11, \frac{9}{2}, 3\}$$

```
In[5]:= L[u + v]
```

$$Out[5]= \{-10, 31, \frac{21}{2}, 9\}$$

This defines the same linear transformation $L : \mathfrak{R}^3 \to \mathfrak{R}^4$ using the Function command.

```
In[6]:= L := Function[{x},
         {3 x[[1]] - 4 x[[2]],
        x[[2]] + 3 x[[3]],
        3 x[[1]] + 1/2 x[[3]],
        x[[3]]}]
```

```
In[7]:= L[u]
```

$$Out[7]= \{-5, 11, \frac{9}{2}, 3\}$$

Here is another definition of the same linear transformation using # notation.

```
In[8]:= L := {3 #[[1]] - 4 #[[2]],
              #[[2]] + 3 #[[3]],
              3 #[[1]] + 1/2 #[[3]],
              #[[3]]}
```

L also can be applied to vector expressions that involve symbolic vectors or scalars.

```
In[9]:= u = {a,b,c};
```

```
In[10]:= L[k u]
Out[10]=
```

$$\{3\ a\ k\ -\ 4\ b\ k,\ b\ k\ +\ 3\ c\ k,\ 3\ a\ k\ +\ \frac{c\ k}{2},\ c\ k\}$$

Here is another application of L involving a matrix.

```
In[11]:= M := Array[Max,{3,3}];
```

```
In[12]:= L[M . u + k v]
Out[12]= {3 (a + 2 b + 3 c + k) -
```
$$4\ (2\ a\ +\ 2\ b\ +\ 3\ c\ +\ 2\ k),\ 2\ a\ +\ 2\ b\ +\ 3\ c\ +\ 2\ k\ +$$
$$3\ (3\ a\ +\ 3\ b\ +\ 3\ c\ +\ 6\ k),\ 3\ (a\ +\ 2\ b\ +\ 3\ c\ +\ k)\ +$$
$$\frac{3\ a\ +\ 3\ b\ +\ 3\ c\ +\ 6\ k}{2},\ \ 3\ a\ +\ 3\ b\ +\ 3\ c\ +\ 6\ k\}$$

EXERCISES 4.1

1. Let $T : \mathfrak{R}^5 \to \mathfrak{R}^4$ be the linear transformation

$$T(x_1, x_2, x_3, x_4, x_5) =$$
$$(x_1 + x_2 + x_3 + x_4 + x_5, x_1 + x_2 + x_3 + x_4, x_1 + x_2 + x_3, x_1 + x_2)$$

    a. Define the linear transformation T in your session and verify that it satisfies the properties $T(\mathbf{u}_1 + \mathbf{u}_2) = T(\mathbf{u}_1) + T(\mathbf{u}_2)$ and $T(k\mathbf{u}) = kT(\mathbf{u})$ for all 5-vectors $\mathbf{u}$, $\mathbf{u}_1$, and $\mathbf{u}_2$ and all scalars k.

    b. Let $\{\mathbf{e}_i\}_{i=1}^5$ be the standard basis for $\mathfrak{R}^5$. Calculate $T(\mathbf{e}_i)$ for $i = 1, \ldots, 5$.

2. Let U be the subspace of $\mathfrak{R}^4$ spanned by the vectors $\mathbf{u}_1 = (1, 1, 1, 0)$, $\mathbf{u}_2 = (1, 1, 0, 0)$, and $\mathbf{u}_3 = (1, 0, 0, 0)$. Let $T : \mathfrak{R}^4 \to \mathfrak{R}^4$ be the orthogonal projection $T(\mathbf{v}) = \text{proj}_U(\mathbf{v})$ of $\mathbf{v}$ onto U.

    a. Define the function T in your *Mathematica* session.

    b. Use vectors with symbolic entries and an unassigned symbolic scalar k to verify that T is a linear transformation.

    c. Verify that $T(T(\mathbf{v})) = T(\mathbf{v})$ for all $\mathbf{v}$.

    d. Verify that $T(\mathbf{u}) = \mathbf{u}$ for any vector $\mathbf{u} \in U$.

3. Find the orthogonal projection of the vector $\mathbf{v} = (1, 2, 3, 4, 5, 6, 7)$ onto the column space U of the 7×5 matrix $M = (m_{ij})$ defined by

$$m_{ij} = \frac{1}{i + j}$$

Verify that the orthogonal projection of $\mathfrak{R}^7$ onto U is a linear transformation. (See Exercise 2 for a hint on how to do this in *Mathematica*.)

4. Let $\mathbf{B} = \{p_1, p_2, p_3, p_4, p_5, p_6\}$ be the basis of P_5 defined by $p_i = (x - 2)^{i-1}$ for $i = 1, \ldots, 6$. Let $T : P_5 \to \mathfrak{R}^6$ be the function defined by $T(p) = (p)_\mathbf{B}$.

    a. Verify that $\mathbf{B}$ is a basis of P_5.

    b. Verify that T is a linear transformation.

    c. Find $T(x^i)$ for $i = 0, \ldots, 5$.

    d. Find $T(a_0 + a_1x + \cdots + a_5x^5)$ in general.

5. Let $\mathbf{u}_1, \ldots, \mathbf{u}_n$ be fixed n-vectors. Let $L(\mathbf{v})$ be the determinant of the $n \times n$ matrix $[\mathbf{u}_1, \mathbf{u}_2, \ldots, \mathbf{u}_{m-1}, \mathbf{v}, \mathbf{u}_{m+1}, \ldots, \mathbf{u}_n]$. Then L is a linear transformation. Verify this for $n = 5$ and $m = 5$ using vectors with undefined symbols as entries.

4.2 Matrices and Linear Transformations

Because any n-dimensional real vector space can be identified with $\mathfrak{R}^n$ (via the coordinates associated with a basis), linear transformations from $\mathfrak{R}^n$ to $\mathfrak{R}^m$ assume a special importance.

    If A is an $m \times n$ matrix, then the function $T(\mathbf{v}) = A\mathbf{v}$ from $\mathfrak{R}^n$ to $\mathfrak{R}^m$ is clearly a linear transformation; such a linear transformation is called a *matrix transformation*. An important fact is that *every* linear transformation $T : \mathfrak{R}^n \to \mathfrak{R}^m$ is a matrix transformation. The matrix A such that $A\mathbf{v} = T(\mathbf{v})$ for all $\mathbf{v} \in \mathfrak{R}^n$ is called the *standard matrix* of T.

This defines a particular linear transformation $T : \mathfrak{R}^6 \to \mathfrak{R}^3$.

```
In[1]:= T[x_] :=
{x[[1]], x[[2]] + x[[3]], x[[4]] + x[[6]]}
```

*You can determine the standard matrix of T by applying the transformation to a vector with undefined entries. In this case, it may be helpful to show the vector T(**v**) in column form.*

```
In[2]:= v = Array[a,{6}]
Out[2]//MatrixForm=
   {a[1], a[2], a[3], a[4], a[5], a[6]}

In[3]:= Tv := T[v]; Tv//ColumnForm
Out[3]= a[1]
        a[2] + a[3]
        a[4] + a[6]
```

The result of applying T to **v** is assigned the name Tv for future reference.

The matrix of T is easily determined from the expression Tv. *The (i, j) entry of A is the coefficient of* a[j] *in the ith component of* T[v].

```
In[4]:= A =
    {{1,0,0,0,0,0},
     {0,1,1,0,0,0},
     {0,0,0,1,0,1}};
```

You can automate the definition of A using the Table *and* Coefficient *commands.*

```
In[5]:= Table[Coefficient[Tv[[i]], a[j]],
    {i,3}, {j,6}]
Out[5]//MatrixForm=
    1 0 0 0 0 0
    0 1 1 0 0 0
    0 0 0 1 0 1
```

*This verifies the equation T(**v**) = A**v**.*

```
In[6]:= T[v] - A . v
Out[6]= {0, 0, 0}
```

The ith column of A is T applied to the ith standard basis vector $\mathbf{e}_i$ (the ith row vector of the identity matrix) for $i = 1, \ldots, 6$.

Bases for the kernel and range of T can easily be obtained from matrix A.

These three vectors, shown here as rows of a matrix,[2] are a basis for the kernel of T.

```
In[7]:= NullSpace[A]
Out[7]//MatrixForm=
    0    -1    1    0    0    0
    0     0    0   -1    0    1
    0     0    0    0    1    0
```

---

[2]We refer to the output as a matrix because it is displayed in MatrixForm. Of course, it is also a set of vectors.

The first, second, and fourth columns of A (the columns corresponding to the leading ones of the reduced row-echelon form) are a basis for the column space of A. Of course, this means the range is all of $\Re^3$.

```
In[8]:= RowReduce[A]
Out[8]=
  1    0    0    0    0    0
  0    1    1    0    0    0
  0    0    0    1    0    1
```

If a linear transformation L is specified by a collection of equations $L(\mathbf{b}_i)$ $= \mathbf{m}_i$ for $i = 1, \ldots, k$, where $\{\mathbf{b}_1, \mathbf{b}_2, \ldots, \mathbf{b}_k\}$ is a basis for V, you can easily create a *Mathematica* function that returns $L(\mathbf{v})$ for any vector $\mathbf{v}$ in V. Note that if $\mathbf{v} = a_1\mathbf{b}_1 + \cdots + a_k\mathbf{b}_k$, then $L(\mathbf{v}) = a_1\mathbf{m}_1 + \cdots + a_k\mathbf{m}_k$.

Here are two collections $\mathbf{b}_1, \ldots, \mathbf{b}_5$ and $\mathbf{m}_1, \ldots, \mathbf{m}_5$ of vectors in $\Re^7$. The vectors $\mathbf{b}_1, \ldots, \mathbf{b}_5$ are a basis for the subspace V they span.

```
In[1]:= Do[b[i] =
  Table[Min[i,j], {j,1,7}],
  {i,1,5}]

In[2]:= Do[m[i] =
  Table[Min[i+1,j+1], {j,1,7}],
  {i,1,5}]
```

Now let $B = [\mathbf{b}_1, \ldots, \mathbf{b}_5]$. If $\mathbf{v} = a_1\mathbf{b}_1 + \cdots + a_5\mathbf{b}_5$ is any vector in V, then $a = (a_1, a_2, \ldots, a_5)$ can be obtained using `LinearSolve[B,v]`.

You can generate B from the list $\{\mathbf{b}_1, \ldots, \mathbf{b}_5\}$.

```
In[3]:= B =
  Transpose[{b[1],b[2],b[3],b[4],b[5]}]
```

Alternatively, the matrix B could be created efficiently using the `Table` *command—the (i, j) entry of B is the ith entry of $\mathbf{b}_j$.*

```
Out[3]//MatrixForm=
  1    1    1    1    1
  1    2    2    2    2
  1    2    3    3    3
  1    2    3    4    4
  1    2    3    4    5
  1    2    3    4    5
  1    2    3    4    5
```

Here is a vector $\mathbf{v}$ in the vector space $V =$ span$\{\mathbf{b}_1, \ldots, \mathbf{b}_5\}$.

```
In[4]:= v = {1,7,9,4,2,2,2};
```

The vector **a** =
($a_1, a_2, \ldots, a_5$) is the
coordinate vector of **v**
with respect to the basis
B = {**b**$_1$, . . . ,**b**$_5$}.[3]

```
In[5]:= a = LinearSolve[B,v]
Out[5]= {-5, 4, 7, -3, -2}
```

w = *L*(**v**) *is now given by*
$a_1\mathbf{b}_1 + \cdots + a_5\mathbf{b}_5 = M\mathbf{a}$, *with*
$M = [\mathbf{m}_1, \ldots, \mathbf{m}_5]$.[4]

```
In[6]:= M =
  Transpose[{m[1],m[2],m[3],m[4],m[5]}];

In[7]:= w = M . a
Out[7]=
  {2, 8, 10, 5, 3, 3, 3}
```

These steps can easily be
combined to make a
Mathematica function.

```
In[8]:= L[x_] := M . LinearSolve[B,x]
```

Note that *L* will apply exactly the same steps to any vector **x** that were applied to **v**. You might wish to verify this by comparing *L*(**v**) with the vector **w**.

Here is a basis **f**$_1$, . . . , **f**$_5$
for a subspace W of $\mathcal{R}^7$ *that*
contains **m**$_1$, . . . , **m**$_5$.

```
In[9]:= Do[f[j]=
  Table[Sum[r,{r,Max[j-i+1,0],j}],
  {i,1,7}],{j,1,5}]
```

If you want the matrix of *L* with respect to **B** and **F**, you can compute it by applying row-reduction to the matrix [**f**$_1$, . . . , **f**$_5$, **m**$_1$, . . . , **m**$_5$].

Form the matrix F =
*[***f**$_1$, . . . , **f**$_5$] *with ith*
column **f**$_i$.

```
In[10]:= F = Table[f[j][[i]],
  {i,1,7}, {j,1,5}]
Out[10]//MatrixForm=
```

1	2	3	4	5
1	3	5	7	9
1	3	6	9	12
1	3	6	10	14
1	3	6	10	15
1	3	6	10	15
1	3	6	10	15

Row-reduce the matrix
[F, M].

```
In[11]:=
RowReduce[Table[Join[F[[i]], M[[i]]], {i,7}]]
```

---

[3]If the vector **v** lies outside the span of **b**$_1$, . . . ,**b**$_5$, then this procedure gives an error message.
[4]Note that `Transpose[{m[1],..., m[5]}] . a = a . {m[1],..., m[5]}`.

```
Out[11]//MatrixForm=
1   0   0   0   0   2   0   1   1   1
0   1   0   0   0   0   1  -1   0   0
0   0   1   0   0   0   0   1  -1   0
0   0   0   1   0   0   0   0   1  -1
0   0   0   0   1   0   0   0   0   1
0   0   0   0   0   0   0   0   0   0
0   0   0   0   0   0   0   0   0   0
```

The matrix of L is the 5×5 submatrix starting at the (1,6) entry.

```
In[12]:= A = Table[%[[i,j]],{i,5},{j,6,10}]
Out[12]//MatrixForm=
2   0   1   1   1
0   1  -1   0   0
0   0   1  -1   0
0   0   0   1  -1
0   0   0   0   1
```

Note that $M = [L(\mathbf{b}_1), \ldots, L(\mathbf{b}_5)]$, so the result is $[(L(\mathbf{b}_1))_{\mathbf{F}}, \ldots, (L(\mathbf{b}_5))_{\mathbf{F}}]$.

This has Mathematica reevaluate $L(\mathbf{b}_i)_{\mathbf{F}}$ for $i = 1, \ldots, 5$.

```
In[13]:= Table[LinearSolve[F, L[b[i]]],
{i,1,5}]//Transpose
Out[13]//MatrixForm=
2   0   1   1   1
0   1  -1   0   0
0   0   1  -1   0
0   0   0   1  -1
0   0   0   0   1
```

EXERCISES 4.2

1. Why is the transpose obtained in %13 the same as that in the preceding calculation?

2. For $i = 1, \ldots, 7$, let $\mathbf{b}_i = (b_{ij})$ and $\mathbf{c}_i = (c_{ij})$ be the 7-vectors defined by

$$b_{ij} = \begin{cases} 0 & \text{if } i = j \\ 1 & \text{otherwise} \end{cases}$$

and $c_{ij} = i + j - 1$. Assume that T is a linear transformation from $\mathfrak{R}^7$ to $\mathfrak{R}^7$ satisfying $T(\mathbf{b}_i) = \mathbf{c}_i$ for $i = 1, \ldots, 7$. Define T in a *Mathematica* session and find its standard matrix.

3. Find the kernel and range of the linear transformation T in Exercise 2.

4. Let $\mathbf{B} = \{\mathbf{b}_1, \ldots, \mathbf{b}_6\}$ be the basis for $\mathfrak{R}^6$ defined by $\mathbf{b}_i = (b_{ij})$, where $b_{ij} = \min(i, j)$. Define a procedure Crd that takes every vector $\mathbf{v}$ in $\mathfrak{R}^6$ to its

B-coordinate vector. Verify that Crd is a linear transformation. You can do this using "symbolic vectors" $\mathbf{u}$ and $\mathbf{v}$. Show that

a. $\text{Crd}(\mathbf{u} + \mathbf{v}) - (\text{Crd}(\mathbf{u}) + \text{Crd}(\mathbf{v})) = \mathbf{0}$

b. $\text{Crd}(k\,\mathbf{u}) - k\,\text{Crd}(\mathbf{u}) = \mathbf{0}$

5. Find the standard matrix of the linear transformation Crd in Exercise 4.

6. Let $\mathbf{B} = \{\mathbf{b}_i\}_{i=1}^{6}$ be the basis of $\mathfrak{R}^6$ from Exercise 4. Let W be the subspace of $\mathfrak{R}^9$ with basis $\mathbf{F} = \{\mathbf{f}_i\}_{i=1}^{6}$, where $\mathbf{f}_i = (f_{ij})$ is the 9-vector defined by $f_{ij} = \min(j - i + 1, 1)$. Let $\mathbf{d}_i = (d_{ij})$ be the vectors of W defined by $d_{ij} = \min(i + 1, j + 1)$ for $i = 1, \ldots, 6$. Let $L : \mathfrak{R}^6 \to \mathfrak{R}^9$ be the linear transformation determined by the equations $L(\mathbf{b}_i) = \mathbf{d}_i$ for $i = 1, \ldots, 6$. Define a function T that takes the $\mathbf{B}$-coordinate vector of any $\mathbf{v}$ in $\mathfrak{R}^6$ to the $\mathbf{F}$-coordinate vector of $L(\mathbf{v})$. Verify that T is a linear transformation from $\mathfrak{R}^6$ to $\mathfrak{R}^6$.

7. Find the standard matrix of the linear transformation T in Exercise 6.

8. Let $L : \mathfrak{R}^7 \to \mathfrak{R}^5$ be the linear transformation $L(\mathbf{x}) = A\mathbf{x}$, where $A = [a_{ij}]$ is the 5×7 matrix defined by $a_{ij} = i + j$. Find a particular solution of the equation $L(\mathbf{x}) = (35, 42, 49, 56, 63)$. Find the general solution $\mathbf{s}[h]$ of the homogeneous equation $L(\mathbf{x}) = \mathbf{0}$. Verify that $\mathbf{s}[g] = \mathbf{s}[p] + \mathbf{s}[h]$ is a solution of $L(\mathbf{x}) = (35, 42, 49, 56, 63)$.

4.3 Applications

The Differential Operators

`[D, f']`

Some of the most important functions in mathematics are linear transformations. One example of particular importance is the differential operator $\mathbf{D}(f) = f'$. From elementary calculus we know that the differential operator $\mathbf{D}$ satisfies the properties

a. $\mathbf{D}(f + g) = \mathbf{D}(f) + \mathbf{D}(g)$

b. $\mathbf{D}(kf) = k\,\mathbf{D}(f)$

This is also true of the identity operator $\mathbf{D}^0 = \mathbf{I}$, the higher-order differential operators $\mathbf{D}^2 = \mathbf{D} \circ \mathbf{D}$, $\mathbf{D}^3 = \mathbf{D} \circ \mathbf{D} \circ \mathbf{D}$, $\ldots$, and all linear combinations $\mathbf{L} = a_0\mathbf{I} + a_1\mathbf{D} + \cdots + a_m\mathbf{D}^m$ of these. (It is traditional to write a_0 in place of $a_0\mathbf{I}$ in this notation, but *Mathematica* does not support the notation.)

In this section we consider differential equations of the form

$$\mathbf{L}(f)(x) = g(x) \tag{4.3.1}$$

where $\mathbf{L}$ is of the form

$$\mathbf{L} = a_0\mathbf{I} + a_1\mathbf{D} + \cdots + a_m\mathbf{D}^m \tag{4.3.2}$$

We assume that the function $f(x)$ is continuous on some interval $[b,c]$ and that all the coefficients a_i are real. Note that, as for all linear transformations, the general solution $\mathbf{s}$ of the equation $\mathbf{L}(f)(x) = g(x)$ has the form $\mathbf{s}_g = \mathbf{s}_h + \mathbf{s}_p$, where $\mathbf{s}_h$ is the general solution of the associated homogeneous equation $\mathbf{L}(f)(x) = 0$ and $\mathbf{s}_p$ is any particular solution of the equation $\mathbf{L}(f)(x) = g(x)$. This makes it particularly desirable to find a basis for the solution space of the associated homogeneous equation, that is, for the kernel of $\mathbf{L}$.

For example, consider the operator $\mathbf{L}$ defined by the equations $\mathbf{L}(f) = \mathbf{D}(f) - f = f' - f$ and $\mathbf{L}(f)(x) = x$. One particular solution of this equation is given by $\mathbf{s}_p(x) = -x - 1$, as you can easily verify by direct calculation. From calculus, the general solution of the equation $\mathbf{L}(f) = 0$ is given by $f(x) = Ke^x$. Hence, the general solution of the equation $\mathbf{L}(f) = x$ is given by $\mathbf{s}_g(x) = -x - 1 + Ke^x$. Here K is a parameter. All possible solutions are obtained by varying K.

The differential operator (4.3.2) is naturally associated with the polynomial $p(x) = a_0 + a_1 x + \cdots + a_m x^m$. This polynomial, called the *characteristic polynomial* of $\mathbf{L}$, is of particular importance in solving the homogeneous differential equation $\mathbf{L}(f) = 0$. In fact, the operator $\mathbf{L}$ is frequently written as $p(\mathbf{D})$; if $p(x)$ has the factorization $p(x) = p_1(x)p_2(x)$, then $\mathbf{L} = p(\mathbf{D})$ has the factorization $\mathbf{L} = p_1(\mathbf{D})p_2(\mathbf{D})$. In particular, if

$$p(x) = \prod_{i=1}^{r} (x - r_i)^{e_i} \tag{4.3.3}$$

where $r_i \neq r_j$ if $i \neq j$, then $\mathbf{L} = a_0 \mathbf{I} + a_1 \mathbf{D} + \cdots + a_m \mathbf{D}^m$ has the factorization $\mathbf{L} = \prod_{i=1}^{r} (\mathbf{D} - r_i \mathbf{I})^{e_i}$.

The solutions of the homogeneous equation $\mathbf{L}(f) = 0$ are the linear combinations of the solutions of the r homogeneous equations $(\mathbf{D} - r_i \mathbf{I})^{e_i}(f) = 0$. From calculus we know that $f(x) = Ke^{kx}$ is the general solution of the differential equation $(\mathbf{D} - k\mathbf{I})(f) = 0$. Hence, if the exponents $e_i = 1$ for all $i = 1, \ldots, r$ in (4.3.3), then the solutions of the differential equation $\mathbf{L}(f) = 0$ are the linear combinations $K_1 e^{r_1 x} + K_2 e^{r_2 x} + \cdots + K_m e^{r_m x}$.

You can solve many differential equations in *Mathematica* using the DSolve command. Consider the example $\mathbf{L} = \mathbf{D}^2 - 4\mathbf{D} + 3\mathbf{I} = (\mathbf{D} - \mathbf{I})(\mathbf{D} - 3\mathbf{I})$. Because of *Mathematica*'s notation for DSolve, it is convenient to define $\mathbf{L}$ using the notation L[f[x]] instead of L[f][x]. $\mathbf{D}^1(f)(x)$ can be denoted f'[x], D[f[x],x], or D[f[x],{x,1}]. $\mathbf{D}^2(f)(x)$ can be denoted f''[x] or D[f[x],{x,2}], and so on.[5,6] Each notation is advantageous in particular situations.

---

[5]The latter is easier to use with Sum.

[6]Derivative[1][f] is equivalent to f', Derivative[2][f] to f'', and so on. In general, Derivative[n][f] is useful when you would normally use $f^{(n)}$ in calculus.

Define $\mathbf{L}(f)(x) = \mathbf{D}^2(f)(x)$ *— 4$\mathbf{D}(f)(x)$ + 3$\mathbf{I}$ for use with* DSolve.

```
In[1]:= L[f_[x_]]  := f''[x] - 4 f'[x] + 3 f[x]
```

Check the definition of **L** *on an undefined symbol.*

```
In[2]:= L[ff[x]]
Out[2]= 3 ff[x] - 4 ff´[x] + ff´´[x]
```

This solves the homogeneous differential equation $\mathbf{L}(f) = 0$. *Call the solution* s_h.

```
In[3]:= s[h] = DSolve[L[f[x]] == 0, f[x], x]
Out[3]//MatrixForm=
   f[x] -> E^x C[1] + E^{3 x} C[2]
```

This defines the "factors" $(\mathbf{D} - \mathbf{I})(f(x))$ *and* $(\mathbf{D} - 3\mathbf{I})(f(x))$ *of* $\mathbf{L}$.[7]

```
In[4]:= L1[f_[x_]]  := f'[x] - f[x]
In[5]:= L2[f_[x_]]  := f'[x] - 3 f[x]
```

Note that the solutions of $\mathbf{L}(f) = 0$ *are linear combinations of the solutions of* $\mathbf{L}_1(f) = 0$ *and* $\mathbf{L}_2(f) = 0$. *Also note that both solutions use the same symbol for an arbitrary constant although the constants are not related to each other.*

```
In[6]:= DSolve[L1[f1[x]] == 0,f1[x],x]
Out[6]//MatrixForm=
   f1[x] -> E^x C[1]
```

```
In[7]:= DSolve[L2[f[x]] == 0, f[x], x]
Out[7]//MatrixForm=
   f2[x] -> E^{3 x} C[1]
```

Now consider the differential equation $\mathbf{L}(f(x)) = x^2$, where **L** continues to have the definition $\mathbf{L} = \mathbf{D}^2 - 4\,\mathbf{D} + 3\mathbf{I}$.

Use DSolve *to obtain the general solution* s_g. *This solution is completely general: all particular solutions are obtained by varying the parameters* C[1] *and* C[2] *in* **s**.

```
In[8]:= s[g] = DSolve[L[f[x]] == x^2, f[x], x]
Out[8]//MatrixForm=
```
$$f[x] \;\to\; \frac{26}{27} + \frac{8\,x}{9} + \frac{x^2}{3} + E^x\,C[1] + E^{3\,x}\,C[2]$$

Replacing C[1] *and* C[2] *by 0 gives one particular solution—call it* s_p. *Note that* $s_g = s_h + s_p$.[8]

```
In[9]:= % /. {C[1] -> 0, C[2] -> 0}
Out[9]//MatrixForm=
```
$$f[x] \;\to\; \frac{26}{27} + \frac{8\,x}{9} + \frac{x^2}{3}$$

[7]Note that you cannot use the notation L[i] here without destroying the definition of *L*.
[8]More precisely, s[g][[1,1,2]] = s[p][[1,1,2]] + s[h][[1,1,2]].

The Wronskian

It is a theorem that the kernel of a differential operator of the form

$$\mathbf{L} = a_0\mathbf{I} + a_1\mathbf{D} + \cdots + a_m\mathbf{D}^m \quad (a_m \neq 0)$$

is an *m*-dimensional vector space. The Wronskian (defined below) gives you a means of verifying that you have all the solutions.

Let **L** be the differential operator with characteristic polynomial $p(x) = \prod\limits_{j=1}^{5}(x-j)$, so the solution space of $\mathbf{L}(f) = 0$ has dimension 5.

Define the characteristic polynomial. You can use it to define **L**.	`In[1]:= p = Expand[Product[x-j,{j,1,5}]]`
	`Out[1]=`
	`-120 + 274 x - 225 x² + 85 x³ - 15 x⁴ + x⁵`

Define **L**.	`In[2]:= L[f_[x_]] := Sum[`
	`Coefficient[p,x,i]D[f[x], {x,i}],`
	`{i,0,5}]`

This solves the differential equation $\mathbf{L}(f) = 0$*. The solution space* $\mathbf{s}_h$ *is the set of linear combinations of* $\mathbf{e}^x$, $\mathbf{e}^{2x}$, $\mathbf{e}^{3x}$, $\mathbf{e}^{4x}$, *and* $\mathbf{e}^{5x}$*. Note the warning message preceding the result.*	`In[3]:= DSolve[L[f[x]]==0,f[x],x]`
	
	`DSolve::dsdeg:`
	`    Warning: Differential equation of`
	`      order higher than four encountered.`
	`      DSolve may not be able to find the`
	`      solution.`
	`Out[3]//MatrixForm=`
	`f[x] -> Eˣ (C[1] + Eˣ C[2] + E² ˣ C[3] +`
	`   E³ ˣ C[4] + E⁴ ˣ C[5])`

This may clarify the solution.	`In[4]:= Expand[%[[1,1,2]]]`
	`Out[4]=   Eˣ C[1] + E² ˣ C[2]+ E³ ˣ C[3] +`
	`   E⁴ ˣ C[4] + E⁵ ˣ C[5]`

`%[[i]]` *is the* i*th summand of* `%`*. This replaces* C_j *by 1 and forms the "basic" solutions into a set B.*	`In[5]:= B = Table[%[[i]] /. {C[j_] -> 1},`
	`  {i,1,5}]`
	`Out[5]= {Eˣ, E² ˣ, E³ ˣ,E⁴ ˣ, E⁵ ˣ}`

The Wronskian is the function $W(x)$ defined by

$$W(x) = \det(M)$$

where the matrix $M = [m_{ij}]$ is given by $m_{ij} = \mathbf{D}^{i-1}B\,[\,j\,]$.

The matrix $M = M(x)$ is called the *Wronskian matrix*. If the elements of B are linearly dependent then the columns of the matrix M are linearly dependent and hence $W(x) = \det(M)$ is the zero function. The converse is true as well.[9] Hence $W(x) = 0$ if and only if the entries of B are linearly dependent.[10] The following tests whether $W(0) = 0$.

Generate the Wronskian matrix.

```
In[6]:= M[x_] = Table[D[B[[j]], {x,i}],
   {i,0,4}, {j,1,5}]
Out[6]=
```

E^x	$E^{2\,x}$	$E^{3\,x}$	$E^{4\,x}$	$E^{5\,x}$
E^x	$2\,E^{2\,x}$	$3\,E^{3\,x}$	$4\,E^{4\,x}$	$5\,E^{5\,x}$
E^x	$4\,E^{2\,x}$	$9\,E^{3\,x}$	$16\,E^{4\,x}$	$25\,E^{5\,x}$
E^x	$8\,E^{2\,x}$	$27\,E^{3\,x}$	$64\,E^{4\,x}$	$125\,E^{5\,x}$
E^x	$16\,E^{2\,x}$	$81\,E^{3\,x}$	$256\,E^{4\,x}$	$625\,E^{5\,x}$

Define the Wronskian.

```
In[7]:= W[x_] = Det[%]
Out[7]= 288 E^{15 x}
```

Check $W(0)$. Because $W(0) \neq 0$, the elements of B are linearly independent. Because s_h has dimension 5, it follows that B spans the solution space s_h.

```
In[8]:= W[0]
Out[8]= 288
```

Initial Conditions

For any differential operator

$$\mathbf{L} = a_0\mathbf{I} + a_1\mathbf{D} + \cdots + a_m\mathbf{D}^m \quad (a_m \neq 0)$$

each solution s corresponds to a unique vector $\mathbf{v} = (s(0), s'(0), \ldots, s^{(m-1)}(0))$ in $\Re^m$. This correspondence is also linear, so all solutions of the homogeneous equation $\mathbf{L}(f) = 0$ can be found from any m solutions $s_1, s_2, \ldots, s_m$ that correspond to a basis of $\Re^m$. Earlier you saw the solutions $e^x, e^{2x}, e^{3x}, e^{4x}, e^{5x}$ of the differential equation $\mathbf{L}(f) = 0$ for $\mathbf{L} = \prod_{i=1}^{5}(\mathbf{D} - i\mathbf{I})$. Because $\mathbf{D}^i(e^{jx}) = j^i e^{jx}$—so that $\mathbf{D}^i(e^{jx})(0) = j^i$ —these solutions correspond (at $x = 0$) to the transpose of the Vandermonde matrix on 1, 2 , 3, 4, and 5.[11] This matrix $V = M(0)$ is invertible; hence solutions corresponding to any vectors in $\Re^m$ are easily found from it. To illustrate, the solution s_1 of $\mathbf{L}(f) = 0$ that corresponds to the vector $\mathbf{e}_1 = (1, 0, 0, 0, 0)$ is found in the following.

---

[9]See, for example, Charles G. Cullen, *Linear Algebra and Differential Equations* (Boston: Prindle Weber & Schmidt, 1979).

[10]This is not true for all lists of functions.

[11]The Vandermonde matrix on $a_1, \ldots, a_n$ has ith row $(1, a_1, a_1^2, \ldots, a_1^n)$ for $i = 1, \ldots, n$.

Define the matrix V. The matrix V^T is a Vandermonde matrix.	`In[9]:= V = M[0]` `Out[9]//MatrixForm=`

$$
\begin{array}{ccccc}
1 & 1 & 1 & 1 & 1 \\
1 & 2 & 3 & 4 & 5 \\
1 & 4 & 9 & 16 & 25 \\
1 & 8 & 27 & 64 & 125 \\
1 & 16 & 81 & 256 & 625
\end{array}
$$

Define the vector $\mathbf{e}_1 = (1, 0, 0, 0, 0)$ in the session.

`In[10]:= e[1] = {1,0,0,0,0};`

If you find the solutions g_i corresponding to all the row vectors $\mathbf{e}_i$ of the identity matrix I_5, then the solution corresponding to any vector $\mathbf{c} = (c_1, c_2, c_3, c_4, c_5)$ is simply $\sum_{i=1}^{5} c_i g_i$.

Solve the equation $V\mathbf{x} = \mathbf{e}_1$.

`In[11]:= a = LinearSolve[V,e[1]]`
`Out[11]= {5, -10, 10, -5, 1}`

Compute the solution corresponding to the vector $\mathbf{e}_1$. Recall that $B = \{e^x, e^{2x}, e^{3x}, e^{4x}, e^{5x}\}$ is the list of "basic solutions" of $\mathbf{L}(f) = 0$.

`In[12]:= s[e[1]] := B . a`
`Out[12]=`
$5\ E^x - 10\ E^{2\ x} + 10\ E^{3\ x} - 5\ E^{4\ x} + E^{5\ x}$

Convert the expression %12 to a function.[12]

`In[13]:= s[1][x_] = %;`

The solution $\mathbf{s}_1(x)$ now satisfies $\mathbf{D}^i(\mathbf{s}_1)(0) = \delta_{i0}$,

where $\delta_{i0} = \begin{cases} 1 & if\ i = 0 \\ 0 & otherwise \end{cases}$.

`In[14]:= Table[D[s[1][x],{x,i}] /.{x -> 0},`
`   {i,0,4}]`
`Out[14]= {1, 0, 0, 0, 0}`

You also can obtain particular solutions of differential equations using DSolve. For example, if the initial conditions are $f^{(i)}(0) = k_i$ for $i = 0, \ldots, m - 1$, the syntax is `DSolve[{L[f[x]] == g[x], f[0] == k0, f'[x] == k1,..., f''···'[0] == km}, f[x], x]`.

This directly obtains the solution $\mathbf{s}_1$ corresponding to $\mathbf{e}_1 = (1, 0, 0, 0, 0)$.

`In[15]:= DSolve[{L[f[x]] == 0, f[0] == 1,`
`   f'[0] == 0, f''[0] == 0, f'''[0] == 0,`
`   f''''[0] == 0}, f[x], x]`

---

[12]Be sure to use = here and not := .

Note that a warning message is given before the solution, and that the solution agrees with %12.

```
DSolve::dsdeg:
    Warning: Differential equation of order higher
    than four encountered. DSolve may not be able to
    find the solution.
Out[15]= f[x] -> EX (5 - 10 EX + 10 E2 X - 5 E3 X
    + E4 X)
```

Exercises on Differential Operators

1. Find the solutions of the differential equation

$$\prod_{i=1}^{5}(\mathbf{D} - i\mathbf{I})(f) = 0$$

that correspond to the standard basis vectors $e_1, \ldots, e_5$.

2. a. Solve the differential equations $(\mathbf{D}^2 - 3\mathbf{D} - 4\mathbf{I})(f) = e^x$ and $(\mathbf{D}^2 - 3\mathbf{D} - 4\mathbf{I})(f) = 0$

    b. Compare the solutions of $(\mathbf{D}^2 - 3\mathbf{D} - 4\mathbf{I})(f) = 0$ to those of $(\mathbf{D} - 4\mathbf{I})(f) = 0$ and $(\mathbf{D} + \mathbf{I})(f) = 0$.

3. Assume $\mathbf{F} = \mathbf{D} - 2\mathbf{I}$ and $\mathbf{L} = \mathbf{F} \circ \mathbf{F} \circ \mathbf{F}$.

    a. Show that e^{2x}, xe^{2x}, and x^2e^{2x} are solutions of $\mathbf{L}(f) = 0$.

    b. Use the Wronskian to show that the solutions in part a are linearly independent. Can you conclude they are a basis for the kernel of $\mathbf{L}$?

    c. What do you conjecture about the solutions of $(\mathbf{D} - r)^n$ in general? Verify your conjecture for $\mathbf{F} \circ \mathbf{F} \circ \mathbf{F} \circ \mathbf{F} \circ \mathbf{F}$.

4. If the characteristic polynomial $p(x)$ of a differential operator $\mathbf{L}$ has a complex root, then the factorization of $p(x)$ over the real numbers has an irreducible real quadratic factor $(x + a)^2 + b^2$. If the factor $(x + a)^2 + b^2$ appears to a power $n \geq 1$ in the factorization of $p(x)$, then the solutions of the equation $\mathbf{L}(n) = 0$ that are contributed by the factor $(\mathbf{D} + a\mathbf{I})^2 + b^2\mathbf{I})^n = (\mathbf{D}^2 + 2a\mathbf{D} + (a^2 + b^2)\mathbf{I})^n$ can be expressed as linear combinations of the solutions $e^{-ax}\sin(bx)$, $e^{-ax}\cos(bx)$, $xe^{-ax}\sin(bx)$, $xe^{-ax}\cos(bx)$, . . . , $x^{n-1}e^{-ax}\sin(bx)$, $x^{n-1}e^{-ax}\sin(bx)$.

    a. Define the linear operator $\mathbf{L} = ((\mathbf{D} + 2\mathbf{I})^2 + (3^2 + 2^2)\mathbf{I})^3$ in a *Mathematica* session.

    b. Verify that $x^ie^{-2x}\sin(3x)$ and $x^ie^{-2x}\cos(3x)$ are solutions for $i = 0, \ldots, 2$.

    c. Use the Wronskian to verify that the six solutions of part b are linearly independent (use E for **e**).

    d. Compare your solutions to the solutions returned by DSolve.

5. Let $\mathbf{L} = \mathbf{D}^3 - 6\mathbf{D}^2 + 11\mathbf{D} - 6\mathbf{I} = (\mathbf{D} - \mathbf{I})(\mathbf{D} - 2\mathbf{I})(\mathbf{D} - 3\mathbf{I})$.

    a. Find the solution space of the homogeneous differential equation $\mathbf{L}(f) = 0$.

    b. Find a basis for the vector space of part a.

    c. Find all solutions of the differential equation $\mathbf{L}(f)(x) = e^{3x}$.

6. Let $p = x^5 + x^4 + x^3 + x^2 + x + 1$ and let **L** be the differential operator with characteristic polynomial p.
   a. Use the `Factor` command to verify that p has an irreducible quadratic factor.
   b. Find all solutions of $\mathbf{L}(y) = 0$.
   c. Find the solution f of $\mathbf{L}(y) = 0$ that satisfies the initial conditions $f(0) = 1$ and $f^{(i)}(0) = 0$ for $i = 1, \ldots, 4$.
   d. Find the solution f of $\mathbf{L}(f) = 0$ that satisfies the initial conditions $f^{(i)}(0) = 0$ for $i = 0, \ldots, 4$, where $f^{(0)} = f$.

7. Let **L** be the differential operator $\mathbf{L} = (\mathbf{D}^3 + \mathbf{D}^2 + \mathbf{I})^2$ and let p be the characteristic polynomial of **L**.
   a. Use the `Factor` command to verify that p has a repeated irreducible quadratic factor over the real numbers.
   b. Find all solutions of $\mathbf{L}(f) = 0$.
   c. Find the solution of $\mathbf{L}(f)(x) = \mathbf{e}^x$ that satisfies the initial condition

   $$\mathbf{D}^i(f)(0) = \begin{cases} 1 & \text{if } i = 2 \\ 0 & \text{otherwise} \end{cases}.$$

Problems on Differential Operators
Hooke's Law and Harmonic Motion
Over a large portion of their designed travel, many springs are linear in that the force required to extend the spring a distance s is a constant multiple of s. The constant k of proportionality is called *Hooke's constant* for the spring, and the equation $F = ks$ is called *Hooke's law*.

Hooke's Law

$$F = k\,s$$

If a mass m is attached to the spring and $s = s(t)$ is a variable, then by Newton's second law of motion, $F(t) = ms''(t)$.

Newton's Second Law

$$F(t) = ms''(t)$$

Together, Hooke's law and Newton's second law can be used to explore the motion of a system of weights and springs.

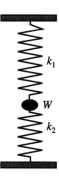

Consider the system shown. If the weight W is pulled to a distance $s(0)$ below its equilibrium position and released, then equating the force given by Newton's second law with that given by Hooke's law gives the equation

$$\frac{w}{g}\frac{d^2s}{dt^2} = -k_1 s(t) + k_2 s(t) - F = (k_2 - k_1)s(t) - F$$

where

- $s(t)$ is the distance of W from the equilibrium position
- k_1 is Hooke's constant for the upper spring
- k_2 is Hooke's constant for the lower spring
- w is the weight of W in pounds
- g is acceleration due to gravity
- F is the damping effect of friction

For simplicity, we assume the springs are massless.

1. Assuming $k_1 = 5$, $k_2 = 3$, $g = 32$ ft/sec^2, $s(0) = -12$, $s'(0) = 0$, $w = 17$, and $F = 0$, find the function $s(t)$ and plot it over the interval $[0, 6]$.
2. Repeat Problem 1 for $F = s'(t)$.

Linear Recurrence Relations and the Shift Operator[13]
```
[RSolve]
```

Let S be the vector space of all functions f defined on the nonnegative integers, and let $\mathbf{d} : S \to S$ be the "shift operator" $\mathbf{d}(f)(n) = f(n + 1)$.[14] Then $\mathbf{d}$ is a linear transformation. This is also true of the identity function $\mathbf{I} = \mathbf{d}^0$, the iterates $\mathbf{d}^2 = \mathbf{d} \circ \mathbf{d}$, $\mathbf{d}^3 = \mathbf{d} \circ \mathbf{d} \circ \mathbf{d}$, . . . , and all the linear combinations $\mathbf{L} = a_0\mathbf{I} + a_1\mathbf{d} + \cdots + a_m\mathbf{d}^m$ of them, where $\mathbf{L}(f)(n) = a_0 f(n) + a_1\mathbf{d}(f)(n) + \cdots + a_m\mathbf{d}^m(f)(n) = a_0 f(n) + a_1 f(n + 1) + \cdots + a_m f(n + m)$. It is customary to denote $a_0\mathbf{I}$ by a_0.

In this section we consider recurrence relations of the form

$$\mathbf{L}(f)(n) = g(n) \tag{4.3.4}$$

where $\mathbf{L}$ is of the form

$$\mathbf{L} = a_0 + a_1\mathbf{d} + \cdots + a_{m-1}\mathbf{d}^{m-1} + \mathbf{d}^m \tag{4.3.5}$$

It is easy to see that an operator of the form (4.3.5) is a linear transformation. Note that, as for all linear transformations, the general solution of the nonhomogeneous equation $\mathbf{L}(f)(n) = g(n)$ is the sum of any particular solution $\mathbf{s}_p$ and the general solution $\mathbf{s}_h$ of the associated homogeneous equation

---

[13]For general information on recurrence relations see, for example, Ronald E. Mickens, *Difference Equations* (New York: Van Nostrand Reinhold, 1990).

[14]You may want to think of f as a sequence $f_1, f_2, \ldots$. Then $f(i) = f_i$ and $\mathbf{d}(f_i) = f_{i+1}$.

$L(f) = 0$. This makes it particularly desirable to find a basis for the solution space of the associated homogeneous equation $L(f) = 0$ (that is, for the kernel of the linear transformation L).

A simple illustration is provided by the operator $L = d - 1$. Any solution s of $L(f)(n) = n + 1$ satisfies $s(n) - s(n - 1) = n$ or, equivalently, $s(n) = s(n - 1) + n$. A solution s_p satisfying the additional equation $s_p(0) = 0$ is given by $s_p(n)$

$$= \sum_{i=0}^{n} i, \text{ as you can easily verify. Now } \sum_{i=0}^{n} i = \frac{n(n + 1)}{2}, \text{ so } s_p(n) = \frac{n(n + 1)}{2}. \text{ On}$$

the other hand, any solution h of the homogeneous equation $L(f) = 0$ satisfies $h(n + 1) = h(n)$, and hence is constant. It follows that the general solution s_g of

the equation $L(f)(n) = n$ is given by $s_g(n) = \dfrac{n(n + 1)}{2} + C$. All solutions are

obtained by varying the parameter C.

The linear operator $L = a_0 I + a_1 d + \cdots + a_{m-1} d^{m-1} + d^m$ is naturally associated with the polynomial

$$p(m) = a_0 + a_1 x + \cdots + a_{m-1} x^{m-1} + x^m$$

This polynomial, called the *characteristic polynomial* of L, is of particular importance in solving the homogeneous equation $L(f) = 0$. The operator L is frequently written as $p(d)$; if $p(x)$ has the factorization $p(x) = p_1(x)p_2(x)$, then $L = p(d)$ has the factorization $L = p_1(d)p_2(d)$. In particular, if the polynomial $p(x)$ has the factorization

$$p(x) = \prod_{i=1}^{s} (x - r_i)^{e_i} \tag{4.3.6}$$

where $r_i \neq r_j$ for $i \neq j$, then the linear operator $L = a_0 I + a_1 d + \cdots + a_m d^m$ has

the factorization $L = \displaystyle\prod_{i=1}^{s} (d - r_i I)^{e_i}$.

The solutions of the homogeneous equation $L(f) = 0$ can be found by solving the s homogeneous equations $(d - r_i I)^{e_i}(f) = 0$. The solutions of the equation $L(f) = 0$ are linear combinations of the solutions of the homogeneous equations $(d - r_i I)^{e_i}(f) = 0$.

It is easy to see that the solutions of $(d - rI)(f) = 0$ (that is, of $f(n + 1) = rf(n)$) are completely determined by the value of $f(0)$. In fact, $f(1) = rf(0), f(2) = rf(1) = r^2 f(0), \ldots, f(n) = rf(n - 1) = r^n f(0)$, so the general solution s_g is given by $s_g(n) = Kr^n$. Hence, if $e = 1$ for all i in (4.3.6), then the solutions of the recurrence relation $L(f) = 0$ are the linear combinations $f(n) = K_1 r_1^n + K_2 r_2^n + \cdots + K_m r_m^n$ of the solutions $f_i(n) = r_i^n$ of the s equations $(D - r_i I)(f) = 0$.

The d notation is not built into *Mathematica*. It is easy to define, or you can use $f(n + i)$ in place of $d^i(f)(n)$.

Consider the example $L = d^2 - 4d + 3I$. Here it is easiest to treat the expression as a polynomial in d. You must first load the $DiscreteMath$ package so you can use the $RSolve$ command.

Load the DiscreteMath *package.*

$In[1] :=$ <<DiscreteMath`RSolve`

Define $\mathbf{L} = \mathbf{d}^2 - 4\mathbf{d} + 3\mathbf{I}$. *It is convenient and customary to write k for k***I**.

$In[2] :=$ L = d^2 - 4 d + 3
$Out[2] =$ 3 - 4 d + d^2

Factor **L**. *(You can probably do this without Mathematica.)*

$In[3] :=$ Factor[L]
$Out[3] =$ (-3 + d) (-1 + d)

You can use RSolve *to solve the "factor equations." Note that the output is shown in matrix form, so the results displayed are the (1,1) entries of the "matrices."*

$In[4] :=$ RSolve[f1[n + 1] - 3f1[n] == 0,
  f1[n], n]
$Out[4] //MatrixForm=$
  f1[n] -> 3^n f1[0]

$In[5] :=$ RSolve[f2[n+1] - f2[n] == 0,
  f2[n], n]
$Out[5] //MatrixForm=$
  f2[n] -> f2[0]

Define the general homogeneous solution $\mathbf{s}_h$ *of* **L**. *Note that* %[[1, 1, 2]] *picks out the second part of the (1,1) entry of* %.

$In[6] :=$ s[h][n_] = %%[[1,1,2]] + %[[1,1,2]]
$Out[6] =$ 3^n f1[0] + f2[0]

Check the solution. You should get 0, *although you may have to simplify the result.*[15]

$In[7] :=$ s[h][n+2] - 4s[h][n + 1] + 3s[h][n]
$Out[7] =$ 3$^{2 + n}$ f1[0] + f2[0] +
  3 (3^n f1[0] + f2[0]) -
  4 (3$^{1 + n}$ f1[0] + f2[0])

The result %7 *expands to* 0.

$In[8] :=$ Expand[%]
$Out[8] =$ 0

Now consider the recurrence equation $\mathbf{L}(f)(n) = n^2$, where $\mathbf{L} = \mathbf{d}^2 - 4\mathbf{d} + 3$. In the following, we define the shift operator **d** to function like *Mathematica*'s differential operator D, hence we will use d[f[n],{n,i}] for $\mathbf{d}^i(f)(n)$. The function d is a linear operator. We will also define **L** as a linear operator.

Load the DiscreteMath *package.*

$In[1] :=$ <<DiscreteMath`RSolve`

---

[15]As noted earlier, Expand is a quicker form of Simplify when the result is 0.

Define d.	`In[2]:= d[f_[n_],{n_,i_}] := f[n + i]`

Define the list **c** *of coefficients of* d^i *in* **L** *(in ascending order).*

`In[3]:= c = {3, -4, 1}`
`Out[3]= {3, -4, 1}`

Define **L**.

`In[4]:= L[f_[n_]] := Sum[c[[i + 1]] d[f[n], {n,i}], {i,0,2}]`

Check the operation of **L**.

`In[5]:= L[f[n]]`
`Out[5]= 3 f[n] - 4 f[1 + n] + f[2 + n]`

Find the general solution s_g *of* $L(f)(n) = n^2$. *Use* `[[1,1,2]]` *to pick out the second part of the* (1,1) *entry of the output.*

`In[6]:= s[g] = RSolve[L[f[n]] == n^2,`
`f[n],n][[1,1,2]]`

$$Out[6]= \frac{1}{4} - \frac{3(1 + n)}{2} + (1 + n)(2 + n) -$$

$$\frac{(1 + n)(2 + n)(3 + n)}{6} - 3n\left(\left(-\frac{1}{4}\right) + \frac{f[0]}{2} +\right.$$

$$\frac{3 f[0]}{2} + \left(-\frac{1}{2}\right) + \frac{3 \ 3^{-1 + n}}{2} f[1]$$

Here `RSolve` *is used to find a particular solution* s_p. *The one chosen satisfies* $f(0) = f(1) = 0$. *It could also be obtained from* %6 *by replacing* $f(0)$ *and* $f(1)$ *by* 0.

`In[7]:= s[p] = RSolve[{L[f[n]] == n^2,`
`f[0]==0, f[1]==0}, f[n], n][[1,1,2]]`

$$Out[7]= \frac{1}{4} + \frac{3^n}{4} - \frac{3(1 + n)}{2} + (1 + n)(2 + n) -$$

$$\frac{(1 + n)(2 + n)(3 + n)}{6}$$

Find the general solution s_h *of the associated homogeneous equation.[16]*

`In[8]:= s[h] = RSolve[L[f[n]] == 0,`
`f[n], n][[1,1,2]]`

$$Out[8]= \left(\frac{3}{2} - \frac{3^n}{2}\right) f[0] + \left(-\left(\frac{1}{2}\right) + \frac{3 \ 3^{-1 + n}}{2}\right) f[1]$$

As always, $s_g = s_p + s_h$.

`In[9]:= s[g] - (s[p] + s[h])//Expand`
`Out[9]= 0`

The Casoratian
The kernel of a linear operator of the form

$$L = a_0 I + a_1 d + \cdots + a_{m-1} d^{m-1} + d^m$$

---

[16]This was found in the previous session by applying `RSolve` to the factors. You may want to compare the results.

is an m-dimensional vector space. The Casoratian gives you a means of verifying that you have all the solutions; it is analogous to the Wronskian for differential equations.

We demonstrate with

$$\mathbf{L} = -120\mathbf{I} + 274\mathbf{d} - 225\mathbf{d}^2 + 85\mathbf{d}^3 - 15\mathbf{d}^4 + \mathbf{d}^5$$

$$= \prod_{i=1}^{5} (\mathbf{d} - i\mathbf{I}).$$

Define **L**. *Let* c_i *be the coefficient of* $\mathbf{d}^i$.

```
In[1]:= L = Product[d - i, {i,1,5}]//Expand
Out[1]=
-120 + 274 d - 225 d2 + 85 d3 - 15 d4 + d5

In[2]:= Do[c[i] = Coefficient[L,d,i], {i,0,5}]
```

Define particular solutions f_i *of the "factor equations"* $(\mathbf{d} - i\mathbf{I})(f(n)) = 0$. *This can be done without* RSolve.

```
In[3]:= Do[f[i][n_] = i^n, {i,1,5}]
```

Take a general linear combination of the factors $f(n)$.

```
In[4]:= LC[n_] = Sum[k[i] f[i][n], {i,1,5}]
Out[4]= k[1] + 2n k[2] + 3n k[3] +
   4n k[4] + 5n k[5]
```

This shows that every linear combination of the functions $f_i(n) = i^n$ *is a solution for* $i = 1, \ldots, 5$.

```
In[5]:= Sum[c[i] LC[n+i],{i,0,5}]//Expand
Out[5]= 0
```

Note that if $k_1 f_1 + \cdots + k_5 f_5 = 0$ then $\mathbf{d}^i(k_1 f_1 + \cdots + k_5 f_5) = k_1\mathbf{d}^i(f_1) + k_2\mathbf{d}^i(f_2) + k_3\mathbf{d}^i(f_3) + k_4\mathbf{d}^i(f_4) + k_5\mathbf{d}^i(f_5) = 0$ for $i = 1, 2, \ldots$. If this is the case, then the vectors $\mathbf{v}_i(n) = (f_i(n), f_i(n + 1), \ldots, f_i(n + 4))$ satisfy the relation $k_1\mathbf{v}_1(n) + \cdots + k_5\mathbf{v}_5(n) = 0$. This implies that the matrix $K(n) = [\mathbf{v}_1(n), \ldots, \mathbf{v}_5(n)]$ is singular for all n.

The matrix $K(n)$ is called the *Casoratian matrix* of the functions $n \to i^n$. The determinant $\det K(n)$ is called the *Casoratian* or *Casorati determinant*.

This defines a generating function for the Casoratian matrix.

```
In[6]:= g[i_,j_] := j^(i - 1)
```

K is the Casoratian matrix. If the functions f_i for i = 1, ..., 5 are linearly dependent, then so are the columns of this matrix.

```
In[7]:= K = Array[g,{5,5}]
```

```
Out[7]//MatrixForm=
1    1     1     1     1
1    2     3     4     5
1    4     9     16    25
1    8     27    64    125
1    16    81    256   625
```

The determinant shows the columns of K are linearly independent, so the solutions $f_1, ..., f_5$ are a basis for s_h.

```
In[8]:= Det[K]
```

```
Out[8]= 288
```

The matrix K is the transpose of a Vandermonde matrix, so its determinant is nonzero.

Initial Conditions

For any difference operator

$$\mathbf{L} = a_0\mathbf{I} + a_1\mathbf{d} + \cdots + a_{m-1}\mathbf{d}^{m-1} + \mathbf{d}^m$$

each solution s corresponds to a unique vector $\mathbf{v} = (s(0), s(1), ..., s(m-1))$ in $\Re^m$. It is clear that, for any solution f, $f(m + i)$ is determined by the values $f(i), ..., f(i + m - 1)$. The choice of the m values $f(0), ..., f(m - 1)$ can be made arbitrarily. Consider the operator $\mathbf{L} = \mathbf{d}^4 + 4\,\mathbf{d}^3 - 3\,\mathbf{d}^2 + 2\,\mathbf{d} - 1$. If initial values $f(0), f(1), f(2)$, and $f(3)$ are chosen and $\mathbf{L}(f) = 0$, then

$$f(n + 4) = -4f(n + 3) + 3f(n + 2) - 2f(n + 1) + f(n)$$

for all $n = 0, 1, ...$ For example, assume $f(i) = i$ for $i = 0, ..., 3$.

This pair of commands defines f to calculate f(n) for any nonnegative integer n.

```
In[1]:= Do[f[i] = i, {i,0,3}];
In[2]:= f[n_] :=
   -4 f[n-1] + 3 f[n-2] - 2 f[n-3] + f[n-4]
```

This shows the values $f(4), ..., f(7)$.

```
In[3]:= Do[Print[f[i]], {i,4,7}]
   -8
   38
   -180
   853
```

The correspondence between $\mathbf{v} = (f(0), f(1), \ldots, f(m-1))$ in $\Re^m$ and the solution f is also linear, so all solutions of the homogeneous equation $\mathbf{L}(f) = 0$ can be found from any m solutions $\{f_i\}_{i=1}^m$ that correspond to a basis for $\Re^m$.

Earlier you saw the basic solutions $f_i(n) = i^n$ of the recurrence relation

$$\mathbf{L}(f) = 0 \text{ for } \mathbf{L} = \prod_{i=1}^{5} (\mathbf{d} - i\mathbf{I}).$$ This basis for $\mathbf{s}_h$ corresponds to the basis $\mathbf{u}_1 =$

$(1, 1, 1, 1, 1)$, $\mathbf{u}_2 = (1, 2, 4, 8, 16)$, $\mathbf{u}_3 = (1, 3, 9, 27, 81)$, $\mathbf{u}_4 = (1, 4, 16, 64, 256)$, $\mathbf{u}_5 = (1, 5, 25, 125, 625)$ for $\Re^5$. The following finds the solution $\mathbf{h}_1$ of $\mathbf{L}(f) = 0$ corresponding to the vector $\mathbf{e}_1 = (1, 0, 0, 0, 0)$.

Define the functions f_i.

```
In[1]:= Do[f[i][n_]:= i^n,{i,1,5}]
```

Put the solutions $f_i = i^n$ into a vector.

```
In[2]:= b[n_] := Table[f[i][n], {i,1,5}]
```

Define the vector $\mathbf{e}_1 = (1, 0, 0, 0, 0)$.

```
In[3]:= e[1] = {1,0,0,0,0};
```

Define the matrix $M = [\mathbf{u}_1, \mathbf{u}_2, \mathbf{u}_3, \mathbf{u}_4, \mathbf{u}_5]$.

```
In[4]:= M = Table[j^(i - 1), {i,1,5}, {j,1,5}]
Out[4]//MatrixForm=
    1    1    1    1    1
    1    2    3    4    5
    1    4    9    16   25
    1    8    27   64   125
    1    16   81   256  625
```

Solve the equation $M\mathbf{x} = \mathbf{e}_1$. The solution $\mathbf{a}$ is the coefficient vector of $\mathbf{e}_1$ with respect to the basis $\{\mathbf{v}\}_{i=1}^5$.

```
In[5]:= a = LinearSolve[M,e[1]]
Out[5]= {5, -10, 10, -5, 1}
```

Compute the solution $\mathbf{h}_1 = \mathbf{b} \cdot \mathbf{a}$ corresponding to $\mathbf{e}_1$.

```
In[6]:= h[1][n_] = b[n] . a
```

The solution $\mathbf{h}_1$ now corresponds to the vector $\mathbf{e}_1$.

```
In[7]:= Table[h[1][i], {i,0,4}]
Out[7]= {1, 0, 0, 0, 0}
```

You also can find the solution $\mathbf{s}$ corresponding to a particular vector directly using RSolve, as demonstrated in the following.

This defines $\mathbf{L}$ and the coefficients c_i as before.

```
In[1]:= Product[d - i, {i,1,5}]//Expand;
In[2]:= Do[c[i] = Coefficient[%,d,i], {i,0,5}]
In[3]:= REQ = Sum[c[i]f[n+i], {i,0,5}] == 0
```

This obtains the solution
corresponding to $e_1 =$
$(1, 0, 0, 0, 0)$.

```
In[4]:= RSolve[{REQ, f[0] == 1, f[1] == 0,
    f[2] == 0, f[3] == 0, f[4] == 0}, f[n],n]
Out[4]//MatrixForm=
  f[n] -> 5 - 10 2^n + 10 3^n -5 4^n + 5^n
```

This verifies the solution.

```
In[5]:= g[n_] = %[[1,1,2]];
In[6]:= Table[g[i], {i,0,4}]
Out[6]= {1, 0, 0, 0, 0}
```

Exercises on Recurrence Relations

1. Find the solutions of the recurrence equation $\prod_{i=1}^{5}(\mathbf{d} - i\mathbf{I})(f(n)) = 0$ corresponding to the standard basis vectors for $\Re^5$.

2. The sum of the first n positive integers is described by the nonhomogeneous recursion relation $s(n + 1) - s(n) = n + 1$ and the initial condition $s(0) = 0$. A similar recursion relation describes the sum of the mth powers of the first n positive integers. Use RSolve to find formulas for the following. (The formulas are traditionally written in factored form.)

   a. $\displaystyle\sum_{i=1}^{n} i^2$ b. $\displaystyle\sum_{i=1}^{n} i^3$ c. $\displaystyle\sum_{i=1}^{n} i^4$ d. $\displaystyle\sum_{i=1}^{n} i^5$

3. Use your results from Exercise 2 to form a conjecture about the nature of the functions $s(n) = \displaystyle\sum_{i=1}^{n} i^m$. Test your conjecture for $m = 10$ and $m = 15$.

4. Assume $\mathbf{F} = \mathbf{d} - 2I$ and $\mathbf{L} = \mathbf{F} \circ \mathbf{F} \circ \mathbf{F}$.
   a. Show that 2^n, $n2^n$, and $n^2 2^n$ are solutions of $\mathbf{L}(f) = 0$.
   b. Show that the three solutions in part a are linearly independent. Can you conclude they are a basis for the kernel of $\mathbf{L}$?
   c. What do you conjecture about the solutions of $(\mathbf{d} - 2)^r$ in general? Verify your conjecture for $\mathbf{F} \circ \mathbf{F} \circ \mathbf{F} \circ \mathbf{F}$.

5. If the characteristic polynomial $c(x)$ of a recurrence operator $\mathbf{L}$ has a complex root, then the factorization of $c(x)$ has an irreducible quadratic factor $((x + a)^2 + b^2)$. Let $\mathbf{L}$ be the linear operator $\mathbf{L} = ((\mathbf{d} + 2\mathbf{I})^2 + (3^2 + 2^2)\mathbf{I})$. Use RSolve to determine the form of the solution of the recurrence equation $\mathbf{L}(f) = 0$.

Problems on Recurrence Relations

1. A famous problem known as the "Towers of Hanoi" has 64 disks with holes in their centers stacked on one of three poles. The disks are arranged so that the largest is on the bottom of the stack, then the next largest, and so on. The problem is to move the disks to another of the three poles— one disk at a time—without ever placing a larger disk on top of a smaller one. You may have seen smaller versions of this problem sold as children's puzzles.

    a. Determine the number of moves required to solve the problem for n disks.

    b. Determine the length of time, in years, that it would require to solve the problem for 64 disks if the disks were moved at the rate of one per second.

2. A variation of the Towers of Hanoi problem has the three poles in a row and the disks on one end. In this version a second condition is imposed: Disks can only be moved to an adjacent pole.

    a. Determine the number of moves required to solve this version for n disks.

    b. Determine the length of time, in years, that it would require to solve this version of the problem for 64 disks if the disks were moved at the rate of one per second.

3. The following famous problem originated with Leonardo de Pisa, also known as Fibonacci. Assume that a farmer acquires n_0 pairs of newborn rabbits. Assume also that each pair gives birth to one additional pair at the end of every month beginning with the second, and that all their descendants do the same.

    a. Assuming none of the rabbits die, how many rabbits are there after n months?

    b. How many rabbits does the farmer have at the end of ten years if he begins with exactly one pair?

Index

(*Mathematica* commands are shown in `Courier` type.)

An ideal supplement to any linear algebra course where students have access to *Mathematica*®!

Designed to be used in conjunction with any standard introductory linear algebra text, this easy-to-understand book begins with a short introduction to *Mathematica*, then proceeds to use *Mathematica* as a tool in working with vectors, matrices, and linear transformations.

Filled with examples, exercises, and applications, this book is self-explanatory, so instructors will need to devote virtually no class time to teaching students to use *Mathematica*.

"The applications in this book were interesting and set good motivation (which is normally non-existent in linear algebra classes) to learn the algebra. . . . Having the computer handle the large computations allows more time for the student to understand the overall mathematical picture. The applications were good in this regard—since *Mathematica* handled the computations, the material focused more on the applications."

Judy Holdener
U.S. Air Force Academy

OTHER RELATED TITLES
FROM BROOKS/COLE SOFTWARE

Software for DOS/Windows and Macintosh computers
Maple V Release 3: Student Edition

Access a powerful computer algebra system inside your word-processing documents!
Scientific WorkPlace 2.0, Student Edition for Windows
Combines the ease of use of a technical word processor with the typesetting power of TeX and the numeric, symbolic, and graphic computational abilities of the *Maple V* computer algebra system.

ISBN 0-534-13068-2

90000

9 780534 130688